Official Portraits and Unofficial Counterportraits of 'At Risk' Students

Helping children find their voices and the power of their writing is crucial for their success as writers, particularly in the current repressive educational setting in which many economically poor children attend school. This book chronicles 5th and 6th grade writers—children of gang members, drug users, poor people, and non-documented and documented immigrants—in a rural school in the southwest US coming into their voices, cultivating those voices, and using those voices in a variety of venues, beginning with the classroom community and spreading outward. Such children are showing up in schools and in research more and more. In their writing, they make sense of who they are as writers and human beings and ultimately learn that their voices carry presence and power.

At the heart of this book is the cultivation of tension between official and unofficial portraits of these students. Official portraits are composed of demographic data, socioeconomic data, and test results. Students tend to appropriate the language of failure about themselves, their school, and the community that is found in their official portrait. Unofficial counterportraits offer different views of children, schools, and communities. The big ideas of official and unofficial portraits are presented, then each chapter offers data (the children's and teachers' processes and products) and facets of the theoretical construct of counterportraits, as a response to official portraits. The counterportraits are built slowly in order to base them in evidence and to articulate their complexity.

Many teachers and soon-to-be teachers facing the dilemmas and complexities of teaching in diverse classrooms have serious questions about how to honor students' lives outside of school, making school more relevant. This book addresses these critical (for student success) issues and presents teaching as the political activity that it is. It offers evidence to present to the public, legislators, and the press as a way of talking back to official portraits, demonstrating that officially failing schools are not really failing—evidence that is crucial for the survival of public schools.

Richard J. Meyer is Professor in the Department of Language, Literacy, and Sociocultural Studies at the College of Education, University of New Mexico.

Official Portraits and Unofficial Counterportraits of 'At Risk' Students

Writing Spaces in Hard Times

Richard J. Meyer
University of New Mexico

Routledge
Taylor & Francis Group

NEW YORK AND LONDON

First published 2010
by Routledge
270 Madison Ave, New York, NY 10016

Simultaneously published in the UK
by Routledge
2 Park Square, Milton Park, Abingdon, Oxon OX14 4RN

Routledge is an imprint of the Taylor & Francis Group, an informa business

© 2010 Taylor & Francis

Typeset in Minion and Gill Sans by
Keystroke, Tettenhall, Wolverhampton
Printed and bound in the United States of America on acid-free paper by
Edwards Brothers, Inc

Library of Congress Cataloging in Publication Data
Meyer, Richard J., 1949–
    Official portraits and unofficial counterportraits of 'at risk' students :
    writing spaces in hard times / Richard J. Meyer.
        p. cm.
    Includes bibliographical references and index.
    1. English language—Composition and exercises—Study and teaching
    (Elementary)—United States—Case studies. 2. Creative writing
    (Elementary education)—United States—Case studies.
    3. Education—United States—Biographical methods—Case studies.
    4. Children with social disabilities—Education (Elementary)—United
    States—Case studies. 5. Hispanic American children—Education
    (Elementary)—United States—Case studies. I. Title.
    LB1576.M4736 2010
    372.62′3—dc22   2009018391

ISBN10: 0-415-87123-9 (hbk)
ISBN10: 0-415-87124-7 (pbk)
ISBN10: 0-203-86679-7 (ebk)

ISBN13: 978-0-415-87123-5 (hbk)
ISBN13: 978-0-415-87124-2 (pbk)
ISBN13: 978-0-203-86679-5 (ebk)

For the children, teachers, and families at Mesa Vista Elementary School. Thank you for teaching me, for revealing your remarkable strength, power, and truthfulness and for your willingness to show others what you know and who you are.

For Sadie and Zoe who taught me how children write.

For Robert Solomon Wilson and the next generation of thinkers and writers.

For Pat.

Contents

Preface

One memory I remember is when my big brother got shot because he had a gun. The new one he got is more smaller. Going with him in his low-rider that has the front windshield broken by a crack head who wasn't in a good mood. At least my brother tells me he will always be there for me telling me to not live like this and not to ever do what he does, never to have a gun like he does. He also says to never sell or do drugs. He said to work for what I want. He also says if I want something bad enough, I will get it. He said if he can go back in time he would change everything. Me and my brother are closer than ever. We stick together. We both grew up without dads.

(Jesus, a sixth grader)

This book is the story of the writers in two classrooms, one fifth grade and one sixth grade, in an economically poor rural school that has never achieved 'adequate yearly progress' status. Mesa Vista Elementary School (all names of the school, children, and teachers in this book are pseudonyms) is located 25 miles from a medium sized southwestern US city. All the children in the school receive free breakfast and lunch, a fact included here as a measure of economic poverty. Most of the children learned Spanish as their first language, either in Mexico or the US. Over 20 percent of the children are homeless, some of their family members are not documented visitors to the US, and most of the students, teachers, and the community have appropriated the idea that MVE is a chronically 'failing' school. Officially, it is a high poverty school, in a high crime area, with low scores. Jesus' piece might confirm the cold data about the school and the community. But it is also the story of two brothers' love for each other. This is the first piece he's written in school about what really happens at home and within it are many of the themes of this book: hope, struggle, poverty, gangs, families, and drugs. Working internally, collaboratively, and across contexts, the children and their teachers undertook to disappropriate the official portrait of failure that became central to their school identities. At the end of our year together, Esperanza, a sixth grader, wrote this brief poem:

> I used to have a brain
> Without words
> But now
> I do.

Esperanza's words capture what happened for many of the children as they learned to write, learned through writing, and learned about writing (adapting Halliday, 1978). There was one guiding principle in all of our work together, a brief sentence that I shared with the teachers before working with the children and with the children once that work began: Tell your truths. I repeated this sentence frequently, almost like a mantra at times, imploring the children to do what many were previously forbidden to do: tell the truths about their out-of-school lives by writing and talking about them in school. One of the most important findings in this work was that the children may seem 'at risk,' and to some degree, they are—of failing in school. But there are *larger* risks that we need to consider, particularly the risks that we face when schools fail children. There is the risk that an intelligent and literate populus, like the children in this study, pose to the status quo; the risk that their truths pose to the comfort of those in power; and the risks that we face when their potentials are left untapped.

There was much testing of the challenge to tell their truths. Some joked, some avoided, and some took risks. Some dove in with a passion and intensity they'd never experienced in school and some observed their colleagues from the sidelines to witness the impact and results of their truthfulness. Eventually, through very different means across classrooms, they presented their truths and the truths of others in their community. The children studied and wrote about adults they love, using digital voice recorders, cameras, and various strategies for interviewing, collecting, and understanding artifacts in their community. They worked with each other in class to explore and compose. The pages that follow are saturated with their work, their thinking, their stories, their poetry, and narratives about their loved ones. There are funny pieces about mischievous fathers and serious pieces about gang deaths, drugs, poverty, stress, love and loss, families whole and caring, and families disrupted into chaos. The work was accompanied by tears, laughter, sharing, privacy, bringing forth and withdrawing, lightness, and intensity. There were clashes and calm periods, teacher angst and angst resolved only to be reborn, and all the complexities of exceeding the borders of safety and history to venture into new areas of thought, emotionality, relationships, and spirit.

The children not only read the word and the world (Freire & Macedo, 1987), they wrote and rewrote their words and worlds as they composed and made sense of different versions of the truths in their lives. They struggled with the difficulties of their home and school lives coupled with the realities of adolescence and the creation of new and different relationships between themselves and their teachers.

Overview

The chapters in this book are a chronological presentation of our work. The analyses that are part of each chapter are ever-deepening considerations of the work and I draw upon a wide variety of literatures because, "Critically conscious research represents multiple, intersecting, and interdisciplinary principles and processes" (Willis et al., 2008, p. 51).

In Chapter 1, I explain how I met the teachers in a summer workshop that I taught and their invitation (or perhaps it was a dare or a challenge) to demonstrate the ways in which ideas from the workshop might be incorporated into classroom lives steeped in required programs and ongoing testing. I provide the hard facts about the district and the school, facts about: poverty, test scores, language, economics, and more. That data forms the foundation of an *official portrait* of the school; counterportraits are vehicles for challenging, interrogating, and undermining the official portrait. But counterportraits are not simply composed and left; rather they are ongoing political projects to disappropriate official portraits of race, identity, language, achievement, and culture.

In Chapter 2, the work of counterportraiture is initiated in the sixth grade classroom as I challenge the students to write their truths, take risks, and tell stories that have never before been told in school. The chapter is an introduction to the sixth graders as writers, thinkers, and children living lives in the "other America" (Polakow, 1993). Each chapter, beginning with Chapter 2, ends with a section on emerging counterportraits as part of the analysis of the data presented in the particular chapter.

In Chapter 3, the theoretical work moves to claiming (or reclaiming) spaces for writers in the two classrooms. Barbara, the fifth grade teacher, wants the children to do something that they will never forget, but wrestles with what that might be, particularly in the environment of a tightly controlled curriculum. In the sixth grade, the writers work on identity pieces, like the one written by Jesus at the beginning of this preface. Yet they don't trust each other. Some of them have family members in rival gangs, some of them know each other from church, and some of them found the safety that silence and being invisible in school provide. Relationships arise as a critical facet of writing spaces—not only relationships with each other as colleagues in writing, but with their teacher, Patia.

In Chapter 4, safety is not such a tenuous issue in the fifth grade because Barbara has worked to create a community of trust. Barbara brings up the idea of 'biography' as a project for the class and she and I discuss the possibility of writing biographies of loved ones, rather than strangers, and of using primary research strategies. We begin by inviting the children to write biographies of each other, teaching strategies of interviewing, listening, note taking, and composing. The children learn new things about each other, deepening their connections as writers as they find out about: prebirth traumas, pet ducks, families' countries of origin, and stories of growing up in Mexico and the US. Goffman's idea of "permeability" (1961) helps explain how a community might change when information from the outside is brought into school. The sixth graders explore growth and change as they write about ways in which their lives have evolved. Their writing suggests moves from places of trust to less trust, from hope to less hopeful, and from secure to less secure (emotionally, financially, and even academically).

In Chapter 5, the fifth graders move from biographies of colleagues to studying someone outside of school. They approach loved ones to collect stories that are not only new to them, but also serve to create an air of excitement and curiosity in the classroom as recordings and photos are brought to school and discussed. The fifth graders invest increasing amounts of time in their biography work. The sixth graders struggle with issues of love in their writing, telling stories of loved ones and hesitating to commit to genres beyond poetry. The theoretical section of this chapter explores the idea of legitimacy in a community of practice (Lave & Wenger, 1991) and extends that consideration into the ongoing counterportraits being composed.

Beginning in Chapter 6 and continuing for the next few chapters, individual fifth grade writers are featured because of the depth and intensity of their work on the biography. The sixth graders are presented *en masse* to demonstrate the variety of writing styles, the intensity of their experiences, and their struggles as writers, learners, and human beings. Theoretically, I submit the idea of 'inertia,' borrowing from physics, as a concept applicable to the view of the children in their official portrait. Within the life of a school, the inertia of the official portrait serves not only to perpetuate a view of the students, their school, and the community, but serves the extant power structure by not challenging the distribution of wealths that yield profit, including: economic, literacy, linguistic, and cultural wealths. In the counterportraiture section of this chapter, I suggest that interrogating and challenging the official portrait is the friction or torque that may influence the inertia of the official portrait. Friction is expressed as finding voice, ending silence, and providing opportunities (venues) for voices to be heard.

In Chapter 7, the sixth graders explore darkness as a theme in their lives. Miguel writes:

Dark Tears

When I look into
my grandma's eyes

I see her folding covers
in my uncle's room.

folding clothes for
someone very special

as tears and praying
was all she did

But tears fall down
and she realizes

He is no longer with
us.

Death is one of the dark struggles that seems to haunt the children on an almost daily basis as friends and relatives die in car crashes and through acts of violence. In the fifth grade, the works of Chuck and Estevan are featured as two writers uncovering their pasts and themselves. The theme of 'struggle' is discussed as it relates to the counterportraits that the children are composing of themselves. I rely upon Bakhtin's (1984) notion of carnival to explain the ways borders and rules are shifting as the writers go deeper into their work.

In Chapter 8, I use the idea of "hybridity" (Bakhtin, 1981; Dyson, 2003), to explain the space that the writers composed in order to write. This is the origin of the subtitle of this book, 'Writing Spaces in Hard Times,' specifically the use of the word 'writing' to mean two things: articulating the space in which to write and committing thoughts to paper (or monitor) within those spaces. A hybrid in nature is typically better equipped for survival; a hybrid space is one in which a writer is cultivated for growth and efficacy.

Chapter 9 is a presentation of some of the pieces that the children presented to the public, a discussion of how they were received, and their work with the Albuquerque slam poetry team. Initially, the students were writing for themselves and each other, but as the audience expanded to other individuals, including families, so did the influence of their work. The impact of their work on future teachers, the poets, and their families is interpreted as expanded spheres of influence.

In Chapter 10, I document the closing down of our year's work as the children reflect in notes, such as Esperanza's earlier in this preface. Reflective of her voice, new understanding of the purposes for writing, and insights into writing as counterportraiture, Verdad wrote, "I would like you to know that people just don't write for fun; they write to express to other people," as part of her final evaluation of the year's work. I use critical literacy to complete the counterportraiture work of this chapter, reviewing how the children interrogated and acted upon their worlds (Lewison, Flint, & Van Sluys, 2002).

In Chapter 11, I present the final layer of analyses looking across all of the chapters. I revisit and explain 'struggles' in greater depth after considering the role of joy, the purposes of school, and the spirit of the child as themes and areas for further research. The appendices contain more of the children's work, some heuristics they used to support their writing, and a discussion of counterportraiture as method and its inherent political nature.

Our year of work changed some people's minds: the children's about writing, their teachers' about the nature of composing in school, future teachers' about 'at-risk, failing children,' family members, and mine about the portraits of children, who gets to compose them, how they are used, and how they might be disrupted.

Acknowledgments

The children and teachers in the fifth and sixth grade classrooms were patient, caring, and daring over the course of our year together. I thank you all for your time, energy, and willingness to tell your truths. Thank you to the families in the 'Mesa Vista' neighborhoods for allowing me to work with your children and affording me insights into your lives, strengths, hopes, and truths. Naomi Silverman continues to inspire many authors, myself included, to take risks in our work, tell our truths, and rely upon her for support throughout the entire process of birthing a book. Thank you to others at Routledge, including Meeta Pendharkar, for your support with all the details. Rae Ramirez, Susana Ibara Johnson, and Zoe Nellie Gastelum helped with translations, not an easy task and one for which I am grateful. Thanks to Chuck Jurich for generous technology support. Thank you to the three reviewers of this book who invested many hours and offered wisdom, feedback, and honesty. Finally, thank you to Dr. Kathryn F. Whitmore for always taking my phone calls, challenging my thinking, and reminding me why we do the work we do.

Prologue

"Peace is threatened by unjust economic, social and political order, absence of democracy, environmental degradation and the absence of human rights."

(M. Yunus, 2006, accepting the Nobel Peace Prize)

Writing Spaces and *Hard Times*

Muhammad Yunus won the Nobel Prize for Economics in December 2006, five months after I met the teachers and children that are in this book. His work to help poor families and villages in remote Bangladesh involved making small low-interest loans to individuals for as little as the equivalent of twenty five US dollars. They used the money to initiate business activities that ultimately led to self-sustenance and an increased sense of dignity and quality of life. Yunus' understanding of poverty and his use of microeconomics (small loans to tiny businesses) resonates with the emotional and cognitive poverty that teachers, children, and communities in this book are experiencing under the constant thrashing of the Elementary and Secondary Education Act (ESEA) (US Department of Education [DOE], 2001a). Consistent with Yunus' lending model, we 'borrowed' small amounts of time from the official mandated curriculum to help children and teachers see themselves not as failures, but as thoughtful writers with important things to say, enhancing their sense of dignity and, perhaps, the quality of their lives. Until Yunus and others like him began their work, economic poverty was a force in motion that seemed relentless in perpetuating itself. Yunus worked to disrupt economic poverty by offering hope enacted through a real and tangible investment. This book is the story of teachers, students, and a researcher working to find hope in the punitive context of the ESEA, euphemistically subtitled *No Child Left Behind* (NCLB).

The economic conditions in which the children in this study live are poor by US standards, though not as poor as those that Yunus serves. The poverties described and analyzed in this book, some of which were acted upon, include economic poverty and also the pernicious educative (Dewey, 1938) poverties that perpetuate the in-school bracketing of children's lives beyond the school. Such poverty includes the silencing of teachers forced to use certain approaches and programs to teach reading and writing because of the political and economic power that certain groups have amassed (Spring, 2002). Publishers and legislation have reduced teaching and schools to pedagogical ghettos for profits at the emotional and cognitive expense of children and their teachers (Altwerger, 2005).

Within this political context, the idea of *writing spaces*, from the title of this book, has two meanings. First, it refers to locations or places in which children get to write; these are physical, social, and emotional places. Second, *writing spaces* means composing those spaces in which the writing takes place. *Writing spaces* means both having (articulating) the space and using (enacting) it. At present, if children get to write in school, the space and time are often co-opted by a program aimed at raising test scores. Professional teachers are degraded and their rights as thoughtful practitioners are dismissed in such spaces. As Yunus suggests, peace for teachers, children, researchers, families and communities is threatened because their right to encourage thought and agency are vulnerable when they are coerced into compliance—"the absence of human rights"—instead of encouraged to be reflective practitioners (Schön, 1983; Shannon, 1989).

The peace that exists as thought collectives in which multiple perspectives about self, language, culture, experiences, and literacy activity are welcomed is not present in many schools, staff development sessions, and adopted programs. This peace is not a quiet place of unanimous agreement on all ideas nor is it the artificial complacency induced by standardized programs and forced compliance. Peace is a contentious, yet safe, place in which we can be pushed to reconsider our most deeply held beliefs as we examine economic, social, political—even spiritual—dimensions of democracy. It is a place of deep and profound honesty and is not always comfortable. Sadly, many teachers and children are ghettoized into a legislated poverty that is perpetuated by the absence of their basic human rights of thought, justice, action, and dissent. This is what I mean by *hard times* in the title of this book. The teachers and children in this book wrote in a different way from the way being dictated by the district and state, intuitively living what Yunus did to address economic poverty by addressing intellectual poverty. We did this in microspaces, small pieces of time in which we lived all the struggles of authentic writers. We had to do so in microspaces because most of the schedule was consumed by prescribed programs with predetermined uses of time and space. In the epilogue, I return to Yunus' work to reconsider the power of *writing spaces* to change lives.

Chapter 1

An Introduction to Searching for Our Truths

"How many legs does a dog have if you call the tail a leg?
Four. Calling a tail a leg doesn't make it a leg."

(Abraham Lincoln)

Lincoln's humor and brilliance shine in this riddle attributed to him (Lincoln, n.d.) and perhaps we smile as we read it because of the play on the nature of *truth* inherent in it. A tail is not a leg simply because someone says it, yet a school is labeled as 'failing' if a test score says it. Apparently, sometimes a tail is a leg, if a legislature says that the definition of 'leg' will, from this point hence, be so adjusted. Similarly, a school may be considered *failing* if the children do not perform on a test at a certain predetermined level if that's the legislated definition of failure. When those in power mandate such truth, it seems to have a domino effect as the public believes it, states and districts act upon it as truth, and eventually children, teachers, and families appropriate a legislated truth as *the* truth. One of the goals of this research was to look at the tail-being-called-a-leg in education and interrogate it. The work begins with teachers asked to tell their truths and to interrogate the worthiness of those truths and then extends into classrooms asking fifth and sixth graders to do the same thing. In this chapter I explain how I met the teachers and was invited into their classrooms and introduce the ideas of the official portrait and counterportraits.

Before the Work Began

One of the outcomes of the Elementary and Secondary Education Act called No Child Left Behind (US DOE, 2001a) is that individuals like me are decreasingly asked to do professional development with teachers. We just don't fit the mold of what is expected when using federal money to address the panic that has set in about not achieving adequate yearly progress as defined in the Act. In early June of 2006 I was surprised when I received a phone call from a doctoral student who was also an administrator and professional developer at a local school district. She was a bit frantic because she had worked for almost a full year to plan a summer conference for teachers from her school district, just north of Albuquerque, and a neighboring district south of Albuquerque. The one-week workshop would run from 8:30 to 4:30 daily and was intended to be an intensive introduction to a view of literacy that the districts were adopting. The teachers would be divided into two groups, one primary and the second intermediate, grades four through six. Her panic rested in the fact that the person originally contracted to work with the intermediate teachers canceled suddenly. I was invited to take her place.

"I'm not sure I know the specific program you want me to teach the teachers. It seems a bit dishonest to portray myself as an expert in any one program," I suggested, hoping she would withdraw her offer. "You know how I feel about programs." She'd taken enough coursework with me to know that I prefer teaching ideas and strategies rooted in teacher reflection and cultural responsiveness (Au, 1993; Ladson-Billings, 1994). Further, my commitment to the idea that teaching is relational work composed of the very specific identities of those involved in the pedagogical discourse made it impossible to recommend any particular program.

"I know all that," came her desperate reply. "I know you. But we're using a set of books that teachers will read, not simply a boxed program from some publisher. You'd like these books. We'd let you do what you want, as long as you have them read and think about some of the ideas in the books. I can get you the books by tomorrow."

I decided I was not going to do it. I was exhausted as we neared the end of a National Writing Project summer institute that I directed and planned a nice long break, in my backyard, reading, and maybe driving to San Diego to read more at the beach once the work was over. After listening to her pleas and thinking about the intensity of a weeklong workshop (a forum I'd grown to appreciate), I relented.

There was a deeper reason for my hesitancy in doing the workshop. Since the beginning of the tyranny when No Child Left Behind became law, I had been witness to teacher trainings. During these sessions, teachers were treated as ignorant and in need of close and frequent supervision and monitoring (Allington, 2004). Further, they were treated as being incapable of thinking for themselves and needing carefully scripted lesson plans. 'Professional development' involved training teachers to read these scripts. They also needed to be trained in the administration of tests that were composed of utter nonsense, including nonsense words and nonsense activities (Goodman, 2006). During these trainings, teachers were not allowed to ask questions. Following Allington and Woodside-Jiron's (1998) lead, when I was a guest during one of these sessions and heard the trainer, for at least the twentieth time, begin, "And the research says . . ." I raised my hand and did not wait to be called on. "What research?" I asked. "I'm a researcher and want to read the work that you're basing this on."

"There's plenty of research," she responded, rather sternly.

"Yes, I'm sure you believe that," I answered. "But I do research for a living and I'm not sure to which work you are referring. Could you please specify?"

"Well, citing the research is not part of our presentation today. We'll have to put that in the parking lot. But you could read the report of the National Reading Panel (2000). However, as I said, we'll have to put that in the parking lot for now."

"I understand," I said. "But just so you know, the Report of the National Reading Panel is not a research study. It is a carefully crafted document to support certain people and marginalize others . . . like me." I sat down.

In the 'parking lot' strategy, the presenter puts up a large sheet of paper at the beginning of her training. She explains the goals of the day and summarizes the agenda, telling the audience (NOT *participants* because there will be very little participation) when they'll get to use the restroom, eat lunch, and the topics to be presented. She points to the large piece of paper and explains that there may be questions as she presents. These are to be written on sticky notes and placed in the parking lot. They will be addressed later in the day. But they never are. The parking lot is actually detention for teacher thinking and questions. It is an immediate response to any action that might derail the very standardized training. It shuts teachers up, placing their thinking not in a parking lot but in a cemetery. They are taught, above all else, that being trained and, in turn, training students, is about compliance (Altwerger, 2005).

I had one week to plan the weeklong workshop. I read the books that the teachers would receive, and integrated some reference to them in each day's plans. I decided that we needed a theme for our work together and the need for this umbrella theme haunted me each day as I worked to compose a mix of theory, conversation, activity, and reflection on activity. I wanted them to have time to plan for the coming year, interrogate those plans, and engage in reflective professional dialogue. A week before that first day, the enrollment was 20, six days before it was up to 30, and by the Friday before the Monday that we started, we'd been moved to a larger room with a microphone system, a screen at each end of the room and 75 registrants. Originally, we were going to begin with some community building, which we'd still do, but it would be far from cozy as I gave up the idea of knowing all the participants as intimately as I'd planned. On Friday, panic set in and still the idea of a theme kept coming up in my mind.

How, I wondered, do I face 75 teachers and explain my truths to them? My truths about the pain and sadness that I see in the eyes of children and their teachers when I visit classrooms. Seasoned teachers tell me of their plans to retire as soon as they possibly can, and many do. Kozol (2007) has seen the same thing in schools:

> When I'm taking notes during a visit to a school and children in a class divert themselves with tiny episodes of silliness, or brief epiphanies of tenderness to one another, or a whispered observation about something

they find amusing—like a goofy face made by another child in the class—I put a little round face with a smile on the margin of my notepad so that I won't miss it later on. In all the 15 pages that I wrote during my visit in this classroom in the Bronx, there is not a single small round smiling face.

[. . .]

I couldn't find a single statement made by any child that had not been prompted by the teacher's questions, other than one child's timid question about which 'objective' should be written on the first line of a page the class had been asked to write. I found some notes on the children moving from their tables to their 'centers' and on various hand gestures they would make as a response to the hand gestures of their teachers. But I found no references to any child's traits of personality or even physical appearance. Differences between the children somehow ceased to matter much during the time that I observed the class. The uniform activities and teacher's words controlled my own experience perhaps as much as they controlled and muted the expressiveness of children.

Before I left the school, I studied again the definition of 'Authentic Writing' that was posted in the corridor. Whatever it was, according to the poster, it was 'driven by curriculum . . .' Authenticity was what somebody outside of this building, more authoritative than the children or their teachers, said it should be.

(pp. 623–624)

The weekend before we were to start the workshop, I began again, knowing that there would be ten tables of at least seven teachers each. I decided we'd begin with a strategy called *what's on your mind?* that we used in the Writing Project summer institute. Participants would begin by writing as a way of bridging from the outside world and all their obligations, responsibilities, worries, and joys, and move to the inside world of the workshop. They'd write, share their writing at their tables, and I'd talk about the importance of starting each day of this week with their lives, their interests, and their professional and personal thinking.

On Monday morning, the first day of the workshop, I faced 75 teachers, turned off the music that I played over the loudspeaker system, and turned on the microphone. "Good morning," I began. A few teachers answered and I smiled; a few people laughed. As I prepared to introduce our first strategy (*What's on your mind?*), already thinking ahead to the theoretical connections I planned to discuss following our engagement, a serendipitous flash of insight finally arrived. In all of the mixed messages, threats, trainings, staff developments and other required duties in a teacher's life, the idea of *honesty* seemed to have taken a back seat, if not entirely dismissed. Our theme would be honesty and, as I set aside my notes for the morning, I looked around the rectangular room at all the unfamiliar faces. "Why," I began, "don't we tell children the truth about what we're doing in school? Why don't we let children tell their truths in school?" I remember those lines almost exactly as I spoke them because in a few minutes we were writing what was on our minds and I wrote what I'd said to begin our week together. "Why do we tell children directly or indirectly that they must leave their thinking, desires, ideas, fears, interests, cultures, and even home languages at the door? What would happen if we embraced those things?" And then I shuffled through my PowerPoint slides to find a cartoon from a Sunday paper that shows a little girl sitting on her couch watching TV. The announcer says, "And that's the news from around the world . . . goodnight." The next frame shows the girl using the remote to turn off the TV and the room is darkened. In the final frame, the child sits with her knees up to her chin in the now dark room; her face is both sad and frightened as her large eyes gaze straight ahead.

I say,

> Our students are living in a complex world. They have things that frighten them, thrill them, and every emotion in between, but we are increasingly forced to ignore these things because we have things we must teach. I can't do that anymore. I have to be honest with children and with you and I hope you (and perhaps your students when you're back in school) can be honest. You don't have to agree with me. There are no grades given out this week [some people laugh]. But the theme for this week is that we work on being honest with children and each other and allow our students to bring into our classrooms everything that is in their economic, social, political, linguistic, and cultural suitcases. Not for the entire day. Just find one place in the day or week—a microspace—where they can be honest and tell the truths of their lives as they understand them.

I show this quote:

> I came to kindergarten so excited and ready to learn. I came prepared with my *maleta* (suitcase) full of so many wonderful things, my Spanish language, my beautiful culture, and many other treasures. When I got there, though, not only did they not let me use anything from my *maleta*, they did not even let me bring it into the classroom.
> (Gutiérrez & Larson, 1994, p. 33)

"We're going to begin with what's on your mind. Everyday when you arrive, we get to spend twenty minutes writing, drawing from what is in your suitcase, with no interruptions. The only things that you need to know about what's on your mind are: Be honest and be willing to share what you write with the whole group or your table. Just tell your truths. We'll live this strategy and other strategies, then you make the connections to your own practice. Let's write."

It's really quiet and we write. And after 20 minutes, five people want to share with the whole group. Some are funny and some are serious and then the others share at their tables. "One more thing," I suggest to them, "just say 'thank you' to the person that shared and go on to the next person. Save conversation until everyone has shared."

During our week together, we study: the reading process (Goodman, 1996; Weaver, 2002), writing, grand conversations (Peterson & Eeds, 1990), and more. But the main focus of our work is that our lives matter and we need a place where we can bring our lives to celebrate, interrogate, study, and share them. One day I read *Fox* (Wild & Brooks, 2000), the story of three friends, betrayal, and the lingering question of whether or not we can forgive those we love when they stretch the limits of our relationship beyond what we formerly found acceptable. They ask that I read certain pages again, show certain pictures again, and talk, laugh, and even cry about the memories and relationships the book conjures up. The teachers suggest the book is not just about friendship, but is also about love, trust, and forgiveness. Some make metaphorical connections to teaching, curriculum, and professional decision-making as they reveal feelings of being betrayed by constantly changing district demands. This conversation helps frame umbrella questions:

How can we live, for ourselves, the literacy life we truly want to live?

How can we support children in doing that?

What is school really and truly for?

I return to these questions regularly during the week. And then it is Friday and our week is over. We spend the last hour of the workshop building a geodesic dome with four foot long pieces of wood, covering it with paper, and drawing out the metaphors of what it means to build something with children: a community, a literate environment, a safe place to think, a safe place to read and write, a safe place to ask questions, and a safe place to honestly interrogate the realities in which we live (Lewison et al., 2002). As I am packing up, in between hugs goodbye and well wishes, a group of teachers approaches me and suggests that the work cannot end here. It is with that request for more that the story of this book begins. Originally, we were going to site a course at these teachers' school (for university credit), but political factors at different school sites made that impossible. We did have a class, open to any teachers in the district, at a more central location. We thought we might have a study group at the school just for the teachers there, but teachers were too busy and could not commit to a weekly or even monthly meeting. The continuing of the summer work eventually came down to the graduate class and, on a more intense level, two teachers at one school that wanted me to visit regularly.

Barbara, the teacher that suggested that the work could not end with a one-week workshop, did not want to take a class. She had only one year (the coming school year) left to teach before she would retire after more than 20 years of teaching. She wanted help in her classroom; she wanted to know what it meant to live with and from children's honest truths for at least part of the day for each day of the school year. My initial response to her was that it "depends on you and the children. It depends on what comes together, who walks through the door, what they have in their *maletas*, what you have in yours, how honest you are willing to be, how much time you are willing to devote." I stopped there because I thought I was scaring her, but I wasn't.

"So come to my classroom and let's see what happens," she said. Barbara, a white teacher, at Mesa Vista Elementary School who felt like, "I still don't have it. I still don't know how to teach like this and it seems so important." During the first semester of the 2006–2007 school year, I visited every Thursday because I arranged to offer the course to the entire district at the district's teacher center on that day. I visited for the day and then drove to the teacher center to teach a class to 18 teachers from six different schools. I spent Thursday mornings in Barbara's class during her literacy time, including having lunch together. During those lunch sessions, we discussed what we saw and did and made decisions about what to do next. A second teacher, Patia, took the graduate class and joined us for lunch. Patia was beginning her ninth year of teaching. She decided to become a teacher after her children were grown up. Some of her family is from Mexico and she was born and raised in Texas, speaking Spanish in her home during her childhood. I went into Patia's classroom in the afternoons, visiting those two classrooms weekly. Having taught young children for almost twenty years, I certainly understood teaching as a private—almost intimate—act, one that many teachers did not want others to witness. But Barbara and Patia were open to my weekly visits, open to arguing with me and sharing ideas and thinking, open to questioning me and each other and the administration, and, most importantly, open to the *maletas* that their students brought to school with them.

One afternoon early in the school year as the children boarded buses to leave for home and after school programs, Barbara said to me, "I want to do something this year that the children will remember for the rest of their lives. I know I have to do the math program and the reading program in the afternoon, but there has to be something that is big and important."

"There is," I said.

"What is it?" she asked.

"I don't know. We have to listen and see."

Then I suggested that my not knowing and her not knowing were essential to our work together because we cannot know without knowing the children and their understanding of what is true for them. That's what I meant by honoring their *maletas*, by being honest, and by searching with them for what it is that matters to them. And we found a lot: sensitive, strong, and perceptive children who understood issues of language, culture, the border between the US and Mexico, economics, and what teachers need to know. In March, we were joined by a third teacher, Roberta, who traveled between all of the classrooms in the school; she was hired to help with the teaching of writing and we were fortunate to have her in Barbara's and Patia's classrooms on the days when I was at the school. Roberta was a student in the language arts methods class I taught the previous school year. She graduated as an elementary education major with a bilingual endorsement in Spanish. This book is about what we all learned together—the children, their teachers, their families to some degree, and me.

Portraits and Counterportraits

I rely upon the qualitative method of portraiture (Lawrence-Lightfoot & Davis, 1997) in this book because that method is a good tool for representing the multiple layers of interactions that occurred in the two classrooms while, at the same time, also demanding consideration of the subtleties of the various contexts that influence those interactions. However, my intent is not to present the portraits of the children and teachers at Mesa Vista Elementary School at one moment in time, suggestive of a group sitting for a photographer's or painter's portrait. The portraits in this book are more consistent with a portrait presented in a book or movie. Rather than a single moment, I present multiple moments and interpretations of those moments. I present the settings, actors, actions, and language use, both oral and written. Lawrence-Lightfoot and Davis (1997) describe portraiture this way:

> As the researcher documents the context—rich with detailed description, anticipatory themes and metaphors, and allusions to history and evolution—she must remember that the context is not static and that the actors are not only shaped by the context, but that they also give it shape. The portraitist, then, must be vigilant in recording changes in the context, some as visible and anticipatable as the shifting seasons . . . [o]ther changes in context are far more subtle.
>
> (p. 57)

It is the organic and constantly changing nature of portraiture that drew me to it as a research tool (see Appendix 1). A portrait is not case studies stacked up next to each other with a subsequent cross-case analysis. It is, instead, constant attention to multiple contexts (school, district, state, etc.) and the individuals and sub groupings within them, consistent with the complexity of life in a classroom (Peterson, 1992).

In this study, portraits are interpreted from multiple perspectives, consistent with critical literacy (Lewison, Leland, & Harste, 2007). From one perspective, the children, teachers, and communities in and around Mesa Vista Elementary School (MVE) are already portrayed in certain ways, in certain official capacities. Later in this chapter, I present components of the official portrait using the data from various local, state, and national agencies, such as the public education department, the United States Census, and the Bureau of Educational Statistics in Washington DC. This (institutional) official portrait is the one that some consider 'objective,' suggesting a deeply complex hermeneutic conundrum because this 'objective data' is presented to the public via the media and official reports as the honest and only truthful portrait of this school. In reality, the official portrait is a homogenized blend of data (also very political) that oversimplifies portraiture. Other data, using multiple perspectives and a variety of literatures, yield different portraits that are more thickly descriptive (Geertz, 1973) and unique. Since the portraits that emerge from the palette of multiple literatures and other data (e.g. children's writing rather than criterion referenced test scores) contrast so deeply with the official portrait, and not being drawn to the idea of only using 'unofficial' because of the less-than-legitimate connotation that the term carries, I use the term *counterportraits*. Counterportraits are composed through narratives, writing, interactions, and settings (contexts) and are supported by field notes and counterliteratures that consider identity, subjectivity, race, languages, interaction, and more. Counterportraits are political acts of defiance and struggle with the ultimate goal of recrafting the official portrait so that it is more robust, inclusive, and comprehensive.

The official portrait marginalizes, disenfranchises, minimalizes, and dismisses many diverse children's lives, relying upon statistical representations of large groups of students, teachers, and schools. Such work is useful and important, but when it becomes a weapon to hurt children and teachers, it takes on a political charge. Counterportraits consider the unique stories that may be used to provide specificity, in contrast to the broad strokes that statistics paint. Halliday's (1978) work on context of situation and Goffman's work (1959; 1961) influenced these analyses. Halliday discusses context of situation as composed of field, tenor, and mode. The field, in this case, two classrooms, is the institutional setting in which language happens. The tenor is the nature of the relationships between the interlocutors and mode is the type of language used, which means oral and written and the various tools through which those are expressed (on a computer, with chalk, etc.).

Understanding the layers of field, tenor and mode in classroom situations offered insights into what children chose to present and what they did not. Within school, students suppress some of who they are and where they are from. They are taught to do this in a number of ways as they make their way through school. Goffman (1959) discusses what people present to each other and what they suppress in their interactions with others. In daily interactions:

> each participant is expected to suppress his immediate heartfelt feelings, conveying a view of the situation which he feels the others will be able to find at least temporarily acceptable. The maintenance of this surface agreement, this veneer of consensus, is facilitated by each participant

concealing his own wants behind statements which assert values to which everyone present feels obliged to give lip service . . . . Together the participants contribute to a single over-all definition of the situation which involves not so much a real agreement as to what exists but rather a real agreement as to whose claims concerning what issues will be temporarily honored . . . . I will refer to this level of agreement as a 'working consensus.'

(pp. 9–10)

Goffman writes that this working consensus results in a certain degree of harmony, though he concedes that it is idealistic to think of this as much more than a somewhat superficial construct that allows for the interactions within a context to occur. Coupled with Bloome's work on procedural display (1983) in which students and teachers strive to continue a lesson at hand even when the students do not understand the concepts being taught and Mehan's work on recitation scripts in lessons (1982), the emerging sense of what occurs in many classrooms, when viewed as sites of social and cognitive interaction, is that there is often little room for honesty in school during the time when the official curriculum (Dyson, 1997) is being delivered. All the players in the classroom, when it is viewed as a dramatic setting, are involved in the unfolding script. Script, in the sense that Goffman uses it, is composed at the site of interaction and responsive to the possibilities that the norms within that context typically allow. Goffman's scripts are malleable, reflective of relationships that may change. His idea of scripts is not to be confused with the artificial script of a scripted reading or writing program, which is much more severely limited and demands little or no teacher thinking. Goffman's script is composed at the point of interaction, but has points of origin in the group's (classroom participants') histories together and multiple combinations of their subjectivities across settings. The teachers and I worked to rewrite the possibilities of this script by engaging the students as writers and thinkers who took on the task of bringing the unofficial (and previously unconsidered) into the classroom as the work of school.

Goffman (1959), perhaps foreshadowing the present work on critical literacy in classrooms, wrote, "Society is organized on the principle that any individual who possesses certain social characteristics has a moral right to expect that others will value and treat him in an appropriate way" (p. 13). He suggests that the power dynamics within interactional settings are rooted in a group's understanding of, and expectations for, what can unfold within a given setting. Although he does not untangle the political knots inherent in such a statement, he does recognize that when disruptions take place, all the players vie for new positions as the focus of power may seem vulnerable. Typically, he notes, those in power are not as vulnerable as some of the players would like, as the dominant force moves in swiftly to restore the old order. During "disruptive events . . . the interaction itself may come to a confused and embarrassing halt" (p. 12).

I did not merely document the work within the classrooms portrayed in this book. I was involved with the teachers and students in ways consistent with our search for honesty and truth. The goal was to interrupt the usual flow of events to such an extent that the students' expectations about what school is for would be reconsidered for a new 'working consensus'. Gilyard (1996) refers to this as "flipping the script." The field may stay the same, but the tenor and mode are disrupted enough to change the context of situation. The context changed because the students' relationships with their teachers and each other and the use of writing in ways they never experienced or even imagined possible in school changed. Changing an "establishment," (Goffman, 1959, p. 240) involves disruption on multiple levels including technically, politically, structurally, culturally, and dramaturgically, changing the students' and teachers' understanding of what can occur.

Within the power dynamic in each of the classrooms, the children assume roles and positions, and from those they present themselves to each other in school. In other words, as players in the classroom drama, they put on masks:

> the word *person*, in its first meaning, is a mask . . . everyone is always and everywhere more or less consciously playing a role . . . this mask is our truer self, the self we would like to be.
> (Park, 1950, pp. 249–250, in Goffman [1959, p. 19], emphasis added)

Yet in school, children may not honestly present their "truer self." Instead, they may put on their compliant or defiant masks in order to survive or resist what they understand is unfolding at school. They assume different positions and roles (wear different masks) with their friends, teachers, and various subgroups to which they belong. We worked to invite into the classroom the selves that they were in other contexts by inviting them to write about who they were, where they were from, who mattered in their lives, and what made a difference to them. We invited into the classrooms the masks beneath the masks we saw each day in an effort to compose counterportraits that are complex and detailed.

The mask that each child wears, the subjectivities that they enact (Moje, 2002), is what they become in school and for each child the pretense to which the idea of 'maskness' is connected is a tense place, saturated with affect, reflection, planning, enacting, and replanning. They compose their masks and may resent what they have composed, resist it, or comply with it as a way of avoiding punishment, meeting with success as defined by the teacher or peers, avoiding or even achieving humiliation, finding positive or negative responses from the teacher or colleagues in the class or their family, or hold it as a temporary place that is still being made. Their mask, then, is a location. It is the signifier of where and how they are living in a certain context.

Some of the children in this study became cynical "as a means of insulating their inner selves from contact with the audience" (Goffman, 1959, p. 20). The audience in the school setting is the other children and teacher in the class-room. Others became angry and withdrew. Some of the students have figured out what the teachers expect the kids to be in school and put on a "front" (Goffman, 1959, p. 35), which is their "idealized view" (p. 35) of what a student should be.

In any portrait or counterportrait certain things are concealed because of our understanding of what constitutes legitimacy in a specific context. Goffman suggests there are five reasons for which something is concealed:

1 it may be "incompatible with the view of [the] activity" (p. 43);
2 students may have made "errors" in school and learned to conceal things because of what happened during those moments (such as when the teacher says a behavior is not acceptable and the student is embarrassed);
3 something is hidden beneath what is presented so the work behind the work does not get shown (p. 44);
4 something someone considers "semi-legal, cruel, and degrading . . . ." (p. 44); and
5 there are standards up to which the actors must live publicly so they are accepted, but privately their lives are quite different, consistent with dysfunctional families that present one image to the world, but whose private lives are undisclosed to the public.

In seeking honesty with the students, we sought to legitimate and honor parts of their lives that were typically concealed at school (for the reasons listed in 1–5, above). Investigating these and making them public contributed to counterportraits that are moving, passionate, and well articulated. In subsequent chapters I return to counterportraits in order to juxtapose them with and put tension on the official hegemonic portrait of 'failing' students. The hope is that as others read the counterportraits included herein, there will be an increased chance that they will be legitimated in other (official) settings, such as departments of education and legislatures at state and national levels.

Mesa Vista Elementary School (MVE): The Official Portrait

Mesa Vista Elementary School's official portrait is not simply one of a failing school, but of a poor community with multiple problems. The broad official strokes are of a community in constant crisis with many health, emotional, economic, language, and education deficiencies. Some of the data presented in this section are not cited in order to preserve the confidentiality of the study site. Federal census, state, and local level data came from reliable sites such as the Annie E. Casey Foundation (AECF), US Census etc.

Mesa Vista Elementary School is located in rural New Mexico and con-sidered to have low population density, in this case just over 1,100 people per square mile. The total land area for the school is ten square miles and it sits almost a mile above sea level. The entire school district had a population just over 11,800 in July 2006, a 17.6 percent increase since 2000. The increase is largely due to the significantly lower price for homes and the proximity to Albuquerque, where there are many jobs. The area is a bedroom community to Albuquerque. The racial composition is: 58.7 percent Hispanic; 37.0 percent White Non-Hispanic; 27.6 percent other; 3.9 percent two or more races; 3.6 percent American Indian; and 1.2 percent Black. In the years 2001–2005, there were over 200 personal assaults in the township, making it among the highest percentage (per capita) for that crime in the state.

The district in which MVE is situated has ten elementary schools, two middle schools and two high schools and there were 8,404 students in the district during the 2006–2007 school year. There are also three 'special' schools (such as the half-day family school that relies upon families to teach reading and language arts, and a technical high school). Elementary schools had 4,688 students, middle schools had 1,446 students and there were 1,947 in high school during the year of this study. The second high school is brand new and only had ninth and tenth graders for the 2007–2008 school year. The district is rural and spread out. The district's website claims "students will learn in a safe and disciplined environment." MVE has at least one, and sometimes two, uniformed police officers on campus. They do not carry guns.

All of the students receive free lunch and there is a breakfast program, included here as an indicator of the economic poverty level. In the larger state context, on a variety of measures, New Mexico is considered one of the poorest states in the US. According to Annie E. Casey Foundation (2007), using updated data for 2006, 26 percent of NM's children live in poverty, meaning that their family's income is at 100 percent of the federal definition of poverty based on income; only Louisiana and Mississippi's children are worse off on this indicator of quality of life. Our state ranks 44th in children living in extreme poverty, meaning their family's income is 50 percent of the federal poverty level. "The federal poverty definition consists of a series of thresholds based on family size and composition. In 2000, the poverty threshold for a family of two adults and two children was $17,463" (Annie E. Casey Foundation, downloaded 9/17/07).

The 2004 data finds New Mexico at 28 child deaths per 100,000, 41st in the state rankings. We rank at 88 per 100,000 for teen deaths, 40th in state rankings. Forty-one percent of our children live in families in which no parent has full-time year-round employment, ranking us 47th in this category. In 2004, 28 percent of children were born to mothers with less than 12 years of education, ranking us 37th. Twenty-nine percent of children five and under live in poverty, ranking us 45th in the US. Over 10 percent of the students in New Mexico live with food insecurity, not knowing the source of their next meal.

The academic statistics seem dismal, too. Twenty percent of our fourth graders scored at or above the proficient level in reading in 2005, putting us at

48th in the nation. That same year, 19 percent of eighth graders scored at or above proficient reading level, putting us at 48th in this category. In 2005, 17 percent of the children in the state, age 17 and younger, did not have health insurance, also 48th in this category.

The report of the Third Annual Nest Egg Index states:

> we ranked the 500 top-performing communities and the 50 states based on their residents' personal savings and investing behavior. By measuring a dozen statistical factors—including participation in retirement savings plans, personal debt levels and home ownership—the Nest Egg Index shows the geographic regions where people are succeeding and facing difficulty with their nest eggs. In this year's results, communities that ranked highly in the Nest Egg Index continue to benefit from strong local housing markets and show a high propensity toward saving and investing in retirement vehicles such as 401(k) or pension plans. And while these communities had higher costs of living than the national average, 19 out of the top 20 also had lower debt levels.
>
> (Wachovia Securities,
> http://www.agedwards.com/public/content/sc/invedu/nest_egg_
> savings/nest_egg_index.html downloaded September 13, 2007)

The scores are indexed to a national average of 100 with 27 states scoring above the national average. Los Alamos, New Mexico scored the highest for any US city at 134.83. However, the state of New Mexico ranked 44th out of the 50 states with an index score of 92.38. This suggests the severe unequal distribution of wealth in the state that has national nuclear labs and high extreme poverty. Those in the defense industry earn six digit salaries, yet all the children at MVE receive free lunch. Los Alamos is the economic aberration in the state with some other pockets of economic wealth, such as in Santa Fe. Statewide, however, the economic wealth and accompanying high educational performance are statistically massaged away by economic and other forms of poverty as evidenced by the high rate of students not completing high school in four years (if at all). In 2005, New Mexico ranked 41st in high school graduation with 61.5 percent of our students graduating in four years. This is an 11.7 percent worsening from the report issued in 1990 (United Health Foundation, 2005, downloaded 11/21/07; this foundation relies on data from the National Center for Educational Statistics).

The Mesa Vista Elementary school boundaries appear atypical because there are two areas designated for MVE. The first area is a large rectangular shaped portion of the district, with the school located in the eastern part of the rectangle. There is a second backwards L-shaped area that is slightly north and west of the rectangle. In between the rectangle and the L-shaped area runs a thin strip that feeds into a different elementary school. It turns out that these lines were carefully drawn so that MVE would serve children from the economically poorer L-shaped area. Although almost all the students take a bus to school, there is one small neighborhood that adjoins the school property and extends across the street from the school with middle class homes, typically between 2,000 and 2,500 square feet. A new superintendent demanded an end to lines that essentially supported segregation by SES. He also demanded an end to K-2; 2-4 and 4-6 schools (another way of segregating for a while). The district would move to K-6 schools, which MVE did at the start of the 2006–2007 school year.

Finding the School

My first visit to Mesa Vista Elementary School involved many challenges, the first of which was finding the school. I left Albuquerque two hours before the scheduled meeting time to discuss with teachers from the entire school what the year's work might be. Driving almost 15 miles out of Albuquerque along the Rio Grande River, I found the exit that the school secretary said to take and found myself passing through a series of rural desert communities with some houses, but mostly trailers. The landscape rolled a bit and there were mountains far off to the east. I drove along blacktop, but many of the side roads were dirt; the countryside was scrub brush and some cactus that could survive the chilly New Mexico winters. I drove another 10 miles, relying upon landmarks and increasingly remote signs. I passed one of the schools in the district, a name that some of the teachers had mentioned during the summer. After 20 more minutes of driving along a rural road, I drove back to that school and found a teacher from the summer workshop. She directed me to the turns I needed to make and I found Mesa Vista Elementary School. The final five miles to the school run through rolling desert hills with dried tall grasses and occasional bushes. There were few houses. I was comforted to find a gas station and convenience store near one of the intersections.

The physical structure of Mesa View Elementary is dramatic, rising from the desert with a brick exterior, beautiful overhang above the front doors to keep out the sun, and silver letters spelling out its name. When I entered, the administrative office and nurse's office were on the left and a beautiful interior atrium full of plants was on the right. Down the hall were the library, cafeteria, restrooms, and counselors office. On the right were two sets of doors leading to a playground. The part of the playground close to the building is a concrete pad large enough for the three-basketball courts that were placed there. Beyond the pad is dirt, brown desert dirt with a few swing sets, but mostly dirt, right up to a fence where there is a small community of homes, beyond which there is desert for many miles. In the far distance, the new high school is barely visible as its windows reflect the sun, and beyond that there are mountains.

Mesa View Elementary is reminiscent of Goffman's "institutional display [in which] the displayed part of the institution is likely to be the new, up-to-date part . . ." (Goffman, 1961, p. 104). Goffman explains that there are "three aspects of reality . . . the concealed [from the students], that which is revealed . . . and that which is shown to visitors" (p. 120). To reach the classrooms, I leave the main building and walk through one set of exit doors. The brick and glass stop. Stretching from the main interior corridor are two long lines of classroom pods constructed of corrugated metal. Each pod consists of four classrooms, typically all at one grade level. Each classroom has one window and two doors, one leading to the playground and one to the small lobby of the quad, both of solid institutional green steel. The window is about two feet high and wide and has a blind that can be raised or lowered. I will learn that the rooms are not well heated or cooled. In the early part of the school year, when the summer desert sun is still quite intense, the rooms start off cool and then get oppressively hot as the dry heat overcomes the cooling system. Later in the year, the rooms are cold in the morning and many of the students will wear their coats indoors. As the day warms and the heating system catches up, the rooms become hot, often reaching 80–85 degrees.

From the district website I learn that Mesa Vista Elementary has not met adequate yearly progress (AYP) in the past five school years, since AYP has existed as a construct for sorting schools. The principal confirms that the school has never made AYP. When the data are disaggregated, students in the following categories had scores that were not proficient, defaulting the school to the "AYP not met" status: Hispanic, English language learners, and children with disabilities. In 2003–2004 and 2004–2005 school years, students in the "economically disadvantaged category" also were not proficient. The 2005–2006 data also shows, on a separate chart, the subgroups that decreased 10 percentage points or more in any of the areas tested. For MVE, one sub-group decreased more than 10 percent: Caucasian (in reading). The school is barely required to report scores in this category because the number of whites is so low; some years they do not have sufficient number of whites to include them in their reported data. The 2006 data showed that MVE did not reach the state goals in math (for English language learners and special education students) or reading (for students in the Hispanic, English language learner, and special education subgroups). The website for the district also lists subgroups increasing five percent or more from 2005. The overall group of 'all students' and the subgroups of Hispanic, English language learner, and FRLP (Free/Reduced Lunch Program) showed this improvement in math. In reading, Hispanic students increased five percent or more from last year's proficiency. Note that the groups may have improved more than five percent but still retain the "AYP not met" status because the gains were not sufficient enough to move them above the cut off line for proficiency.

Although the 2006–2007 school year results (the year of this study) for MVE were not on the district's website at the time of this writing, the results were posted at the school on the first day of the next school year (2007–2008) when I made a follow-up trip to the school in August 2007. Large graphs (18"×24") were posted in the main corridor outside the school library, just down the hall from the main entrance and the office. Some grade levels did meet AYP for some of the categories; however, the "students with disabilities" and "English language learner" categories were not proficient and once again the school received the "AYP not met" status.

Homelessness

I learned about the economic poverty in which the children at MVE live by visiting official websites, reading their writing, supporting their research into their families, and visiting their homes. Street (1995) explains that the belief that literacy can cure poverty is wrongheaded and that we would offer our economically poor individuals greater hope by getting them out of poverty; then we'd see a rise in literacy—not just scores but actual engagement in official literacies. Moll, Amanti, Neff, and Gonzalez (1992) found many ways in which community members relied upon each other to navigate the literacy that comes home from school and also documented the wealth of literacy activities in which economically poor families engaged. Although this study is not specifically about poverty, it was always present as children attempted to wear the mask of 'regular kid,' meaning middle class, but knew they had little or no financial security. Some (condescending) people in the district refer to two large sections of the MVE area as "Little Juarez" because so many of the families come from Mexico and are economically poor. At this point, as a way of contextualizing the socioeconomic lives of the children you are about to meet, I briefly consider the official portrait of homelessness and how the children of MVE fit into it.

The principal of MVE shared with me a one-page form entitled "Student Residency Questionnaire" that is in English on one side and Spanish on the other. At the top of the form one of the sentences reads, "The answers to this residency information help determine the services the student may be eligible to receive." The first question asks where the student is presently living and has four choices: in a shelter (for abused, homeless); with more than one family in a house, mobile home or apartment (other family rents or owns house, mobile home or apartment); in a motel, car, campsite or park; with friends or family members (other than parent/guardian). There is a separate box that may be checked if none of these apply. Although all of the families had not yet returned their forms in the first month of school, of those that had returned them over 120 students are considered homeless. This is over 20 percent of the students at MVE, which has a student population of just over 500.

Section X of the Elementary and Secondary Education Act (US DOE, 2001b) lays out the criteria for homelessness. In Section 723, we learn that the goal of the Homeless Assistance act is to "create and disseminate nationwide a public notice of the rights of homeless children and youths." Further, a report is to be issued that describes the children's and youths' "state," meaning the conditions of their homelessness. The Act demands that states develop specific plans for homeless children and outlines financial support to enact approved plans. The plans may include items from a list of "authorized activities" that includes "tutoring . . . enriched educational services . . . professional development [for teachers] . . . referral services . . . for medical, dental, mental, and other health services . . . early childhood programs . . . before- and after-school mentoring and summer programs . . . needs [due to] domestic violence . . . school supplies, . . . and emergency assistance needed to enable homeless children and youths to attend school." It is also expected that states will work to find affordable housing for homeless children and youths and the adults responsible for them.

The definition of homelessness is specific:

(i)   children and youths sharing the housing of other persons due to loss of housing, economic hardship, or similar reason; are living in motels, hotels, trailer parks, or camping grounds due to lack of alternative adequate accommodations; are living in emergency or transitional shelters; are abandoned in hospitals; or are awaiting foster care placement;

(ii) children and youths who have a primary nighttime residence that is a public or private place not designed for or ordinarily used as a regular sleeping accommodation for human beings;

(iii) children and youths who are living in cars, parks, public spaces, abandoned buildings, substandard housing, bus or grain stations, or similar settings; and

(iv) migratory children . . . who qualify as homeless . . . living in circumstances described in clauses (i) through (iii).

(US DOE, downloaded 9/23/07 from
http://www.ed.gov/policy/elsec/leg/esea02/pg116.html≅c1031)

But all of the children in this book live somewhere. They have a place in mind (sometimes two or three places) where they know they will go at night. The leaky trailer, the overcrowded rooms, the unpredictable moods and dramas that will unfold are, for them, the way things are in a home. Officially, some of them are homeless. The counterportraits to be presented in the following chapters are of children that live in the US and in Mexico. Although they are federally defined as homeless, they are transnational (Guerra, 1998), translingual, and transcultural as they live in two places or live in one place with strong ties to roots in another. They have stories that, they come to find, matter. They matter because they offer a rich rather than poor portrait of strong rather than weak and intelligent rather than low performing students. It is to those officially ignored stories—counterportraits—that I now turn.

Chapter 2

Writers Reveal Themselves

little by little his sense of self and identity was chiseled and fragmented and crumbled in small but irrevocable ways . . . [he] began to bend his shoulders . . . his dazzling smile became progressively a sad and lamentable frown.

(Pedraza del Prado, 2008, p. 50)

In this chapter I explain my deepening involvement with the children and their teachers in the search for truths. I began to understand the ways in which that search was contextualized and bounded in the individual classrooms and the lives of the children and teachers and to see the ways in which school and life experiences "chiseled and fragmented." I also saw moments of confirmation and affirmation (the first glimmers of counterportrait activity) embedded within the constantly looming shadows of the official portrait of failure with which the children and teachers lived.

Becoming More than an Observer

It is early October and I have visited Mesa Vista Elementary since August. On a typical day, I divide my time between two very different worlds, one a fifth grade classroom and the other a sixth grade classroom. Some mornings, when the fifth grade class goes to their computer class, I visit the sixth grade to observe. When the two teachers and I meet for lunch, we discuss what we noticed, questions we have, and ideas for teaching and learning. When I arrive at the sixth grade today, the 27 students are sitting in rows, facing the front of the room. I sit at the back of the class as they switch from math to literacy at 10:45. Patia, the sixth grade teacher, raises her voice, "This is my classroom." Her voice gets louder, "Do you hear me? My classroom." Then she says it in Spanish even louder. The class is for English as a second language (ESL) students and Patia has told me that she has the expectation that no Spanish will be spoken as part of the official curriculum; she will use it to support newly arrived students if they speak no English and to reprimand almost all the students individually or collectively. The child that is the focus of her anger slumps in his chair. His name is Ricardo. I'll get to know him quite well as a sensitive and warm writer, and a fighter who will face any adversary. Standing close to 6 feet tall and weighing over 160 pounds, he's huge for a sixth grader.

Patia is taking the graduate class that I am teaching in the district on Thursday evenings. She was also in the weeklong summer workshop that I taught and was one of the teachers that wanted me to visit her classroom once school resumed. During graduate class sessions, she often describes how noisy and uncooperative her sixth graders are. She's not shy about telling her colleagues how much she has to yell at her students, something I witnessed at many visits. Patia does not support bilingual programs, even though she and all but two of her students speak Spanish at home and, quite often, to each other in school. She believes that English is the language of the United States and her students need to learn it; Spanish, she believes, is acceptable at home, but not for school. She uses only English language textbooks. Her students are not allowed to turn around, chew gum, have a water bottle on their desk, get up without permission, or a host of other things that Patia gets to do. Even in August when the school year begins, the students complete math worksheets in preparation for the state test in March (based on the state standards). When one student gets the answer, she or he calls it out and the rest of them color in the bubble next to that answer. Reading instruction involves a basal and worksheets, too. The school purchased a supplemental computerized reading program for students scoring below grade level so there are eight computers in each classroom. These machines (in both fifth and sixth grade classrooms) will become instrumental in our work.

As the basal lesson ends and the kids are going to lunch, Patia and I have a minute to talk. "Show me what they've written this year," I offer.

"They write all day," she says.

"Did I see any of that writing?" I ask.

"Well, yes, you did."

"Oh . . . do they ever write longer pieces, than say a sentence on their worksheets?"

"Wellll," she explains, "when we get closer to Halloween, they'll write scary stories."

I learned in the summer workshop and again early in the year that Patia wants me to be honest with her. She welcomes questions and questions me; she welcomes challenges to her practice and challenges me, typically in the form of a question. I will learn that she is dedicated to her students' learning. I may not agree with everything she does and she does not always agree with me, but we talk honestly to each other. She heard me say "tell your truths" a lot during the summer and she tells me hers with an intensity that I appreciate.

The next week I arrive and she's screaming at them. She tells me, over their heads, that, "For the next six full weeks all the kids in the school will NOT be allowed to talk or whisper or communicate in any way during lunch."

"Why not?" I ask.

"They're too noisy. They talk too much, all the time."

I've seen and heard this level of noise. Patia struggles to keep their attention during reading lessons and when she asks them to complete assignments independently, they often spend the time talking. She walks over to me so we can talk.

"You're upset today," I say to her.

Silence.

"Can I teach today?" I ask. "I won't if that offends you. I'm just curious about . . ."

"Go ahead," she says. "You'll see."

"I know. They're a really hard group."

Their last year's teacher is in the graduate class too. He said he screamed more than ever at this group of kids.

So there I am in front of the class. I'm the only white person in the room. I'm the only bald person in the room. I tell the class both of these facts. They look a bit stunned after the first. Some giggle after the second.

"The problem with school," I begin, "is that we have to be liars here. We have to say and do and be things that just are not true. That's what I hated about school. And things happened in my house and I never ever ever would think to tell these things in school. Today, for 15 minutes, you get to write your own truth. You don't have to read it, you don't have to show it me."

"What about her?" one of the students asks, moving his chin towards Patia.

"You don't have to show her, either. You can read it to us, if you want, but you don't have to."

Silence.

"You can't talk at all during this time," Patia says sternly, startling me. I had reached for my pencil and no one was talking.

Patia calls out a boy's name and speaks somewhat harshly to him in Spanish about being serious.

Fully intending to share my truths with the students, I write:

> School was a lonely place for me. My mom was so sick when I was younger, having cancer before many kids even knew what the word meant. She had three different surgeries, times when we were left alone as my dad went to the hospital. We were so scared. He hired a woman to come and cook for us, but we didn't have money for that and the three of us (my two sisters and me) couldn't figure out how we could afford that. We didn't like her cooking. We found out later that my uncle paid for it. No one in school knew, no teacher or other kids knew. I was alone with this fear.

After fifteen minutes, I ask who would like to read and no one does. So I read my piece and ask for any comments or thoughts about it. No one says anything.

In class that night, we were going to read *Chicano Borderlander* (Martínez, 1994), so I took out a copy and read it to the class.

Chicano Borderlander
Oscar J. Martínez

A Chicano Borderlander
I am
Part Mexican, part American.
Two currents feed my soul:
one southern, mestizo, Third World,
one Northern, Anglo-Saxon, First World.

Straddling two nations, two cultures,
belonging to both, belonging to neither,
One moment totally sure of who I am,
the next baffled by my duality.

Bilingual, bicultural, binational,
embracing two social systems,
assuming multiple identities,
criss-crossing ethnic boundaries,
negotiating and taming opposing worlds.

Spare me the hellish choice
of taking sides
between the United States and Mexico.
One is my home, the other my nurturer.

On the border,
conflict of the heart of the nation
has but one cure:
recognition of jointness
and jointness in resolution.

"What do you think of this poem?" I ask.

"Read it again," one of the boys calls out. I don't know their names that well and voices seem to jump out, such as this request to reread. I read the poem again.

"I don't understand it," a girl calls out.

"What's bilingual?" another asks.

"Yeah, and what's bicultural and binational?"

I give them the copies I was going to give the graduate class and read the poem again. Then, I talk about the poem, adding a few times, "This is just what I think. It's not the right answer. There is no right answer. It's how I understand Oscar Martínez's truth about who he is and where he's from. You might think it's different. Do you? What do you think he means?" I'm talking to fill the eerie silence, but also to demonstrate (Smith, 1983) how to respond to a poem.

Silence.

I talk about my own life in two worlds, as Jewish kid and a poor kid, and a kid who felt like he didn't understand things a lot (like my mother's sicknesses).

"That's more than two worlds," someone calls out.

"Yes," I laugh. They do too. Some of them, anyway.

"Any thoughts?" I ask.

An eternity passes, maybe fifteen seconds.

"It's about us," comes a voice from the back of the room.

"How?" I ask.

"We live in two worlds and one is in English and one is in Spanish."

"Who else?" I ask.

Some others talk, making references to lines in the poem that they're rereading. "I like the part about being Mexican and being American," one of the girls says.

"Read that line," I say.

She reads it.

More silence.

"How come you chose that line?" I ask.

But questions can be considered punishment for children in school, something I remember as I am doing all this asking. Authority figures ask things like, "Why did you do that?" or "Can't you be quiet?" Questions don't always demand answers and when they do many children fall into recitation scripts in which they expect there to be one right answer (Mehan, 1982).

One of the boys talks about being between two countries, still having family in Mexico and visiting them when they can, and a few tell briefly about crossing the border at El Paso. Patia asks the class, "Why do people have to call us Hispanic or Chicana? I'm not a Chicana. I'm a Mexican American. Why is it such a big deal? Why is it so difficult to call me that?" The kids are quiet. Her tone was harsh and almost accusatory, but I'm not sure if she was angry with me, the poet, or some people trying to label her. At this point, the tone of the room was changed by her anger as kids seem to withdraw physically, their bodies sinking, and cognitively as they become silent.

Then, one of the students calls out a reference to his own writing. He doesn't read it but he says he wrote like Martínez, "about being in two worlds and not wanting to choose one."

"You want to read it?" I ask.

Silence.

No offers to read and there are no further thoughts expressed out loud about the Martínez poem.

"It's almost time for you to go to lunch," I say. "Reread what you wrote, think about what I wrote and think about the poem and what people in here said. Write more. Write until it's time to go eat."

Before returning to my own writing, I scan the desktops around the room and see that many papers are blank because many of the students hadn't written when I gave them time. I begin to write more and when I glance up, I see they're writing. Verdad happens to look at me at the same time I'm surveying the room and I smile. Her face is intense, not returning a smile. There were a few whispers, but I couldn't hear what was being said. "Remember!" comes the teacher's voice. "He said to write, not talk! Write!"

"If you want me to read yours, I'll take it with me and give it back next Thursday with some comments," I say. "It is time for you to go to lunch."

Patia tells them to stay seated until she tells them to line up. "When I call you, then you go. You have to be quiet." She calls them by rows to line up.

First Pieces of Writing

Twenty-four children gave me pieces to read. I wrote back to each child, right on their pieces, writing more than they wrote. Their short pieces focus on being from Mexico and living in the US, much like Martínez's piece. They weren't sure of how much to reveal nor what would happen to those revelations. Their tentativeness was resonant with my own because we were all exploring new writing ground. Patia's influence on the pieces is pronounced as, for example, in the case of Vianca who first weighs through her teacher's ideas before reaching her own truths.

> I'm sad because the Americans call us, the Mexicans, all kinds of names and I'm sad too because my family fights a lot and I'm sad too because I always hear my friends talking about their dad and I don't have a dad.

Mercedes' family is very religious and believes that school is a privilege that every student should take seriously. Her first piece reflects those values, but also her desire to present more of her fashion-mindedness in school.

> What I don't think is fair at school is that we have to wear uniforms to school. We only get one day to wear jeans but you have to wear a uniform shirt. I would like it if we could wear jeans all week. It would be better because a lot of people try to do their best at school but a lot of them won't. That's one thing I don't like because there is a lot of kids which want to come to school and the kids who don't pay attention shouldn't come to school.
>
> Mercedes

The Martínez poem resonated with Verdad's experiences in school, including getting into trouble for defending her roots in Mexico. Her passion for justice rises on more than one occasion and leads her to take actions that consistently get her in trouble.

> I hate when I get in trouble at school. I don't like when they made some game of Mexicans that are crossing the boarder and they shoot people. This is what happened to me at school, in [another town] one day: We were playing soccer and some kids just started to call us stupid Mexicans. We got mad. They told us bad words and other stuff. D—, a friend of mine, even gave a black eye to some kids named —. Just for calling us stupid Mexicans. We got in trouble and they did, too. We were really mad at them.

Corazon liked the format of the Martínez poem and, to some degree, appropriated it as she composed her piece. She is witness to violence that she can neither explain nor understand. She is one of the few to title her piece and does so in a way that challenges her teacher's desire to not be called Chicana.

Chicanos

> Part Mexican. Part American. Two cultures disturbing one another for many years.
> When is the fight from one culture to another going to end?
> Probably in one year or probably never.
> Americans being rude to Mexicans and Mexicans hating Americans for no reason.
> When will this end?

Ricardo's narrative introduced him to me as a writer that has a strong sense of family and identification with Mexico.

> I feel like I'm on the border in many ways. I am Mexican-American. My dad is Mexican. My mom is American. I want to go see my grandma in Mexico because I have only seen her once when I was 6. But I feel like I have to stay here in America.

> Sometimes I wish Mexico was right next to my house so I can visit whenever. So sometimes I feel like a Mexican-American. Sometimes I just feel like an American. Sometimes I feel like a Mexican. But I like to think that I'm both.

After using her first sentence to defer to her teacher's concerns about what one is called, Esperanza writes a border story, another of many that I will hear and read as the children explain their lives in multiple worlds. Many of the details, the stuff that happened between the lines, are things that Esperanza told me she didn't know, such as whether or not large sums of money were found and paid for her mom's release. The children live with (or perhaps choose to limit their writing to) partial stories, contradictions, and misunderstandings, an idea I discuss further in Chapter 5.

> I am a Mexican American. One time my mom had to go to Mexico because my grandpa was very sick and my mom did not have papers so my dad told my mom to go.
>
> When my mom went to Mexico, she took my little brothers. And did not take my sister or me. When she was coming, they caught her and they called my dad. She was in jail. They wanted a lot of money to let her go. They let her go and my uncle went for my brothers. At the end, they gave the papers to my mom. Now she could go to Mexico. That was very happy.

Lorenzo is a very resistant writer and, according to Patia, has handed in little written work and is easily distracted by friends in the class. Not only is he sensitive to border issues, but he also has a sense of globalization and workforce.

> I feel that it's not fair that they don't let the Mexicans across the border. They're the ones that do all the work here, like building houses and everything like that.

Carlos seems to also appropriate the teacher's point of view, complaining about what he is called. He goes deeper as he contemplates hatred.

> Why can't people call us Mexicans? They have to call us like Chicanos. Why can't they call us Mexicans or by our names. How would they like it if we would call them something else and who cares if we come from Mexico and even if we talk Spanish only. We are stuck in a place with hate.

This first round of writing was both powerful and exhausting for me as a researcher and teacher. Being in front of a classroom full of children is not the same as teaching at the university and I found myself full of doubts about how to manage and connect with so many writers. Kozol (2007) describes this too, as he visits a first grade classroom and the teacher challenges him to teach about nonfiction. He discusses talking animals, clearly not following the teacher's request accurately and she points it out to the children, who vote him into time out. I wasn't literally in time out, but the children's lack of trust in each other and in me, as evidenced by their unwillingness to read their pieces, was isolating.

Initiating Data Analysis

I saw my roles in the classrooms as twofold; I was there to help teachers learn about teaching writing, and I was, eventually, there as a researcher. As a helper, I could read and respond to any of the children's pieces. As a researcher, it mattered that many students with families from Mexico are not documented as legal visitors to the US and fear any form that must be completed. The Human Subjects forms are extremely complicated and intimidating to many families because of all of the specifics that must be included and the language used (even in Spanish). The requirement of multiple signatures, one for written pieces that children produce and one for photographs and video, and the multiple forms, one for the children and another for adults, added to the intimidation. Eventually I obtained almost half of the students' permissions.

As I typed the students' work, I began to look for points of analysis—and there seemed to be many. As the year progressed, many of these points reemerged as issues important to the children's lives in and out of school. I knew I had to consider: one teacher as a very loud presence, the writing and sharing voices of the children, the nature of the school context as a place to present one facet of self (a mask), the power of a community of writers to produce and inhibit writers, living in an English school world and a Spanish home world, and more. The idea of analyzing data into categories by "comparing incidents applicable to each category . . . integrating categories, [and] . . . delimiting . . . theory" is the constant comparative method (Glaser, 1965, p. 439) of qualitative research. I relied upon that method and domain analyses (Spradley, 1980) to understand issues that arose during this first writing session with the sixth graders, keeping in mind that I wanted to compose portraits. Following subsequent meetings with them, I further analyzed the data, either finding new categories, confirming the importance of categories, or disconfirming categories as inaccuracies, incomplete, or not fully substantiated. Analyzing the data this way led me to extensive reading as I searched for other researchers and theorists that would help me understand what unfolded in the classrooms. A more complete discussion of method is presented in Appendix 1.

The number of pieces of writing from this first writing session felt like an immense responsibility. I wanted to honor every piece for which I had research permission by including them in this book. I also wanted to provide a sense of the many issues the children were willing to write about and the variety of voices I faced each week. These multiple voices are the essences of counter-portraits and their continued emergence and elaboration during our writing time are offered here and explained further in subsequent chapters as evidence that the children understand their positions and roles within, and beyond, the school context. I could not sequester shorter pieces to an appendix, essentially isolating them from the other pieces composed at a given time in a specific context, although I did so for some longer pieces (Appendix 2) so that chapters would not be overly burdensome to read. Each writer may be tracked individually by referring to their names in the index to locate the succession of their pieces over the course of the book.

Teacher as Screamer

Patia yells at her students often, reminding them "this is my classroom" and demanding that they comply with her demands for silence, attention, and completion of assignments. Some students comply while others resist passively or actively. Since her yelling was first presented in this chapter, it is necessary to interpret it to some degree. It's important to keep in mind that Patia wants her students to succeed and, concomitantly, feels extreme pressure from administrators that they perform well on many evaluations and tests that occur within the reading program, are part of the state criterion-referenced tests, and many more. Although she sometimes discusses students' levels on some of these assessments, she reported that she was never taught how to use them to inform her instruction. Barbara, the fifth grade teacher, confirms this lack of connection between the assessments and instruction, explaining that, "They want us to use data-based instruction, but they don't tell us how to do that. We just keep testing and testing." The pressure Patia feels visibly shakes her as her eyes widen and she talks at lunch about how the expectations being placed on her are unreasonable. The pressure she feels often manifests itself as anger, demands for silence and performance, and impatience when she is in her classroom. She is a casualty of the focus on adequate yearly progress.

Patia's anger is not simply unfocused rage, although it may be misfocused. She has appropriated, to some degree, the official portrait of her students and the school. Her concerns, similar to many teachers at the school, are rooted in the stigma that saturates failing status. The urgency she feels for her students' success is about their performance on state tests and what she believes those tests may imply for their futures. She wants them to succeed in the years ahead; her fear is that the tests indicate they cannot. That fear is expressed in screams; the strictness she exhibits as a teacher is connected to her feelings of professional vulnerability. She fears others see her as failing and as incompetent. She tells the students it is her classroom as a way of gaining control over their behavior and over their attentiveness to, and success in, schoolwork. They are in her world, one dominated by the official portrait but conflicted with the urgency to prove it wrong. Yet, her screaming may mean even more. A teacher's use of harshness, not listening to the children's points of view, and stating her own perspective with loud strength and conviction are vehicles for compliance or silencing (Fine, 1996) the voices of speakers and writers. Publicly embarrassing those that are hesitant, different, or even those that agree but do so beyond the boundaries of acceptable behavior (for example by standing up because they're so excited about agreeing) further silences those voices. The students' understanding of the official curriculum (Dyson, 1997)—

what is acceptable in school—increasingly narrows, for some, to the point of not knowing the limits.

There is no abundance of descriptions in the professional literature of teachers yelling at their students, but children are yelled at, publicly embarrassed, and described in extremely negative ways by some teachers. Polakow's (1993) interview with seven year old Heather's teacher is among the saddest, as the teacher angrily states:

> This child does not know the difference between right and wrong—she absolutely does not belong in a normal classroom with children . . . . I've given up on this child—she's socially dysfunctional—three times now we've caught her stealing free lunch and storing it in her desk to take home!
>
> (p. 138)

Polakow explains that Heather's mother is frequently hospitalized, has lost her job, and, quite often, there is no food in the house. Heather takes food home so that she can eat on weekends.

The situation is somewhat similar for first grader Pam (Norton, 2005), whose novice teacher is required to allow a demonstration teacher to teach the class, except that Pam fights back. The demonstration teacher screams at Pam for getting a chair when all the children were told to sit on the floor. Pam does not want to get her clothes dirty because her family can afford only two school uniforms. Norton writes, "Pam's actions affirm her poor and lower-class identities and seek to disrupt the violence that devalues and erases lower-class perspectives . . . " (p. 121). Further, yelling is "an inequitable classroom management strategy that adult educators use to inflict violence . . . and maintain inequitable hierarchies" (p. 123). Norton's words, although deeply troubling because of their accuracy about yelling as a violent act, haunt me because I was witness to such acts and, although I was honest with Patia about how troubling the yelling was, I was not instrumental in helping it stop. Patia was committed to yelling as a way of managing her classroom. Norton explains that young children's responses are often dismissed as belligerence, inappropriate behavior, and failure to comply with the rules that teachers have set up in their classrooms. She writes that "teacher yelling is unfair, a violent erasure of children's identities, and in inequitable pedagogy that privileges adults . . . educators who yell at children maintain hierarchical relationships of power since power is maintained within most schools so that children can't yell back at adults . . ." (p. 124).

A strong voice and swift acts of punishment may get results that the power figure finds acceptable or even pleasing, but the deeper levels of learning may be obscured. Dyson (2001) discusses the case of Megan, a young girl whose brother, David, has just fixed her toy vacuum. David wants to play with it, but so does Megan and after a conversation with their mother, Megan decides that perhaps boys can play with vacuum cleaners. However, Dyson raises the question of whether Megan has "temporarily acquiesced to a higher power" or been truly "internally persuaded" (p. 6), the latter being an idea from Bakhtin (1981, p. 346). School children often acquiesce to avoid further trouble with their teacher, to gain the teacher's acceptance, or to avoid other repercussions. In the sixth graders' first pieces of writing during our work together, there is evidence of appropriation of the teacher's perspective. The focus on test preparation in this classroom, daily from the very first week of school, may have overflowed into this writing experience as the children search for the 'right answer' in order to move to the next piece of work put before them. Later experiences will bear this out as the children struggle with what to write, seeking to please me, the teacher, and each other—all as means of avoiding (or perhaps ignoring, bracketing, protecting, or suppressing are more accurate descriptors) their own voices as writers. The power dynamics of school demand that Patia's students comply, which grows out of Patia's compliance with the effects of the official portrait of Mesa Vista Elementary School.

Strictness, Power, and Microaggressions

A teacher works at the nexus between the official portrait and possible portraits. She has the power to cultivate potential or to convince students that they really are who others say they are. Any act of violence contributes to an unknown volatility that may erupt at any point in socially acceptable or unacceptable ways. When children's home lives are punctuated with violence and school is consistent with that, we are setting children up, but not for 'at-riskness.' They are not as much at risk as we are. For, as I hope you will see in the coming chapters, there is a huge amount of talent, thoughtfulness, insight, and sensitivity that we are at risk of losing or at risk of being used in harmful (even self or other destructive) ways if it goes untapped.

The concept of 'microaggressions' comes from Critical Race Theory and applies to some of the children in this study because of the ways in which they are treated. Microaggressions are defined as "subtle, stunning, often [seemingly] automatic, exchanges which are 'put downs' of blacks by offenders" (Pierce, Carew, Pierce-Gonzalez, & Wills, 1978, p. 66). Racism, Pierce et al. argue, is rarely manifested in overt acts of aggression but in small, subtle exchanges that, in their totality, work to create a subjectivity of "lesser" for the receiver. Others have reported on microaggressions against Chicana and Chicano scholars (Solórzano, 1998) and against black students on mostly white campuses (Solórzano, Ceja & Yosso, 2000). This book is not primarily about race, but race matters here, as do primary language, primary discourse, socioeconomic status, culture, and the fact that children are required to be in school, where they live, seemingly (to them), at the discretion of teachers. The children in Patia's classroom are subjected to microaggressions in the form of yelling. Yelling 'chisels' away and tears at the children's sense of self, identity, and relationship (both with peers and the teacher) as they are humiliated as the target of the yelling. Yelling is a way to control bodies, demanding children be in a certain place and a certain way. It is a way to enforce and reinforce power over content, the use of time, and of controlling the classroom agenda, demanding that the children marginalize their needs and interests. Metaphorically, even the walls of the school screamed at the children as their test results from the previous year assume a central place in the main hallway. These microaggressions (and others) contribute to the children's appropriation of their official portrait by chiseling away at their beliefs about what school can do (it's supposed to help you reach goals, have a better life, etc.) and who they can be as students (smart, productive, and competent).

But my goal is not to portray Patia as intentionally mean. When she discusses her grandchildren, her own family, and different parts of her personal life, she becomes softer, more animated, and typically reaches out to gently touch others in the conversation as a way of bringing them into her passion about the people she is discussing. Grumet (1988) explains some of the tension between motherhood and teaching, noting that, "[w]e have burdened the teaching profession with contradictions and betrayals that have alienated teachers from our own experience, from our bodies, our memories, our dreams, from each other, from children, and from our sisters who are mothers to those children" (p. 57). Thus, it is not only the students whose subjectivities reflect a socially constructed fragile and vulnerable state. Teachers, most of them women, find themselves living narratives and painting self-portraits counter to those they imagined when they first entered the profession. Patia, too, is the target of microaggressions as day after day she is told to follow programs upon which she is told she may not reflect and from which she may not deviate. The goal of this book is not to cast blame, but to deepen our understanding of the ways in which subjectivities are expressed or marginalized in the portraits composed for, in and by schools. Some of the portraits that are ultimately composed contribute to microaggressions against the very ones that were, according to some, supposed to be nurtured and nurturing in schools. I write *according to some* intentionally because not everyone believes that schools (or even families) should be nurturing places.

Lakoff (2002) writes about two views of the child, suggesting that some view the child from the "strict father" perspective, meaning that children must be taught to be compliant to all authority, but particularly those in the family and school. The other perspective is that of "nurturing parent," a view of the child as a unique individual in our care as parents and, in the case of this study, teachers. Lakoff notes that this is not a perpetual dichotomy because different contexts and relationships may place a child in one or the other of these views at different times. I would argue that for children in poverty the most consistent view of the child is one in which she or he is seen from the strict father perspective. Patia has this view. Schools, for such children, exist to teach compliance and to indoctrinate them into the school-as-future-workforce model. It is mostly in referencing children living in economic poverty that we hear "chastening concerns as to their future economic value, their 'utility' and their 'productivity'" (Kozol, 2007, p. 20). Documents such as the renewal of the Elementary and Secondary Education Act (US DOE, 2001a) specifically detail expectations for economically poor children, whom the act refers to as "disadvantaged" (in its very first lines and in large font). The act is strict in terms of expectations, including adequate yearly progress on statewide tests and the types of reading programs that the children must endure.

Children not living in economic poverty may experience such programs, but their lives beyond the walls of the school and the opportunities afforded to them counterbalance school. Further, advantaged children are not typically in failing schools (yet) so their teachers have more room to make professional decisions about curriculum. Even when strict programs that make little sense (Altwerger, 2005) are instituted at more privileged schools, parents may not defer to the school's program and demand that their children receive more intellectually stimulating (nurturing) experiences in school. This leads to the quite predictable overabundance of "gifted" children in higher income and less racially diverse schools (de Valenzuela, Copeland, Qi, & Park, 2006). The strictness with which Patia administered curriculum, perhaps seeming harsh to some, is nonetheless reflective of an articulated view of childhood that continues to be part of children's experiences in school, particularly those from diverse and economically poor populations.

Strict Schools and the Search for Joy

It is in school settings like MVE that teachers are required to use strictly scripted reading and writing programs. Such programs reduce teachers to readers-of-the-script status, as they deliver programs that often make little sense to children (Meyer, 2001). Shannon (1989) refers to such teachers as technicians because their roles as substantive thinkers have been confiscated by restrictive and oppressive layers of demands from their district, state, and federal levels.

Typically, it is 'for' economically poor children that legislation and programs are composed because these children are constructed as the defective scape-goats responsible for many of our society's ills. Every effort must be made to teach them to read in order to remedy the ills and the evil they perpetrate on society. Street (1995) explains the wrong-headedness of such thinking as he suggests that teaching children to read does not change the economic realities in which they live. However, changing the economic realities leads to conditions more conducive to learning to read and to the betterment of social conditions. For example, a single mother that makes sufficient salary at one job so that her family has medical and dental coverage, her children have enough to eat and are clothed, and her family has a decent place in which to live, may provide the deeper and more spiritual care that a child needs to succeed not only in school but as a productive and thoughtful member of society. However, among the poor, many do not have sufficient income from two or even three jobs to create such a context for their children.

It is, supposedly, 'for' the economically poor that there exists the strict environment that treats all children the same, claiming that such treatment is equity in its purest form. All children get the same curriculum and, therefore, all are expected to succeed (Ohanian, 1999). Yet the reality is that economically poor children are deprived of experiences found in higher socioeconomic schools. Under the guise of a commitment to enhanced school performance, field trips at MVE are severely limited and often questioned as to their relevance to student performance. Most trips are only allowed after the year's testing is over. The children and teachers are also expected to comply with the district curriculum and any interference with curriculum may be viewed harshly, as part of the "zero-tolerance measures [found in] many urban, low-income schools" (Lewis & Solórzano, 2006, p. 63). I would add that this is true at rural low-income schools as well. Lewis and Solórzano present one of the most dismal accounts of school for the economically poor suggesting that schools are "creating one of the central preconditions for sustaining an ever-expanding prison industry: a criminalized population" (p. 64). In their analysis, school serves as a pipeline for prisons. They go so far as to use the metaphor of school as concentration camp and suggest that:

> A discourse of war, terror, and siege justifies or legitimates the transformation of the school into a [concentration] camp like space where a culture of violence and neglect is not curbed but sustained, where students are not taught but rather policed or simply expunged from the educational system, and where behaviors that disrupt the 'normal' functioning of learning become the dysfunctional norm.
>
> (p. 66)

I didn't find such severe conditions at MVE, but my fear is that rural, diverse, and economically poor children may find school coming closer and closer to such a model. As teachers are forced to set aside their often altruistic reasons for becoming teachers, such as their deep sense of caring (Noddings, 1984), they find themselves doing and saying things that are consistent with the description above (see also Grumet, 1988). Lewis and Solórzano discuss a school in Boston that was locked down after a shooting. "Seventeen students were arrested, lockers were raided, the school was placed on lockdown, and suspects were detained . . ." (pp. 66–67). When students are not safe at school and risk being shot, we would expect severe responses. However, we need to locate ways of doing so that "train, normalize, or rehabilitate [rather than] punish [innocent] students through the shock-and-awe tactics of war" (p. 67). The war and camp metaphors are powerful ones because they are suggestive of the trauma that students experience when they are treated in such harsh ways and the post traumatic effects we might anticipate later in their lives.

Put simply, school, for the economically poor, rural, bilingual children in this study, is not a joyful place unless teachers struggle to find or actively open spaces to teach reflective of their caring and nurturing selves. The idea that learning could or should be joyful is reflective of the nurturing parent view of the child, but is not found in the many documents that shape the contexts in which children's and teachers' school portraits are painted:

> The truth is that in all the documents I read that come from Washington, or from the various state capitals, or from the multitude of government-supported institutes where goals are set and benchmarks for performance of our students are spelled out in what is usually painstaking detail, I never come upon words such as 'delight' or 'joy' or 'curiosity'—or, for that matter, 'kindness,' 'empathy,' or 'compassion for another child.' Nothing, in short, that would probably come first for almost any teacher working with young children.
>
> (Kozol, 2007, p. 14)

This study became a search for joy as much as for truths. Joy involves sustained commitments, learning, sharing, presenting, viewing, sweating, crying, wondering, searching, finding, not finding, and many of the categories into which the immense amount of data in this study were organized and are presented in the chapters in this book. For the writers in this book, joy meant unraveling and critiquing their lives, the lives of others in their community, and the way the community is and what it does. Joy meant truth-seeking and truth-telling; this was hard work, not always happy, but *joy* seems to be the word that captures the feelings within the sense of accomplishment that was felt. This was no easy or romantic task. It involved pushing by me and the teachers and each of the students—pushing to make meaning and make sense of what they were finding out about themselves and those they loved. For some, joy meant finally having the opportunity to present who they were, where they were from, where they lived, with whom they lived, and how all of those pieces composed who they were. Part of the joy was in uncovering what school could be *for* in opposition to what it has been *for* historically. Most of the fifth and sixth graders learned to read and write before I met them. In our work together, we learned to read the world (Freire, 1991) and write it (even rewrite it), and to use that reading and writing to understand and make their presence known. It is within that presence and within the full spectrum of emotions that their writing carries, that we began to find the joy that comes with consciousness, possibility, and telling one's truths.

The Counterportrait Up to This Point

The official portrait of the writers in this book was presented in Chapter 1 as a litany of failure, deficits, and inadequacy. Two important events occurred in the sixth grade that contributed to the initiation of counterportraits. First, my role shifted from observer and lunch conversationalist to being pedagogically active. Patia's willingness to allow this precipitated the second event, which was the children engaging in a different way of writing. They wrote brief personal narrative compositions that originated in experiences and feelings that were welcomed as part of what can happen in school. Homes and lives outside of school became legitimate as a local official curriculum. This was a shift away from the official program occurring in classrooms in the district, and it was illegitimate in the larger contexts of the other sixth grades, the school, district, state, and national officialdoms focused on test performance. It was also the beginning of counterportrait work. Counterportraits are not necessarily explicitly stated by students or teachers. Rather, they are moments of voice or action that challenge or interrogate the official—sometimes internally and locally (as in our first writing together) and sometimes in more far-reaching contexts, described later.

The counterportrait, to this point, includes the beginnings of specificity (writing activity specific to one classroom context), which runs counter to the broad and sweeping generalized strokes of official curriculum rooted in a deficit view. The move away from standardization is a move towards counterportraits. Counterportraits begin with the risks of introspection and reflection that were needed for the sixth graders to compose these first pieces. The specificity of counterportraits also involves the potential and eventual realization of unique and individual pieces of writing. Three of the children wrote about being hated, Carlos putting it succinctly, "We are stuck in a place with hate." The children named part of the emotional climate in which they live and, in so doing, named a truth in their lives. They peeled back the official portrait, including the voice of their teacher, to look into themselves and the contexts in which those selves dwell. Thus began our journey into the composing of complex counterportraits. In the following chapters, I continue to present their writing processes and products to demonstrate their agency in composing counterportraits as sites of possibilities for seeing themselves differently, and for being seen differently by others.

Chapter 3

Claiming Spaces to Write

> I want the freedom to carve and chisel my own face, to staunch the bleeding with ashes, to fashion my own gods out of entrails. And if going home is denied me then I will have to stand and claim my space, making a new culture—una cultura mestiza—with my own lumber, my own bricks and mortar and my own feminist architecture.
>
> (Anzaldúa, 1999 p. 44)

Anzaldúa's passion for a space to create, a location in which she could compose something new, suggests some of the potential I felt as I read the sixth grader's pieces in the last chapter. Policies rooted in the official portrait of Mesa Vista Elementary School articulate and put borders around writing spaces in which teachers and students must dwell, particularly because MVE is a school that has consistently performed poorly on high-stakes tests. Such articulation presents itself as scripted programs that leave little room for teacher input or writing that grows from students' lives. Writing activity is severely limited because reading and mathematics take center stage. Pressures to perform on tests shape the writing activity within the classroom by influencing the time available for writing and the specific qualities of instruction: genres, conventions, vocabulary, topics, length, format, use of technology, and more. Adopted curriculum and state standards lead to a compressed and limited writing space—a direct result of the official portrait. In counterportraiture, those within the compressed spaces push back to expand writing spaces; they may do so intuitively, consciously, or by following the lead of someone they trust and with whom they can think. They resist deferring to that which is imposed. Resisting the pressures from the outside means making decisions about: how time is used, relationships, taking risks, and truth telling. Space, then, is a political location and awareness of what articulates the space and how it is used will influence decisions by teachers and students about what is written, how it is written, for whom it is written, and who will have access to written pieces.

The Sixth Graders' Space

On a late autumn morning, I approached MVE with another poem in hand to share with the sixth graders. "Hey, Dr. Meyer," Juliana's voice rang across the courtyard, "you coming to our class today?"

"Yes. I love sixth grade."

She smiles and looks at Verdad and they run off to their classroom, having dropped off the garbage bag full of remnants of the breakfasts that the class had eaten.

Linda Christensen (2000) reminds us to "make our students feel significant and cared for" (p. 21) and that caring is one of the foundational pieces in helping students to develop an understanding of their lives, their positions in the world, and a sense of agency within that world. Such understanding may serve them in changing those positions in ways that move us all towards "a more just society than the one we now live in" (p. 21).

Counterportraits are evidence of a changed position and counterportraiture is the unfolding political project that changes positions in an individual's and other's minds. Such work needs a place to happen and the opening of those spaces is the focus of this chapter. Using G. E. Lyon's poem *Where I'm From* (reprinted in Christensen, 2000) as the point of origin, I once again presented the students with the idea of telling their truths. Lyon's poem is a wonderful mixture of things that the sixth graders could understand (fudge, dirt under a porch, trees, and strong coffee) and things with which they struggled (Billie's Branch, carbon-tetrachloride, forsythia, auger, and Imogene and Alafair). They moaned about the parts that made no sense.

"What do you understand?" I asked.

"It's about a girl . . . you said George is a girl."

"She is a woman," I restate.

"That's not a girl's name."

"What **do** you understand?" I request, again.

"She ate dirt," someone yells out and there's a round of laughter.

"Yeah, what's that all about? Why'd she do that?" I ask.

Silence.

"Well, we don't know," I answer my own question. "It doesn't say. She didn't tell us why. She just said that she did it. The important thing is that it's a memory, something she remembers, something that tells her who she is and she is telling us. She's letting us know, 'look, I ate some dirt.'"

More silence.

"What else do you get . . . do you understand in the poem?"

The answers start to come forward as the children read lines or parts of lines to the whole class. She had a back porch, the dirt tasted like beets, she made a lamb at Sunday school, and her grandfather lost a finger (but we don't know what an auger is). There were pictures under her bed in an old dress box.

I point to the last three lines and say, "Look, look at the bottom. The third to last line says, 'I am from these moments.' I wish she just ended the poem there.

I get all the stuff you just told me about dirt and a finger and all that. That is where she's from. That's what happened in her life. It's all real and it all makes sense, even though there are some words you may not know and I may not know, I still get the idea of the poem. But now she writes, 'snapped before I budded—leaf-fallen from the family tree.' What does that mean?"

Silence.

So I read those last two lines again.

"She left her family," someone volunteers.

"What else?" I ask.

"She left her family," another one says.

"I heard that the first time," I say, "but I'm not sure that is the only explanation. It can mean more than one thing. There's no right answer. We have to sort of guess."

"Maybe she got thrown out of her family," comes a voice from the back of the room. A typically quiet student had volunteered.

"Maybe," I say. "Like maybe there was a fight or . . ."

"She ran away with a boyfriend," someone completes my sentence and there's some laughter.

"I know," I say. "Any of those are good ideas."

"Snapped," says one child. " 'Snapped before I budded' means someone took her picture."

"Ohhhh, like with a camera," I say. "What else?"

"I think she may have died," comes a tentative voice.

"She could have died," I agree. "She is off the family tree because she died."

"But who wrote the poem, if she died?" comes a challenge.

"I have no idea. What do you think?" I ask.

"Someone is writing like they are her, like she died but then they tell her story," someone suggests.

"This is a lot of ideas, isn't it?" I ask.

"What's the right one?" asks one of the students.

"I have no idea. I'm not even sure if we did or didn't say the one that was on the poet's mind when she wrote it. It's for us to read and think about. And it's for us to wonder about where we came from, too." We were, for that moment, transacting with the poem (Rosenblatt, 1978), as each volunteer offered something different to explain the lines. Each contributor was drawing upon his or her experiences, not just with school, but with life, to create a meaning for the poem that was theirs. Still, the slow-in-coming explanations were bounded by the social realties of the setting. They'd learned that school is the search for the one known answer (Mehan, 1982) and that the answer must fit not only the teacher-demanded parameters, but also the social fabric of their relationships with each other (Lewis, 2001). This classroom, as with any other cultural forum, had norms, like any other community of practice (Holland, Skinner, Lachicotte & Cain, 1998).

"So we have to write one?" asks one of the students.

"You will get to write one, soon," I say, "but first I want to show you what other kids wrote, kids a lot like you, in a sixth grade class near where I used to be a professor."

I show them the *Where I'm From* poems that Tami Filbrandt's (1999) students wrote. Her students' lives resonate with the students in Patia's class. Filbrandt's sixth graders are living with family members in gangs, in poverty, in houses with leaky roofs, and with unstable family constellations because of money, jobs, murder, prison terms, drugs, and health issues. Some of them are recent immigrants and some are homeless just like the MVE kids. I distribute copies of the poems that Filbrandt's students wrote and I read them as the sixth graders follow along. They hear about kids whose families migrated here for safety, but don't feel safe. They hear about gangs, drive by shootings, drugs, lies, religion, and friends that you can count on and ones that you can't. There was a lot of talk as the students pointed out to each other things in the poems that were much like their own lives. "These kids told their truths and they didn't get to do that in school very much before this," I said. "I just thought that if the kids in Ms Filbrandt's class can write poems like this, you can too. So, let's write." There's a scramble for paper and pencils and Patia yells that they should be quiet when they write and not walk around and not talk to friends. I will not dwell excessively on her yelling; suffice it to say that the writing conditions were typically punctuated by it.

The poems that they wrote stand alone as examples of who the sixth graders think they are and where they see themselves as coming from on one particular day. I introduce each one briefly as a way of helping readers learn a bit more about the children whose writing you'll be reading throughout this book. The analysis that follows the poems focuses on the space that we created as writers in the classroom and how that space is composed. What came to fruition within that space is presented first so that the poems are in the forefront, not presented as a backdrop. I added one final comment before they wrote. "I have your writing from last week and I wrote back to you if you gave me your piece to read." I wrote each child a rather lengthy letter about what they'd written, why it was important, and quoted their words as examples to prove that they are thoughtful and truthful in their writing. "Remember, as you write," I pleaded one last time before they began, "Tell the truth." First they read what I wrote to them, some choosing to share with their friends. Then, they shifted to write their poems. During the next few times that we met, they wrote, revised, typed, and formatted their work on one of the eight computers in the classroom. Once typed, the students played with font and format, but I reformatted them so that they would fit this space.

Mercedes brings in a mix of food, family, the dangerous neighborhood in which she lives, and care. The key phrase for the analysis is 'brings in' because she does just that, bringing into the classroom her feelings and thoughts of things outside of school.

Where I'm From

I'm from the tamales and Mexican food.
I'm from the people who get hurt everyday.
I'm the girl who helps my mom clean the house everyday.
I'm from the people who take care of me every day.

Mercedes

Miguel provides a scattergram of images, almost a montage of the events and people that are part of his life. He pays tribute to the paper that serves as the backdrop for his composition, seeming to acknowledge his literate self. His final lines leave us with an image of him surrounded by anger.

I Come From

I come from playing sports
I come from an immigrant family
I come from my mom's tired eyes
I come from people selling drugs
I come from not choosing to do or sell drugs

I come from my mom crossing the border
I come from my mom making food for us
I come from horse racing, rooster and dog fighting
I come from leaks in my house
I come from education

I come from my family
I come from feeding my pets every day
I come from a lost little puppy
I come from a Mexican culture
I come from a paper holding my thoughts
I come from my parents getting mad at each other

That's where I come from

Miguel

Vianca's piece suggests her family's belief in the American dream and some of the struggles that are part of the journey towards the realization of that dream. She brings in the reality that families fight, worry about money, and are not always composed of a mom and a dad. In a later piece, Vianca expresses her anger at her dad's absence from their lives and imagines how much easier their lives would be if he were present. In her closing, Vianca alludes to her mother's battles with epilepsy and depression, conditions that prevent her mom from working. Vianca and her mom live with Vianca's grandmother.

Where I Am from

I am from my family
that's trying to give
me a good life.
I'm from a family
that is trying not to
fight a lot.
I'm from a family
that is not poor and
not rich.
I'm from a dad that
doesn't care of his
family.
I'm from a mom that's
trying to be happy, not
sad.

Vianca

Juliana sat for fifteen minutes, writing nothing. I asked her if she wanted to talk about anything before she wrote and she began to cry.

"I'm sorry," I said almost urgently. "I didn't mean to upset you. I guess writing the truth, or even thinking about it, can hurt."

She wrapped her arms around her paper, leaned into the dark cave she'd created, and began to write. A little while later, I looked over at her and she was smiling. I asked if I could read what she'd written and, without thinking, I read it aloud.

"I come from a drunk dad," I read. That's all she'd written.

From across the table, one of her colleagues in the class said, "It's true. He drinks a lot. I've seen him drunk."

Juliana struggled with the writing, cried as I read it, and smiled when I looked at her after reading it. It's honest, her truth. She continued writing until our time was up.

But there is a second version; one that happened, I believe, when Juliana acquiesced to my response to the poem after I visited her home. I saw the very small and rusty trailer in which the family of three girls, a mom, and a dad live. But behind the trailer is a beautiful home, built by her dad, of about 2,500 square feet with separate bedrooms for the girls, a huge dining/kitchen area, and a master suite for her parents. Back at school, the week after the visit, I told Juliana how impressed I was with her dad as a carpenter and builder. "Don't you want any of that part of him in the poem?" This comment turned into a lesson for me as Juliana, ever desiring to please adults and her friends, or perhaps worried about the *right* answer, acquiesced and revised her original into the second version, below.

"I'm sorry," I began, looking at her new piece. "Your first poem was your truth and I feel like you changed it because of what I said. That was wrong of me. I'm really sorry."

"It's okay," she said.

"No, it's not, not really. You can change it back if you want. That first one seems like your real truth."

She didn't change it back and I learned once again how important it is to conference lightly (Murray, 2004) and to treat pieces of writing as truly fragile and writers as vulnerable to the powerful forces of my (or any authority figure's) perceptions.

> I come from a drunk dad.
> I come from arguing with my mom everyday.
> I come from the neighborhood, the
> one that smokes and drinks and does
> bad things.
> I come from strong enough to do better
> choices than that.

And after conferring with me . . .

It's All About Family

> I come from a drunk dad, but although he is
> a drunk dad, he is a hard
> working man.
> I come from a nice, cool, helpful, and
> Understandable mom.
> My mom argues a lot with me. She thinks my
> Cousin Leslie is a bad influence for me.
> I come from a cool sister, Liliana. She keeps my
> Secrets because I keep her
> Secrets. My sister takes me everywhere
> I want to go in the school
> Year because
> This summer of 2007 she is going to
> Go get a job at Cliffs.
> I come from a little sister that wants
> To be like me and do things like me,
> That one that bugs me all the time.

Corazon's family is grieving the loss of her brother to a gang, portrayed as a second family, but the poem gets a little confusing when, in the middle, she writes about being from two families herself, leaving us wondering about what two families she is referring to. The confusion over families may be evidence of the tensions within or across families and also the feeling of helplessness that Corazon feels. She feels little sense of agency and positions herself as the little girl that endears herself to all, suggesting that she uses gender-related qualities to try to massage away some of the very tension that she views as irreconcilable.

Where I'm From

I'm from making
My mom proud of
My grades, I'm from
My brother joining
Gangs and calling
Other people family
Being thankful of
His Westside homies,
I'm from my 2 families
Fighting against each
Other, and from me
Being in the middle
Of those families and
Not being able to do
Nothing about their
Conflict, I'm also from
Being the little girl
Of both families.

Corazon

Verdad is often the object of Patia's anger as Patia consistently finds her not doing what she's been told to do; yet she seeks Patia's approval and praise. Verdad crumbles under the yelling, turning stoically silent, focusing her eyes towards the floor, and refusing to respond to her teacher's questions because, I conjecture, they seem more like reprimands than genuine inquiries. Pulling her arms around her paper so that no other students can see her writing (the process and the product), she composes pieces that are con sistently honest, truthful, and saturated with the angst that accompanies poverty, tragedy, and keeping too much inside. Ultimately, though, in her walk, her interactions with others, the intensity of her eyes, and her willingness to physically fight for who and what she believes, she is proud. She'll share with me, but not until the last few weeks of school does she share with others. This change came about dramatically when we worked with the Albuquerque slam poetry team (Chapter 9). Her use of "dark soul" (something she'll return to in a later piece), suggests a space in which she can neither see nor be seen, hear nor be heard.

I Come From

I come from my mom's dark eyes
I come from a Mexican family that crossed the border to survive
I come from my dark soul
I come from a immigrant family
I come from my dark silence
I come from my parents fighting because of my progress report
I come from my sister running away because of my parents fighting
I come from a Mexican family and I'm proud

Verdad

"Can it be funny?" Ricardo asks me privately after the class begins writing their poems.

"Is that the truth?" I ask. "Is part of where you are from really funny?"

"Yes," he whispers and grins, drawing me closer. "I ate paper towels."

"What?" shrieks the boy to his right who's been eavesdropping.

"Shhh," I say. "Don't tell anyone. Let him write it, ok?"

Ricardo, his friend to his right, and I all shake our heads in agreement as we anticipate a poem that will make the class laugh. Ricardo's work, this time, will ease some of the intensity and tension that occurs when curriculum's authentic roots stretch into the real lives children lead outside of school. Although buried in the poem are dead pets and gang graffiti, we're left with a warm feeling of family and events that made his colleagues smile and nod at the new, the familiar, and the funny.

Where I'm From

I am from the brown paper towels
I ate on my kitchen counter.
I am from the toys I used to play
with all day long.
I am from the back yard I would spend hours playing and getting dirty.
I'm from the first bike I rode.
I'm from the movies I would watch
over and over again.
I am from the first video game I played
Mario Kart 64.
I am from my nephew's newborn face.
I am from the times my nephew and I waged war on Worms Armageddon for
the computer.
I am from the scar on my leg.
I am from my dogs and cats who are dead now, Tyson, Patches, Chico,
Simon, Sunny, Shadow, Rocky, Bandit, and Whiskey.
I am from the Westside and JMV Graffiti

on the street signs.
I am from the walks my dad, Tyson, and I would take in the desert hunting
for rabbits.
I am from these memories.

Ricardo

Jesus will miss a field trip because of a fight with Ricardo. Jesus rarely shared a piece of writing with others in the class or his teacher, but would slip me pieces as I was about to leave for the day. I'd read his pieces on the spot, hug him, and tell him that his writing was important, moving, and honest. He rarely answered with words, but would shake his head or throw a quick nod in my direction as a way of letting me know he understood. Patia yelled at him mercilessly on many days. Jesus was also big, though not as big as Ricardo. Jesus weighed 120 pounds and was almost five feet five inches, towering over his teacher by three to four inches. When Patia screamed at him, his shoulders sagged, he looked down, and his eyes filled with tears. Either no one noticed or no one dared mention his eyes, fearing what could happen on the playground if Jesus was the brunt of any teasing. What follows is one of the longest pieces he wrote all year, but it is also the piece that attached him and me. I always asked about his brother, learned about his sister (and her baby, Jesus' niece), and their mom. After the school year ended, I visited the family a few times to help with some things beyond the range of this study. Jesus' strength as a resister is apparent in the lack of work he produced for Patia or me. But in his home, I was witness to his gentleness, his love of his three-year-old niece and six year old sister as he read them books, played in a tiny swimming pool with them, and watched over them.

I am from gang signs growing up in a neighborhood with people who don't care who you are if you say something you might get jumped. One memory I remember is when my big brother got shot because he had a gun. The new one he got is more smaller. Going with him in his low-rider that has the front windshield broken by a crack head who wasn't in a good mood. At least my brother tells me he will always be there for me telling me to not live like this and not to ever do what he does, never to have a gun like he does. He also says to never sell or do drugs. He said to work for what I want. He also says if I want something bad enough, I will get it. He said if he can go back in time he would change everything. Me and my brother are closer than ever. We stick together. We both grew up without dads. My brother taught me what he knew and what he is learning. This life is hard and I'm trying to not live it. My brother said by seeing all this and not wanting to live it, will help me not live this life. I'm from pasole, quesadillas, enchiladas, and chili. I could go on forever but I don't have the time.

I invited the students to share drafts on our first day of working on the poems and on the days following when we met to write. The few that shared looked down into their papers and their strong voices evaporated into the not-yet-safe setting in which we wrote. Ricardo, barely audible, did receive the laughs he'd anticipated because word that he was writing a humorous piece had spread quickly through the classroom. The issue of safety remained contentious for the year that we wrote, but we had moments when the students found that writing and sharing made them strong, not weaker, and made others see them in a different (from official) way.

Finding the Space to Write

In her writing about the poet Jimmy Santiago Baca, Slavitz (1992) offers insights that connect to the writers at MVE.

> some writers . . . elect lives of bland monotony, of strict outer orderliness as counterbalance and defense against the inner wilderness of their explorations. For others, however, there may not be the luxury of choice. But choice they do make, and one of notable courage. Engaging what has been given, apparently irredeemable circumstances of insecurity and deprivation, in this darkness they seek their vision and find their art.
>
> (p. ix)

Hidden between the lines of Slavitz's introduction to Baca's autobiography is her understanding of the complex nature of writers making choices. She writes "there may not be the luxury of choice," yet in the very next sentence writes, "But choice they do make." Choice is directly related to truthfulness and the nagging question that haunts many writers: how truthful will I be? For the children at MVE, a complex web of experiences and relationships ultimately drove their truthfulness and their willingness to compose as "they seek their vision and find their art." These changing relationships (Halliday's [1978] tenor) influenced who they could be in school. After a brief consideration of Gee's (2000–2001) understanding of identity, I will discuss the spaces (Halliday's [1978] field) for writing in school with the understanding that an individual's identity may be enhanced, welcomed, strained, or denied within the many relationships that form at school.

Gee explains that identity is "the kind of person" (p. 99) you are or get to be, but that is not stagnant. "The 'kind of person' one is recognized as 'being,' at a given time and place, can change from moment to moment in the inter-action, can change from context to context and, of course, can be ambiguous or unstable" (p. 99). Gee suggests that there are four "ways to view identity" (p. 100): nature, institution, discourse, and affinity. "When an identity is underwritten and sustained by an institution [school], that institution works, across time and space, to see to it that certain sorts of discourse, dialogue, and interactions happen often enough and in similar enough ways to sustain the [institutional] identities it underwrites" (p. 105).

Our work was identity work, which considered the spaces in which identities (or subjectivities) are 'sustained.' This is continuous with the discussion of masks and the ways in which masks are related to contexts. Gutiérrez, Rymes, and Larson (1995) explain that there are multiple possible spaces in school, determined by relationships, language, and power. The *first space* in a classroom is the dominant voice of the teacher, albeit that voice may be merely a conduit for a publisher's program and not necessarily an authentic presentation of the teacher. *Second space* refers to the ways in which language is used by students outside of the classroom, in their homes and communities. The qualitatively larger the differences between first and second space, the more one might predict a mismatch between what happens in school and life outside of school. *Third space* is a collaboratively and consciously constructed:

> radical middle . . . a **space** where two *scripts* or two normative patterns of interaction intersect, creating the potential for authentic interaction and learning to occur . . . a **space** for shifts in what counts as knowledge and knowledge representation is created . . .
>
> (Gutiérrez, Baquedano-Lopez & Turner, 1997 p. 372;
> **bold** are emphases added; *italics* are emphasis in original)

Third space is a place of tension because of varying educational histories and agendas and fundamental linguistic, class, social, and cultural differences between teachers and their students. It is fragile and easily violated as participants test and evaluate the complex issues that exist when the dominant appears to relinquish some power in order for the oppressed to gain voice and presence. Gutiérrez, Baquedano-Lopez, and Turner (1997) refer to third spaces as "contested spaces" (p. 374) because of the struggles that exist there. This space is not some compromise reached, but rather is more a hybrid with its own unique 'genetic' makeup. In this case, 'genetic' is a metaphorical referent to the potential expression of identities not formerly available or viewed within a particular setting. It's not a little of one thing and some of another, but is a unique and new way of being within a given context—the classroom.

It is my contention that the use of the word *space* suggests dimensionality. Gutiérrez, Rymes, and Larson (1995) ultimately define third space as "the social **space** within which counter-hegemonic activity, or contestation of dominant discourses, can occur for both students and teachers" and further that it is where the "*how* of both a social and critical theory can be implemented" (p. 451, **bold** emphasis added; *italicized* emphasis in original). Third space is a place of mutual respect and care, composed of multiple portraits that are increasingly revealed and clarified. It is a space with multiple points of origin that is mutually composed with attention to the ways in which each detail influences and affects every other detail. It is saturated with relationships, such as mine with Juliana. I was only beginning to learn about her and her life, and she was investigating who she was as a writer in that relational space. I didn't realize how sensitive to teachers' words she was and she didn't understand how willing she was to bend her words to be compliant. We were figuring each other out, and the space in which we were writing and learning. The 'kind of person' each of the poets was in school was recrafted when first space and second space gave way to the third space in which we wrote. And that space was a mutually constructed location in which each of us made decisions about the truths and identities we would present.

The Fifth Graders' Space

Barbara, the fifth grade teacher, taught for over 20 years and decided to retire at the end of the school year for two reasons: she wanted to be closer to her out-of-state grandchildren and she became increasingly frustrated with the demands placed on her and the children in the No Child Left Behind environment. She was very organized, kind, compassionate, and also demanding of her students. Most rose to her demands because they sensed that her caring was at the core of her teaching. When she asked questions about the classroom community, something that was very important to her, they considered her questions seriously and typically responded honestly. Barbara's husband is a minister and, although she never discussed any particular religion with the children, her strong faith radiated with her genuine curiosity about what the children thought. The students in her class learned that when Barbara asked a question about how they treated each other or were treated by others in the school, she expected honest answers so that they could discuss issues that arose.

During one of my visits, there was a kickball competition between the classes and Barbara's class wound up playing Patia's class; the fifth graders lost. Even though the sixth graders won, they yelled at each other about errors, poor kicks, slow fielding, and slow running. Barbara's class appropriated some of that language and, when they lost, many of the fifth graders began yelling at and accusing each other because of the loss. When they returned to the classroom, hot and tired, they sat at their desks angry and frustrated. The 22 desks were organized in an open rectangular horseshoe (with the opening at the front, facing the board) and some desks inside the horseshoe in rows parallel to the board. The desks inside the horseshoe touched each other. Although the room retained this pattern of desk organization for the year, individuals were moved regularly because Barbara wanted the students to sit with a variety of their colleagues over the course of the year. The hot sweaty faces in the room faced their teacher as she sat in the high barstool chair that she liked to sit in during discussions or while she taught. She typically would jump off the chair to write things on the board, grab a book, or help a child. When she read to them, something she did daily, she'd stay seated as they enjoyed her reading. She used different voices and dialects and read with expression texts that she knew would draw the class in. Over her many years of teaching, she'd acquired a substantial collection of children's books and owned multiple copies of books that she'd invite groups to read.

Barbara sat in her chair and looked at them. One striking feature of this seasoned teacher was her intense and bright blue eyes. She looked at the class and asked, "What happened out there?"

Many voices chimed in at once accusing some people of making errors, others of running too slowly, others of running the wrong way around the bases, others of not fielding well, and still others saying that they didn't care who won and that they don't like kickball. "There was so much anger out there. I saw that in the sixth grade team you were playing," Barbara began. "Why did they get so mad?" she asked, skillfully taking the focus off of her own students' performance and placing it on the sixth graders. Some of the fifth graders talked about the sixth graders' attitudes towards each other, how they yelled at each other. "They hurt each other's feelings," Barbara added. "They really weren't kind to each other at all. They didn't cheer for each other or tell each other what they did well; they only screamed at each other about their mistakes."

She looked around the silent room and then softly asked, "What happened to our class?" and before she could finish came, "We did the same thing," from one of the kids. "I know," she said. "But I want to know if any one didn't try as hard as they could. Everyone isn't great at sports and part of sports is competition and I understand that," she said. Most of the kids in the class knew that Barbara's husband also taught at the high school and had been a football coach for many years. She even interviewed him as part of the biography work that the class did during the year. "Who didn't try that hard?" she asked.

One of the boys called out the name of one of the girls in the class to begin what he thought would be a gripe session about the athleticism of the kids in the class. Barbara turned to the girl and asked, "Did you give one hundred percent? Did you do your best?" The girl's eyes were filled with tears as she squeaked out, "Yes." Barbara explained, "If someone gives one hundred percent, it's all they've got. They gave all they had. Can someone give one hundred and ten percent?"

One of the students asks, as he answers, "No?"

"Of course not," Barbara says. "She gave her all. That was it. And one team lost. Our class lost. But we did our best. When two teams play in professional sports, someone wins, but everyone did their best. They may do better at their next game, but in that game, they did their best. In this kickball game, you did your best."

"But," she continues. "I'm a little worried about how you spoke to each other out there and the things you said to each other. You didn't seem like you were having a good time because some of you were so angry. Just because the sixth graders were so angry, you didn't need to be. What do you think?"

Barbara helped the class to "flip the script" (Guilyard, 1996), meaning they took an event and worked collaboratively to rewrite it in a way that served their greater good, which was, in this case, a sense of support, even peace, between the members of her class. Some students didn't agree with her and struggled to make sense of what she was saying. Particularly some of the boys wanted to win and weren't content with diminishing the importance of winning, but it was clear that they were struggling as they asked Barbara about whether or not it was better to win. The conversation continued, lasting almost 20 minutes as they worked together to understand how everyone felt, including Barbara. Some of the boys did not relent, holding onto their view that some of the girls "lost it for us."

I was witness to these same types of discussions during writing workshop, as Barbara worked with the class to address issues such as: what makes a good lead in a story; what makes a good ending; how do you know if the character is described well; how can you tell where a story takes place; what makes action interesting and understandable; what confuses us about pieces of writing; and what are the characteristics of a nonfiction piece. She used her collection of children's literature as well as the students' work, working with the whole class or individuals, to help children become better writers. For most of my time during fall 2006, I was an extra person available for conferring with the children about their writing. Some days Barbara invited me to teach a strategy lesson, such as discussing with the entire class the effect that a piece of children's writing had on me. I brought to the class some of my own writing about bullies, scaring my sisters and getting into trouble, and the story of how I wrecked my only bicycle and knowing my family couldn't afford a new one. I talked about parts of each piece that were a struggle to write or were still not quite right. The children offered ideas and we often found ourselves talking as I imagined 'real' authors talking at some café or conference. We talked about the 'big' issues that writers face as well as spelling, punctuation, and grammar.

The Biography Assignment Begins to Evolve

Barbara, Patia, and I ate lunch together each day that I was there. During that time, we'd try to discuss what happened in Barbara's class and what I had planned for Patia's class. Barbara knew that I was doing more teaching in Patia's class, but Barbara was comfortable with that because her fall writing was planned out as she worked on poetry writing and short descriptive pieces. Quite often, the politics of the school consumed our brief lunch periods as more tests were imposed on the kids, stricter guidelines were being enforced about addressing the standards, and other pressures of being a 'failing' school were felt. Still, Barbara persevered trying to hold onto writing as one place where she could allow kids to express themselves and engage in thoughtful discussions.

Barbara's scripted reading program involved strict adherence to a three-part daily session: skills work with the teacher, skills work at the computer, and reading books alone and taking tests about the books on the computer.

Barbara's classroom, like Patia's, was equipped with eight computers and a printer in order to have one-third of the class at the computer during their literacy instruction time. The fifth grade teachers grouped their students homogenously during this time and some of Barbara's students left while students from the other fifth grades arrived for reading instruction. The reading program consumed an hour and a half of every school day. The sixth grade teachers followed the same program, timing, and use of homogenous grouping for the four sixth grade classrooms.

The math program was also prescribed and carefully directed by coaches and the fifth grade teachers, like their sixth grade counterparts, worked to be in the same place in the text. There were one or two recesses each day, a special class (such as computer or physical education), and lunch, all of which meant that Barbara's students were with her for less than half of the day. Writing was one place during the day that Barbara felt that she could use some of the creativity that she longed for herself and her students to express.

"I want them to do something that they'll remember for the rest of their lives," Barbara said one day while the students were at computer class. She was anticipating this year as her last teaching in New Mexico and wanted to leave a lasting impression on the students. She showed me a folder of ideas for having children study biography as a genre, things she'd collected over many years of teaching. I looked through the various forms in the folder, all geared towards children reading about someone and writing a report, similar to a five-paragraph essay, as the culminating project. She'd done this in the past and there were a few samples of children's work, which she'd use as exemplars, in the folder.

I must have put on a strange face because she asked, "What?" as I thumbed through the folder. We'd gotten to the point of being quite honest with each other.

"Well, this isn't something I'd remember," I began. "I'm sure I did a report on Edison or Einstein in fifth grade, but I didn't remember anything about it. I copied it out of the encyclopedia, had to recopy it two or three times and then glued it to a piece of folded construction paper. And, I'm sure it never made it home."

"You threw it out?" she asked.

"Why wouldn't I? It didn't mean anything to me. It seems to me that a good biography is something that the biographer is really interested in, even has passion about."

"How do we do that?" she asked.

"I don't know."

We sat for a while and just thought about what we'd said. We had other conversations like this. During one such discussion, we talked about children having choices as writers, working collaboratively with others, writing about what they know, and conferring with teachers about much more than conventions (Atwell, 1998; Calkins, 1994; Graves, 1991; Harwayne, 2000). Barbara asked if she could watch me confer with some of the children about their writing. During my next visit, Barbara watched as I met with a student to discuss what she was writing, how she felt about it, where it was strong, and where she wanted to work on it further. I asked questions and listened, offering input where I thought it might be useful.

"What about all those spelling mistakes?" Barbara asked me after the child left the conference.

"Not yet," I answered. "That's editing; we're revising first." We talked about the difference. The next week, I watched her confer with a child and we, including the child, talked about how that went. "I still have to write it over?" came Consuelo's voice after a discussion of her piece. "Ohhh, I understand," I said. Barbara and Consuelo looked at me. "This is about time," I said. "Kids want to finish their pieces and move on. But if they really love their piece and want it to be better, then . . . well, maybe they learn to NOT love their pieces in school because of the pressure to finish something." We realized that we might have to lighten up the pressure that is put on the children to complete a piece of writing.

But, back to the week at hand. As I sat in the silence between Barbara and me, considering how biographies could be meaningful, the children came back from computer class. I watched them come in and thought of all the stories they'd told me informally, on the side, outside of the official momentum of the curriculum, and I had an idea. At lunch I asked Barbara what she thought of having the children write a biography of someone that is important to them, someone whose story it would be important to preserve for a reason that the children identified. Barbara liked the idea and Patia said that she wanted to do it, too. The biography project was born that day and we spent many days in late October, November, and December figuring out the details and trying to imagine how to ignite the children's passion for collecting and writing the story of an important person in their lives. Things changed along the way and it was messy, forcing Barbara to relinquish some of her strict adherence to organization, but also forcing me to become increasingly organized.

As will become clear in the following chapters, the work was very different in the two classrooms. Barbara found time for her fifth graders to work on their biographies during the week when I was not present as well as during the time I was in the classroom. Patia's students rarely had time to work on the project when I wasn't there. She typically stepped to the side while I taught, but often told the students to be polite and to do what I asked. In contrast, Barbara, the children, and I worked in collaboration to develop rubrics and other organizational and assessment tools that the children could use to understand the scope of their work. In the sixth grade, things went in a very different direction because the students weren't involved in sustained work on their projects while I was gone. In some ways the sixth graders had already begun the project with the poetry that they'd written, most of which was autobiographical or biographical.

Writing Spaces and the View of the Child

Earlier, I discussed Lakoff's (2002) idea of the views of a child: the strict father view and the nurturing parent view. Patia is very strict. Barbara views her students as sources of information and inquiry and sees her classroom as a setting in which social exchanges enhance learning. Children's questions and misbehaviors are seen as important indicators of their development and Barbara uses these as information in planning her teaching. Lakoff purposely genders the second view as *parent* because of the caring nature that more progressive mothers and fathers bring into their relationships with their children. Strictness, on the other hand, is typically a male attribute in child rearing, Lakoff argues. The classrooms look quite different because the content that they teach is contextualized in the teacher's view of the child. That view will affect how they talk to the children, how they present their expectations as teachers, the nature of their authority in the classroom, and the social context in which they play a key role by expressing the tone of their teaching (Van Manen, 2002). The view of the child in the NCLB (US DOE, 2001a) environment is from the perspective of the strict father and is consistent with Patia's view. Her view of the children in her classroom is confirmed by the district, state, and national view of children as NCLB is enacted. That law exerts pressure on all teachers and their students to comply with the NCLB strict teacher view of children (see, for example, Coles, 2000 or McQuillan, 1998). Teachers, also regarded strictly, must adhere to mandated curriculum and demand that students do the work provided by the basal publishing companies.

Barbara complies with certain parts of the adopted programs because students travel to other classrooms and she has responsibility for the students that arrive at her classroom. She enacts that responsibility by covering the pages in the program's teachers guides. But during other parts of the day and week, Barbara acts upon the flexibility that she feels she has when her students are not traveling to other classrooms and she does not have students from other classrooms in her classroom. During those times, she does not use the basal reader, has her students read from novels and picture books, and her students engage in sustained periods of writing time. Patia's students, when they were all together in her room (and not grouped for math or reading), tended more to experience school as a succession of worksheets and textbooks because of the pressure Patia felt to comply in order to raise test scores. She did have them write "what's on your mind" pieces from time to time. These two teachers contributed to the nature of the writing spaces in their classrooms which was reflective of the view of the child and teaching that each held and enacted. Each teacher acted differently in reflection of her response to broader (district, state, federal) views of the child and teaching and their need, willingness, and desire to adhere to or disregard those broader views.

Counterportraits So Far

The counterportraits of the writers in these two classrooms began at different points during the year, but they initiated within the classroom contexts, the individual children and teachers as they came to see themselves contrary to the official portrait they had appropriated. Engaging in the composing of counterportraits demands the opening of new spaces in which to compose or recompose both self as a writer (the children) and teacher. Claiming spaces for writing involves teachers, students, and the myriad of possible relationships that can occur within a classroom. It is also rooted in the many relationships that exist beyond the walls of the classroom, as close as the playground or as distant as home, church, district office, state and federal departments of education, other social and cultural groups, and other countries. It would be an oversimplification to suggest that Barbara is the good teacher and Patia is the bad one, with the former creating spaces for writers and the latter denying such spaces. Both classrooms had spaces for writing. In portraiture, context matters, as Lawrence-Lightfoot and Davis (1997) suggest:

> Like all researchers working within the phenomenological framework, portraitists find *context* crucial to their documentation of human experience and organizational culture. By context, I mean the setting—physical, geographic, temporal, historical, cultural, aesthetic—within which the action takes place. Context becomes the framework, the reference point, the map, the ecological sphere; it is used to place people and action in time and space and as a resource for understanding what they say and do.
>
> (p. 41)

Each teacher's pedagogical location matters, but location is not limited to a physical setting. Location is a metaphor for the meanings that Lawrence-Lightfoot and Davis ascribe to contexts. It matters that Patia has taught for nine years, worked in a community center before that, was born in Texas into a bilingual family, and calls herself a Mexican American. It matters that she's divorced and has grandchildren. These things that *matter* are rooted in, and contribute to, her view of children, herself, and the spaces she'll make available to and with her students. It matters that Barbara is an experienced white teacher who is about to retire and married to a (locally) well-known coach and minister. Her location, as a metaphor, also matters as does her view of the child. She, too, recently became a grandmother. Roberta, the teacher hired in March to help school-wide in the teaching of writing, views children from a nurturing perspective. All three teachers live in the district, although Barbara and Patia have never visited the homes in which their students live. Roberta knows the community well, having been a Head Start teacher for a number of years and, in that capacity, required to make regular home visits.

By understanding the complexity of the spaces (contexts and relationships) in which teachers teach and students live as writers in school, I hope to bring to the foreground the ways in which the children composed themselves as writers and to juxtapose their composing processes with the ways that they are portrayed in their official portrait. That process has already begun as evidenced by the sixth graders' writing pieces that are unique for their in-school writing experience. Through weekly visits, my goal was to support and be witness to the composing of counterportraits that present writers as rich in potential and possibilities, rather than defective and beyond hope. Lawrence-Lightfoot and Davis (1997) capture the spirit of this type of work, which focuses on:

> empathetic regard [that] circles back to the pioneering work of Rollo May and Carl Rogers and underscores the merging of emotional and intellectual content, of inquiry and intervention, and of the insight and catharsis that can develop in relationships in portraiture, particularly when the research encounters are sustained.
>
> (p. 151)

Counterportraiture requires canvases—spaces—in which the composing of portraits that challenge the official portrait may occur. In this chapter, the sixth graders moved more deeply into a poetic space that was nurturing. The fifth grade setting, already quite nurturing, was interrogated by the fifth grade teacher as a possible space for writing activity that would leave an enduring impression. We were, metaphorically, stretching the canvas to create spaces in which the possibilities for counterportraiture may be realized. These are spaces in which the official portrait that showed them as failing, their school as failing, and the conditions and greater contexts of that 'failure' as irrelevant, may be disappropriated.

Chapter 4

Rewriting Self and Writing About Others

> There are indeed many precautions to imprison a man [or woman] in what he [or she] is, as if we lived in perpetual fear that he [or she] might escape from it, that he [or she] might break away and suddenly elude his [or her] condition.
>
> (Goffman, 1959, p. 76)

Teachers and students in this research took precautions about relationships and curriculum because of fears, habits, and histories inherent in living in the strict NCLB world for seven years. Even a genre may be a prison for some writers as they struggle to conform to requirements of length, language, space, form, structure, and function of that genre. In this chapter, the fifth and sixth graders move towards telling life stories in ways that elude the condition of 'at risk' or 'failing.' As I present various writers and the contexts in which they write, their in-school masks become more evident, as do the ways in which those masks are created and may hold them as prisoners within well-defined expectations and ways of being in school. We interrogate those masks, the sixth graders cautiously and the fifth graders more explicitly. The sixth graders engage by escaping some of the parameters of what constitutes a biography; the fifth graders engage by exploring the genre in a more traditional sense. Both paths lead to writers knowing more about themselves and others. In this chapter I present and discuss the work of both groups of children as we moved toward understanding the masks that others and we wear, and the ongoing need to deal with issues of safety and community.

Sixth Graders' Non-Biography Biography Work

The colder weather made both classrooms a bit more difficult to be in. In the mornings, we wore our jackets in the classrooms and in the afternoons, when the heat kicked in with full force, we often shed as many layers as possible. During December, the sixth graders continued practicing for the state criterion-referenced tests (given in March), followed the basal programs (hard copy and computer based), and had little time to read or write biographies, but Patia was always welcoming of the work when I was there. Early in December, still concerned about their unwillingness to share, I considered the success that Krogness (1995) had with improvisation and other acting strategies working with resistant adolescents. I searched the web for theater games (http://www.creativedrama.com/theatre.htm and http://fuzzyco.com/improv/games.html were useful sites), and developed some community building activities.

"We're going to start a little differently today," I began. "I noticed that many of you are working on poems, but still quite unwilling to read them to each other. That's about trust. Today, we're going to try to feel more like a community that can trust each other. One way to do that is to play together."

"We're gonna play games?" came a voice.

"Sort of," I said. "But these are games that actors use when they are learning to act. They're supposed to loosen up our minds and help us feel a bit more comfortable with each other." I was getting used to the silence that the kids presented when I offered an idea that was new, different, threatening, or challenging. I asked them to find the piece that they were working on (the next draft of some of the work presented in previous chapters) and to keep that out on their desks. I asked them to move the desks to the sides of the room so we had a space in the middle. The noise that instantly burst forth was near deafening as children shouted orders to each other and desks and chairs fell over, collided, and were dragged. Patia stepped in quickly, "Dr. Meyer asked us to make a space in the middle. You have to do that quietly."

It was instantly quiet. I said, "I think that it may be too hard to get a big space in the middle." Then I asked specific kids to move their desks to the middle and put them really close together and other kids to move their desks to the perimeter of the room. We had a space for a circle with an island of desks and chairs in the middle.

"Okay, let's make a circle," I said. The circle that resulted was remarkable because every girl was on one side of the room, between the outside furniture and the middle island and every boy was on the other side. Two large gaps opened between where the last boys and the last girls stood at each of the two ends. I looked at the lines and laughed out loud.

"What?" one of the girls asked.

"Look! It's all girls on one side and all boys on the other."

Silence.

"Okay," I said. "Everyone hold hands." All eyes immediately went to one or the other end to see if the boy/girl pairs would join hands. "Just kidding!" I said.

No one laughed.

"Just move a little closer together near the ends and bend the lines a bit more so it's a bit closer to a circle," I pleaded. "No one has to hold hands."

They move closer together.

"Thank you. This is fun, so far, right?"

Silence.

I asked them to pretend to have a ball in each hand with their arms at their sides. When I said, "Throw!" they had to throw one of the balls as fast as they could and put their arm back down to their side. They laughed. "Why's that funny?" I asked.

Silence.

"Let's do it again," I suggested. So we did. No one laughed.

We played "Zip, zap, zoom," a game that started with me saying "zip" and looking left. The person to my left said "zip" and then the person next to them, until it came back to me. Then we said, "zap" going in the other direction. "Zoom" was said when I looked at someone and then they had to say the "zoom" to another person and no one could 'get' the word twice until we all had it once. No one could remember who went, disagreements erupted, and I laughed. "It's supposed to be fun. It's really hard to remember who's gone once so when it happens that someone gets zoomed twice, it's just funny. It's okay to laugh about it." No one did.

Then we tried to say the *Pledge of Allegiance* by going around the circle with each person saying the one word in the correct sequence. I started, saying, "I," and the boy next to me said, "pledge," and it became apparent that no one was sure of the words. "Well that didn't work, did it?" I asked. I answered my own question and we went on to the next warm-up.

"Okay, now walk slowly around the circle. The rules are you all face to the right and walk and you cannot touch anyone. Look at me so you know how fast to walk." They walked and I began to walk slower and slower until I was walking in slow motion. Some laughed, were chided by Patia, and then continued following me. "Really slllllloooowwwwww," I said. Then I laughed. "It's fun," I said. "It's okay to laugh. Now walk like we're really happy, like we got some real good news." I walk with a spring in my step and smile and some others smile as we all walk a bit faster. "Okay, now on tiptoes." Then we moved to walking like we were afraid, then dragging a piano, then listening to great music on headphones, and ended by going very slow once more. We moved to a mirroring exercise during which we did all the motions that a partner did. I asked them to do them all in slow motion. There were arm and leg movements, facial contortions, and even some ear wiggling going on. And there was some laughter, which I acknowledged as being important. "A community has to be able to laugh together, or cry, or wonder, or challenge."

Silence.

"We're going to move to some that are more creative," I offer and then explain that I had some actions written on slips of paper. "When I give you one, you go to the front of the room, perform the action with no words or sounds, and choose people that have their hands raised to tell us what it is." I had them: bowl, look into a microscope, make a bed, pack a suitcase, wash their face, peel a hot egg, decorate a Christmas tree, play football, and more. We did them quickly and interest seemed high so I ventured to the next idea.

We moved the furniture back to being in rows and I went to the front of the room to explain that the last activity was to get ready for a more complicated scene. Pairs or groups received a slip of paper with a description of a scene on it and they had to act it out and make up dialogue to go along with their actions. I gave one pair a scenario involving a phone call in which they ask someone to a movie, but she can't go. I put two girls together for this and made it clear that they were friends, with one calling the other, but the second girl's mom won't let her go. "You have to act out why her mom won't let her go and talk for a while before hanging up." I brought two old telephones for this.

Another scenario was four people on an elevator and one collapses and does not talk, but is breathing, when the elevator gets stuck between floors (a few students had never been in an elevator). I present one of these scenarios to provide some insights into what happened to the group as we progressed from the warm-ups to the more complicated scenarios. A foursome approached the front of the room, "We're on an elevator. Well, we're getting on an elevator," Verdad said. They reach the front of the room and spread out along the edge of the whiteboard.

"You're too far apart," I say. "There's not that much room on an elevator."

They move closer together and stand still. Nothing happens. We wait; there are some giggles on the elevator and in the room. "Well, what do you do when you get on an elevator?" I ask.

"I don't know," Ricardo says.

"Well, you could press a button to get to the floor you want," I suggest, wondering what they'd rehearsed.

Verdad reaches out and presses an imaginary button. Mercedes puts her hands over her mouth to suppress her laughter. Miguel and Ricardo just wait. Then, in a subtle motion, they all look up. "Wow," I can't contain myself, "They are looking at the numbers above the door of the elevator. That's what people really do on an elevator." Verdad looks at me and I know that I need to be quiet. One of the actors passes gas loudly (for real, not part of the scene) and the class erupts into laughter.

"Oh, I wouldn't want to be on that elevator," I say. "It's too crowded and that smell will stay there because the door is closed." They calm down.

Verdad bounces her knees a little to suggest they are moving. The others follow suit. Then she stands stiff and the others do that, too. No one says anything. Verdad looks sternly at Mercedes who says, "It's stuck. It's stuck," almost whispering.

"Stuck!" Ricardo screams and the class erupts in laughter. He ignores them. "Stuck," he says again. "Oh nooooo," he yells, grabbing his shirt at his heart, twirling around, and falling to the ground. The other three occupants of the elevator look at him but do not move.

"That's it," Verdad says.

"Well, ummm, what's going to happen to this poor elderly gentleman?" I ask. Ricardo looks up. "I'm dead."

Again the class laughs.

"That's the end?" I half-say, half-ask.

"Yes," Mercedes says.

"Okay," I offer the class. "This is a really sad ending. Good job," and, as we did with the others, I clap and some of the kids clap too. As the two boys walk to their seats, they are offered high fives by their friends in the class; the girls slip quietly onto their chairs, but I look at Verdad and she smiles. There was, for that moment, a subtle shift as they enjoyed each other, rather than fearing ridicule or criticism that often derailed authentic work.

I ask the actors to bring their poems and stand in a circle again. "You're really good performers. How do you feel?"

I know before I say it that I will not get any response to that question. It's one of the many questions I've learned to answer myself, hopefully demonstrating some possibilities for responses that they may, someday, offer. "You're good performers and you took your roles seriously."

Ricardo says, "It was fun to die." There's laughter.

"If you write these scenes down, then they're plays. You could all write plays if you wanted to; I know you can because I just saw you put them on. And you also trusted each other a little more. Writers and performers have to trust each other. You have to know that no one will make fun of you or laugh at you or hurt you. That's important when we're doing this kind of work and when we're writing and sharing our writing." I'm about to make a huge leap. "So now, who wants to read what you have on your paper?"

"All of it?" Carlos asks.

"That's a good point. Let's do this. Everyone gets to read one line. Look at your paper and read one line when it's your turn. We'll just go right around the circle. Who will go first?" Juliana volunteers and reads one line. The person next to her does too. Isaac reads a line. One of the boys asks, "Can I just read one word if I don't want to read the whole line?"

"Sure," I reply.

That was probably a mistake because, of the remaining ten or so writers, a few only read one word (like 'the' or 'and'). They got some laughs, but I try to make it into a gentle lesson. "When a person reads such a safe word, like 'the'" I begin, "it means they're not feeling safe enough to read what they wrote. They don't want to share their truths, their honest feelings. We have to all think of ways to make everyone feel safe enough to read their whole pieces, OK?"

Of course, there's no response.

"We're just about out of time," I say. Some of the kids look at the clock. "I'd like to know what you thought about today so I'm going to give you a quarter of a piece of paper and ask you to write me a short letter or a note. Tell me what you thought about today."

"I've learned that if you really have courage and trust your class mates, you can act and do lots of different stuff without having to feel embarrassed," wrote Corazon.

Isaac wrote, "I really don't want to take an elevator anymore. I wonder if you hold a fart too much it may stink even more."

Lorenzo asked, "Why do you make us do funny things? I felt embarrassed."

Verdad wrote, "I feel really embarrassed. I feel that everyone is looking at me. I feel really sick. I feel that I want to go home right now. Sincerely, Ver[dad]."

Carlos wrote, "I really liked what we did today."

Juliana recapped a bit of history of the performance, writing, "When we were practicing for the elevator, R—started to talk in his phone like really loud and fast and I was so upset. I was acting like I was mad and then I slapped him."

"Thanks for being here because we have lots of fun when you come. I hope you enjoy coming in the class. You are a good friend. Your friend, Mercedes."

Mercedes and Vianca sit near each other and wrote generalized notes to me, rather than specific to the day's events. Vianca wrote, "I'm so glad that you come to our class. Thank you for making us laugh and for being funny."

Jesus used my first name, "Rick, I like the things we did today. They were fun. We should do things like that more often." Ricardo, seated near Jesus, also used my first name, "Rick, I liked the acting part in the elevator. It was cool to act dramatic and all that stuff. We should do that again. I really thought it was fun. Thank you."

These notes suggest that some of the students understood the bigger picture of the day: that we were a slightly changed community, one that could engage and enjoy with each other. They were a little more forthcoming, took risks, trusted each other a bit more, laughed more together (rather than at someone), and learned that it's not a great idea to fart in an elevator. Verdad and Lorenzo were embarrassed and shared their truths with me, another move towards safety and trust. Verdad's may have signified some joy in performance and accomplishment, but was also a reminder to me that she was not willing to completely let go of a deep sense of distrust.

Lemke (1995) wrote:

> We participate in many communities in our lives. We have multiple grounds of affiliation to multiple communities. We construct multiplex personal identities which combine elements of our lived experience in these different communities, our different social practices. We enact the moments of our lives with resources from the whole combined repertory of practices we acquire through participation in diverse social groups and categories.
>
> (p. 150)

Perhaps during the theatre activities, we experienced some facets of the masks that students wear at home, at play, and in other places in their lives. They drew on more of their 'resources' and took risks in presenting themselves to each other. Their school masks were temporarily changed, as were the 'social practices' that constitute the repertoire of possible behaviors for the school setting. We had a different kind of moment in a very well established space, the effects of which remained to be seen.

Moving Towards Increased Sharing

Over the next few weeks and into January, the sixth grade writers were more willing to share lines or even entire poems during our time together. A few began writing stories about their lives because poetry didn't seem to offer them enough space for the details they wanted to provide. I searched for ways for all of them to sense that the narratives of their experiences were important to write and met with some success in early February when I rediscovered Koch's (1970, with the children of P.S. 61 in New York City) work. I introduced one of Koch's strategies by talking about the changes that I'd seen in them and some of the changes they told me about. I talked about growth in height since August and also growth as writers who were descriptive and, most important, truthful. I introduced Koch's strategy of using the sentence frame: "I used to _____, but now _____." I wrote on the board, "I used to have hair, but now I don't."

When some of the children laughed, I said that I intended it to be funny and appreciated their laughter. Then I wrote, "I used to have a father that could blow up like a volcano, but now I don't." I talked about my father's temper and that, since he died, I don't see that anymore.

"You get the idea. Be funny, be serious. Now go write for fifteen minutes."

After 15 minutes, I asked everyone to read one line of their poem, but before they did that I suggested rereading the entire piece and selecting one that was really good. "What if we have two really good ones?" asked one of the boys. "You can read all of them, if you like," I said. "We have time." Everyone read at least one line. Over half of the class read their entire pieces. The poets that wanted me to type their first drafts for our next meeting submitted them to me. Some of those drafts are presented below, with written miscues corrected.

I used to trust my friends, but now I don't.
I used to not argue with other girls, but now I do.
I used to have a puppy, but now I don't.
I used to have a family, but now I don't.
I used to have a trusting sister, but now I don't.

Corazon

I used to have a cat, but now it's gone.
I used to paint, but now I don't.
I used to believe there was a ghost, but now I know it's a lie.
I used to have a cat, but now it's gone.
I used to have a best friend, but now I know there are no best friends.

Mercedes

I used to be in fifth grade, but now I am in sixth grade.
I used to have two dogs, but now I have one.
I used to have bad grades, but now I have good grades.
I used to hate math, but now I like math.
I used to have a bike with air in the tires, but now it's flat.
I used to have bad grades, but now I have good grades.
I used to believe in trust, but now I don't.
I used to want to be perfect, but now I know that no one is perfect.
I used to want peace, but now I know violence makes the world go 'round.

Jesus

I used to have a cool dog, but now it's gone.
I used to have two talking birds, but they are gone.
I used to have an uncle, but he's gone forever.
I used to like my uncle, but now there's no one to like.

Isaac

I used to have six puppies, but now I only have three.
I used to think all cool, but now I don't.
I used to beat up my big brother, but now I don't.
I used to fight with Esperanza, but now I don't.
I used to think all cool, but now I don't 'cause it's dumb.
I used to talk back to my mom, but now I don't 'cause it's disrespect.

Lorenzo

I used to have nobody to play with, but now I have my nephew and friends.
I used to have pets, but now they're dead.
I used to like school, but now I don't like it so much.
I used to think life was easy, but now I know it's hard.
I used to think everyone was peaceful, but now I know that some people are violent.

Ricardo

I used to have a cat, but now I don't. He died.
I used to have good times with my cat, but now I don't.
I used to have bad grades, but now I don't.
I didn't used to listen to the teacher, but now I do.
I used to be by myself, but now I have friends.
I used to sleep in my room, but now I don't sleep in my room.

Esperanza

I used to talk back to my parents, but now I don't because my parents get mad.
I used to have a cat and a dog, but they died.
I used to go to the store a lot, but now I don't.
I used to misbehave in school, but now I don't.
I used to have good grades, but now I don't.

Juliana

I used to have a dog, but now it's dead.
I used to have a cat, but now it's gone.
I used to play with my dog, but now it's gone.
I used to drink pink milk, but now it tastes bad.
I used to eat vegetables, but now they taste bad.
I used to have a dad, but now I don't know him.

Vianca

I used to have a dog, but now it's not with us anymore.
I used to go shooting a lot, but now we hardly go.
I used to have a garden, but now it died.
I used to have a bike, but now it doesn't work.
I used to believe in Santa Claus, but now I know it was our parents.
I used to think the war was over, but now I know it is still going on.
I used to have a motorcycle, but now I don't have it any more.

Miguel

I used to have a cat, but now I don't.

Carlos

I used to talk back to my parents, but now I don't talk back to my parents.
I used to have a dog, but now I don't have a dog.
I used to have a grandma, but now I don't have a grandma.
I used to have a grandfather, but now I don't.
I used to have a motorcycle, but now I don't.
I used to have a favorite uncle, but now I don't.

Verdad

Using domain analysis (Spradley, 1980), I grouped together words or topics (Spradley calls them "terms" [p. 89]) because they are in a semantic relationship with a cover term. For example, the children wrote about things (terms) like pets, bicycles, motorcycles, hobbies, ghosts, Santa Claus, and food. One semantic relationship between all of these is that they are all things found and discussed outside of school. Domain analysis proved useful in considering what the poets revealed. They wrote about kinds of relationships, including: aunts, uncles, grandmothers, grandfathers, mothers, fathers, sisters, and friends. They also wrote about qualities of relationships, including: trust, arguing, respect/disrespect, peace/violence, 'good' friends, 'bad' friends, and being, thinking, and talking cool. The poems were another work in which these writers explored and revealed themselves. Thus, they are biographical and autobiographical pieces. Their writing did not contain all of the conventions of expository biography, but the biographical and autobiographical content suggest the biography genre. These differences led me to refer to the sixth grader's pieces as non-biography biographical (or autobiographical) work. The sixth graders' writing challenged (Goffman's [1959] "eluded") the conventional biography genre by bending its traditional literary parameters.

To demonstrate to the writers the power of their work, I composed a slideshow presentation that included lines I selected from their poems with photos I found from the web. I added music and presented it to them at the start of my next visit. They were excited and some asked how their families and friends could view it, an idea to which we would return later in the spring semester. I suggested to them that one reason their lines in the slideshow meant so much to them was that they knew the stories behind those lines. Then I discussed the difference between showing and telling in writing. I invited each of the writers to choose one line from their poem and show the story behind that line. I explained that details of some of these events are crucial, not to live in the pain, but to interrogate it, understand it, find commonality with others (when they felt safe enough to share), and to wear their experiences as strengths from which they could make decisions that serve them well. The pieces that they submitted to me at the end of the day were another set of genre-bending non-biography biographies. About half of the writers shared their entire piece with the whole class before I took them to type. The elaborated pieces are presented below, with the line they selected to elaborate rewritten at the top of the piece.

I used to have a family, but now I don't.

The whole story behind this is talking about my life of how where I was five years old my mom had a really bad argument and moved. Our family was torn apart. Now that I'm 12, I don't have any trust in my dad at all. I try to but I can't. Sometimes I'm actually scared to talk to him because for some reason he hates my mom. And sometimes doesn't stop [talking] bad about her that's why I used to have a family but now I don't.

Corazon

I used to have a favorite uncle, but now I don't.

Because I don't have a favorite uncle. The story is that I don't have a favorite uncle is because they killed him. They killed him because he didn't pay those people some money. So they decided to kill my uncle. Now my uncle is in heaven where he is supposed to be.

Verdad

I wrote a comment to each student as a way of revaluing (Goodman & Marek, 1996) them as writers. I won't include them all, but here is my response to Verdad, which I gave to her the following week:

> This is a beautiful and very sad piece of writing. I can see how much you love him and I know that you miss him a lot. I'm glad that you picture him in heaven and also glad that you were brave enough to write about him. This is a story that many people should hear, but not just because it's sad. They should hear it so they know that such things happen and it's not right. They should hear it so they maybe think twice before deciding to do harm to others. You are a good writer with a strong voice.
>
> Dr. Meyer

I used to have a best friend, but now I know there are no best friends . . .

because I used to say Vianca was my best friend, but we got in a fight. After that we didn't talk to each other for a while. Then Vianca started to talk to me but I ignored her for a couple of weeks. Next, we made each other faces, but we got tired and started to talk to each other but we ain't best friends.

Mercedes

I used to want peace, but now I know violence makes the world go 'round.

The story behind this one is that I would have not learned what drugs are or even what they looked like. I wouldn't have had a clue about who was probably bad just by looking at them. People say not to judge a book by it color but that's the first way I judge all persons. If there was peace on earth, cops would not have a job. Also, the life cycle has to have violence. It's what makes the earth go 'round. Another thing I hate to see is when two people act like if they like each other, but then again if there was peace on earth, maybe I would have met my dad.

Jesus

I used to like my uncle because he would play with me. He would take me in his fast cool car. I would do anything he asked me to do. I even washed his car when it was dirty. Even in the inside. I would wash it good. I used to like the car. But a car accident changed everything.

His name was M— A—. He was 32 when he passed away. He passed away in 2006, December 19. Every time he said, "If I ever die, I am going to in my car." Every time I see an Eclipse, it reminds me of him. His Eclipse was gray with blue lightning. I wish I went to his funeral, but I missed it. He would tell me memories when I was a baby. I only saw him once a month. My grandma feels it was her fault because she is the one who gave it to him. I had good memories with him but [ended this way, with no punctuation]

Isaac

I used to think all cool, but now I don't.

Because my brother always tells me that I shouldn't because one of these days someone is going to kick your butt and almost kill you.

Lorenzo

I used to watch movies all day, but now I play video games all day.

When I was about 3 or 4 years old I started watching movies. I don't remember the first movie I saw. I would watch one maybe four times over. I remember I would watch them from the morning until I went to sleep. My mom would come and watch them with me. One of my favorite movies was "Brave Little Toaster Goes to Mars." But then when I was 6 years old I saw my sister playing a video game. It was a Nintendo and an old one. She was on the last level on a Mario game. I remember when she made it to Browser, the main villain in the game and how she defeated him. I just sat there watching like a zombie with my mouth hanging open. When she turned it off, the first thing I said was, "Can you do it again?" The next day about in the afternoon she was at the TV holding the controller. But this time it was a Nintendo 64. After she was done playing she said, "Here, you play." I got the controller and started playing Mario Kart 64. I wasn't very good. I kept driving and bumping into the wall but I was still having so much fun. I still watched movies but after time passed I stopped watching movies and started playing games. Finally one day I started playing games all the time. Now I am a video game pro. I still watch movies just not so much.

Ricardo

I used to have a cat, but now I don't.

I don't have a cat because some dog went to D—'s house because D— has a girl dog. And one morning my mom went to throw the trash and saw that he was dead. I got so unhappy that I didn't want to see those dogs again.

I had four years with him. He was very special because he had a green eye and the other one was blue. He was with a gray spot on his head. I used to have a lot of fun with him.

Esperanza

I used to talk back to my parents, but now I don't because they get mad.

One day my mom did not let me go to the movies with my friends. I got really mad and told her, "only cause in your times there was no movies." She ignored me. One day it was a day before Christmas in the morning. She told me put the turkey in a pot and put it in the oven. I am going to the store before the family comes. Well I didn't and when she came back and did not see the turkey in the oven she got really mad and did not let me go out for a week. She said, "You go to school, come back, eat and go to sleep." So that's why I don't talk back to her now.

Juliana

I used to have a dog, but now I don't because it's dead.

One day me and my cousin G— were playing with my dog named Spot. We were playing ball with him. My mom called us and told me and my cousin that we had to go to my auntie's house walking. When me and my cousin were walking, we were talking about things. Then when we're half way we saw my dog Spot coming to the road. A car was going very fast, my dog was running. Then he got run over.

Vianca

I used to believe in Santa Claus, but now I know it is our parents . . .

because the night before Christmas I went to the bathroom like around 2:00 a.m. and I heard a crumbling sound in my parent's room and I looked through a crack and saw them bringing the presents to the living room. So I stayed still in my hiding spot and I saw them putting the presents under the Christmas tree and when they were done I went to my room and went to sleep. The next day, I woke up and saw a lot of presents under the tree. So at night when we were going to open our presents and when they said, "Merry Christmas. Santa brought you these presents," I thought in my head, "Yeah, right."

Miguel

I used to have a cat but now I don't.

One day my brother slept on the cat and the cat used to sleep on the couch. That day my brother slept on the couch. He smashed the cat and the cat died.

Carlos

Once again, I analyzed their writing (Spradley, 1980) in order to uncover some of the broad areas about which they wrote. The nature of the *I used to, but now* format carries an inherent theme of transitions and, except for Ricardo, every one of the transitions that these young writers recalled from their lives involved changes from a happier or more secure state to one of increased instability, sadness, or loss. Corazon's piece involves the transition of her family to a state of separation, but also includes a move from a trusting state to a non-trusting one. Verdad and Isaac both write about transitions from life to death, both in violent ways and with an air of senselessness. Mercedes moves from a state of 'best-friendness' to one that is tentative at best and certainly not as reliable as she previously had. Jesus and Lorenzo write about transitions from stability to vulnerability and from peacefulness to the reality of violence. Pets, which children rely upon to give love to, and to get love from, are vulnerable, even unreliable. Esperanza, Carlos, and Vianca all lost pets through acts of violence, seemingly reaffirming Jesus' insights about the cycles of life. Juliana learns of power, something she learns again and again in and out of school, as her agency is unsettled and her voice is silenced through her mother's final words of punishment. Even the magic of Santa fades. Each of these students transitions to a less secure, less magical, and in some ways less loving place, and bravely reports those transitions in their writing.

Ricardo stands alone as he writes about transitions from movies to video games; Ricardo's life is more stable than many of his colleagues'. Recall that he wrote about eating paper as a younger child and reaped the rewards of his colleagues' laughter. In writing about video games, Ricardo took the familiar and composed from it in such a way that the other writers smiled. Ricardo captured snippets of life that they've all lived or could understand and made them unique and worthy of commitment to paper. In some ways his writing underscores and accentuates his position in this classroom community, as he is truly a gentle giant who, in his writing, can make the familiar unique, curious, or funny. That is a position he will assume until a point, but when persistently challenged or threatened, he unleashes power that draws blood and leaves welts because he will not be compromised. His writing is a thin line, like a river, that flows between his own dark secrets and fears and the choices he makes about who and what to present as his truths. He has a smart way with words and is known for his general intelligence, as any member of the class will inform trusted visitors that Ricardo is one of the few sixth graders that will be taking algebra next year.

Fifth Graders Begin Biography Writing

During the month of December, the fifth grade class began discussions of biographies. Barbara found biographies with the help of the school librarian and the students were asked to read as many as they could. Barbara had regular discussions with the class about the biographies, focusing on what they learned about the person in the book as well as the style in which the author wrote the piece. Most of the books were picture books, which the fifth graders liked reading because they are faster to read than a chapter book. There were very few Chicano/a biographies, with the exception of Caesar Chavez and a few athletes. They read about men and women, actors and actresses, songwriters, doctors, lawyers, civil rights workers, athletes, and scientists.

Barbara copied leads from ten different books onto a handout for the students. They met in small groups to read them and discuss which leads were good, including a consideration of what made them good. They met back as a whole group and contributed to a list on the board of the qualities of a good lead in a biography. The list included: rhythm, catchy, asks question, makes you think, humor, details that tell us information about a story, shows and does not tell, puts a picture in your mind, creative, descriptive, refreshing, pleasant, gives a feeling, makes me want to read more to find out what happens, and quotation (from the person). The children copied this list for use as a reference during their own composing of a biography.

As a way to begin some biography writing, we decided to have the children write biographies of each other. These initial practice pieces could be used as the "about the author" section of the longer biographies the students would write next.

"OK, so how do we start?" Barbara asked me one morning in early January as the children returned from their computer class.

"I'm not sure, what do you think?" I asked.

"Well, I thought you could get them started . . ." she suggested as children greeted me and found their seats.

Genuine inquiry (Short & Harste, with Burke, 1996) involves creating curriculum (Short & Burke, 1991) that didn't exist before, in ways not necessarily done before. I suggested we do this with a conversation that might then lead to the children beginning their own biography research work. Barbara moved to the whiteboard behind me as I stood near the front of the room. She wrote key words in categories that she created as the children and I spoke. I began, "You've been reading all these biographies," pointing to the long line of them standing upright on the ledge of the board. "Now you get to write one of your own. You'll write a biography of a classmate, but first we need to talk about biographies." This was not a great way to start as students immediately raised their hands and asked if they could write their friend's biography and if the person whose they wrote had to write about them.

"We'll get to those questions later," Barbara suggested. "First let's let Dr. Meyer talk with us about biographies."

"What is a biography? What do you understand it to be?" I asked.

"It's a story about someone and it's true," Consuelo said.

Barbara wrote "Biography" on the board and underlined it. Under it, she wrote "story about someone (true)." Another student offered that biographies are nonfiction, and that word was added to the list.

"Does the person have to be dead?" asked Ramona.

"No," I said. "You'll write a biography of a person in the classroom, someone who is alive."

"Good," she said.

Barbara added "person can be alive" to her list under "Biography."

"But it can be someone from history," Debi said. Then she referred to a few that she'd read from the collection at the front of the room. Barbara wrote "can be history" on the board.

"Anything else?" I asked. No one had any more ideas so I suggested that we move on to how you could get information to write a biography. Suggestions included: the Internet, interview (ask questions), from books, ask friends, ask relatives, read old newspapers, magazines, encyclopedias, and atlases. Barbara wrote these under a new category on the board "How do you get information?"

"Does it have to be something that you write down, like a book?" Chuck wanted to know.

"Wow. Great question. What do you all think?" I asked.

Students volunteered that it could be written, a movie, photographs, a CD, or tapes. Barbara started another list called "Can be" and listed these things under it.

"What do you need to know to write or make a good biography?" I asked next.

Having been in writers workshops all year, the students knew 'details' were important and called that out. Barbara added another list to the board called "Know" and she wrote "details" under it. Someone else suggested "information about their lives" and another offered "how they change lives" and those two items were also added. "How will you get those details?" I asked.

Isabel said we have to ask the person questions. I asked, "What makes a good question?" A new topic "what makes a good question?" went on the board. The students couldn't think of any ideas, so I suggested the following ideas that Barbara posted on the board: probing, digs for more information, not a yes/no question, makes a person think, and follow-up questions (asking that the person tell you more). I said that yes/no questions don't yield much information, but asking 'why' afterwards may get more. I also told them that I always take notes and even ask people to slow down so I can get all the facts. Then Barbara asked what they would ask someone to get some interesting details about their lives. She wrote "Good questions" on the board and wrote these items, which the children suggested: when did your life begin/where?; hobbies; heroes; how have you changed people's lives?; what do you want to be when you grow up?; tell me about your family; how have you helped someone?; how did you get here?; what are you afraid of and why? The question about how people got here came up because so many of the children have border and immigration stories to tell, either of their own travels or those of their immediate family.

Composing Classmates' Biographies

Barbara and I gave the students pads of paper and Barbara assigned them each a partner. The fifth graders chose which questions to ask their partner, and the energy level in the classroom rose as fact-finding gradually changed to intrigue and conversation. For the first time since I'd been visiting, some of the children began to speak in Spanish to each other in the classroom because their histories made more sense in that language, particularly their history outside of school. Christensen (2008) explains the importance of welcoming students' home dialects and language in the school setting:

> We signal students from the moment they step into school, whether they belong or whether we see them as trespassers. Everything in school—from the posters on the wall, to the music played at assemblies to the books in the library—embraces students or pushes them away. Approaching students' home languages with respect is one of the most important curricular choices teachers can make.
>
> (p. 23)

Stories of immigration, family members, pets, hobbies, interests, and worries were told. When Barbara and I reminded the students to take notes, the conversations slowed down as the students worked to take copious notes on the person they were interviewing. Those whose discussions took place in Spanish worked together to have an English translation of their findings.

Luisa worked on a biography of Consuelo (and later they switched when Luisa became the subject and Consuelo was the biographer). She elicited from Consuelo both funny and remarkable stories about Consuelo's life over the past nine years. Barbara encouraged the children to refer to the list that they'd generated about the characteristics of a good lead for a biography. Consuelo and Luisa spoke about making the short biography interesting and funny. Here is Luisa's final piece:

> Consuelo [Last name] was born on March 28, 1966 in [town], [state]. Consuelo's family names are Luis, Leticia, Luis, and Vanessa. When Consuelo was two years old, she would chew wood because she had sharp teeth. But her Auntie Sarah knew that Consuelo would chew wood. That's why she daren't put wood on the ground. Also, Consuelo's favorite artifacts are her life, her education, her Play Station 2, her computer, her Game boy, and her soccer ball.
>
> Consuelo saved her mom's life. Her mom was going to give up, but Consuelo said, "Don't give up, mom."

Luisa's awkward use of the word 'artifacts' comes from a lesson that I gave about things that are important to someone. I wanted the children to have a name for items they would see or collect (through photography) when they began their study of an adult. Since they were acting like researchers, I thought the word artifact would serve the purpose well and introduced it by presenting artifacts from my life. I showed them photos of my parents, a pair of running shoes, a cookbook, and a children's book to represent things (artifacts) that are important to me (family, running, cooking, and reading).

The briefness of the writing hides the depth of conversations that occurred between these two writers. They learned many stories about each other as they laughed together, stared at each other in disbelief, and helped each other with the details of their final pieces. Barbara used the school's digital camera to take photos of the writers to be placed on the same page as the written biographical text.

Atwell (1998) discusses the importance of giving children time to write. In the fifth grade classroom, two hours passed quickly as the writers engaged in thinking biographically and finding their biographers' voices. This is somewhat evident in Luisa's piece as she seems to step back to discuss her friend, Consuelo. Other students found their biographical voices as well. Marisol began her 200-word piece about E— by writing, "It started in the Presbyterian Hospital in Albuquerque, New Mexico on August 3 in the year 1966." Later she writes that he "has changed people's lives by talking to them and making them feel better." She includes funny stories about no one believing his father fell off a ladder and poignant moments like the death of his grandfather. Equally as rigorous as her final piece are Marisol's notes about E— (see Figure 4.1), the source from which she ultimately drew as she composed her final piece about him.

Ramona wrote about A—, that "she is a normal kid, with good grades." She also found out something that no one knew about A—, that she has pet ducks. This caused much commotion as the children asked questions about where the ducks slept, what they ate, and if they were allowed in the house. At a deeper level, A— was a star for a few moments and events like this one started to happen more frequently as biographers' excitement about their findings overflowed into the classroom. The effect was noticeable as students started to talk across fairly well established social groups and interest in each other soared. The community of the classroom, which was already safe under Barbara's leadership, became a bit more casual and somewhat more close-knit. For example, when Debi read from the biography that she was writing about her friend being "afraid of spiders because they can bite you and kill you [and] afraid of boats because she can't swim," discussions about fears—both silly and very real—permeated the biography work. Chuck wound up writing that the person he was studying "is kind of scared of boats because they can sink." Chuck also wrote that his friend wants to grow up to play for the Denver Broncos and work on a SWAT team.

When we met while the children were at computer class, Barbara expressed concern that the children weren't getting enough of the details of their findings into the penultimate copy of the biography. We decided that we needed some vehicle that the students could use to be reflective about their processes as writers as well as their final pieces. What ensued became more and more typical over the course of the year as one of us engaged the children in some thinking, writing, or strategy discussion. When they returned, Barbara led the class in a discussion of what should be included in a biography, writing the list of their ideas vertically on the board. Then she turned on the overhead projector and copied the list, using it to generate a rubric by putting a 1, 2, and 3 at the top of new columns. Some of the children spontaneously began copying the rubric, an idea that spread quickly as they discussed what words to place in each cell to reflect the point value of that cell. The completed rubric, which I typed that evening and distributed the next time I was in the fifth grade classroom, appears in Figure 4.2.

His life first
started in August
3, 1999. He was
born in the Pres-
pretarian in
NM. His hobbies
are basketball, but
soccer, basketball,
drawing, playsta-
tion. His heroes
are his mom, his
two sisters Adan
and Senaka Fredy
Gemma, Claudio,
and his dad
and Jr, and
his aunt Gylma,
and husband
tregorio, and
Hector V. He has
changed peoples
lifes by talking
to them making
feel better and

got baseball cards
dad never token
card out plastic
favorite baseball
player Nolan Ryan
doesn't like team
loves New York Yaks
favorite team dad
Red Socks betted
on team and
lot every time

fitball cards dad
didn't like cow
boy liked washing
ton Red Skins the
wash, Red Skins
beat Cowboys onces
and cowboys beat
wash, Red Skins
once

Key change
Grandpa before de
had since 2001
never knew abart

when he was
3 or 4 years dd
his dad was
checking the
heater and then
he got shocked
he went down
the ladder and
he dropped to
the floor care-
fully cause he
was playing around
and he called
my mom and he
thought we belived
but we didn't
believe that he
fell and when
he got up we
started laghing.

When they went
to las Veglas, Ne
vaga they were
swiming and
didn't want

	3	2	1
Details/Description	Describes what happened to person	Little information	No details about person
Tells a story	Tells a story	Unfinished story (incomplete)	No details about person
Lead	Interesting; makes you want to read it; catchy	Name, born	Doesn't talk about person
Ending	Sentence that ties back into the lead; wraps up the story	That was this person's life; story just ends	"the end"
Grammar Punctuation Capitalization Spelling/use spell check CONVENTIONS	No errors (mistakes)	A few errors	Many errors
Title	Name and a grabber	Name only	No title Nothing to do with the person
Read out loud	Good voice, expressive, point of view, personal touch	Some facts, expression, personal touch	Boring, no expression, all facts
Photographs	Baby pictures, married, life pictures, artifacts, newspaper clippings	Blurry	No pictures, poor quality, none

Figure 4.2 Rubric for biographies.

Barbara, Patia, and I met at lunch and discussed the rubrics. I suggested that the children had so much experience with rubrics that they could engage in conversations about their biographies and give themselves a grade. The next time I was in the class, the students met in small groups and had discussions about their pieces. We called these "writers support groups" and the children were not allowed to be in a group with the person whose biography they were writing. They appropriated the language of the rubric, saying things like, "I think yours has a lot of detail, so that's really a three." Debi said, "My lead is not that good so I think it's a two." When a colleague in her group of three asked why, she explained that it was "sort of interesting but not that catchy." The discussion within and around the development of the rubric, followed by using it as a tool for assessment, led to the children thinking about what makes a biography work. In some ways, the product (the rubric) was a reification of the discussion. Building it with the children was inseparable from building their deepening understanding of biography as a genre, way of thinking, and way of demonstrating learning. Its local and collaborative construction, rooted in conversation, is its strength.

"So how do I grade these?" Barbara asked me as the groups read, discussed, and rated their biographies.

"It seems to me the students are doing that right now," I responded.

After some discussion, we reached the idea that a good indicator of how reflective they were about their own writing might be to have the students write a letter to Barbara explaining what their grade on the biography should be. "For example," Barbara said to the class, "if you have all twos, you can't give yourself a one or a three. It's really a two. But if you have a lot of threes and a few twos and maybe one one, that would be a three. Now, write me a letter that tells the number grade, a one, two or three, you should get and tell me why you should get that grade."

Some of the children wrote:

Dear Mrs. Carter,

I think I deserve an A because I missed two words and a letter. I got a 2 on the title, a 2 on my lead, a 2 on my details, a 3 on my stories, and a 1 on my ending.

Sincerely,

Chuck

Mrs. Carter,

I got a 2 on my title because it said [student's name] so they gave it a two. Then for my details I got a 3 for them and for the ending I got a three. I think I should get a A- for my biography because it had detail but it was a different subject every time. I read the biography.

Sincerely,

Debi

Dear Mrs. Carter,

Based on my rubric, for details I get a 2, for stories I get a 3, for ending I get a 1, for lead I get a 2, for conventions I get a 2, for title a 2. My details give a little info. I tell one full detailed story. My lead says when she was born and my title was only the name. My ending is a one because it just ends. I think I should get an A-.

Sincerely,

Ramona

Dear Mrs. Carter,

I think I should get a B+ because I got mostly 2 and a few 3 because I thought I should get a 3 on stories, grammar, and photographs. That's why I think I should get a D !

Your Student,

Andres

Dear Mrs. Carter,

I think I should get a 100 percent which is an A+. I should get that grade because I only made two mistakes and I think I did a very good biography. I did everything but two mistakes and that is why I say I should get that grade. 100 percent which is an A+.

Sincerely,

Marisol [last name]

Barbara and I both noticed that the students connected the 1-2-3 scale to traditional letter grades. Although the grading process was complete, Barbara still noticed that some of the students' pieces were not entirely conventional in uses of grammar and punctuation. She wanted the pieces "to be perfect," and suggested we meet individually with the students to have them learn where they needed to edit their pieces. I observed one such conference as Barbara went through the piece and marked each place that needed correction. "It's too much for them," I offered. "Let's just edit for them, and maybe teach about one thing we want them to focus on, like periods or spelling the word 'they' correctly, but just tell them to fix the rest using our edits." The fifth graders learned to be thoughtful biographers by engaging in writing about each other. They became a more cohesive community with an increased awareness of each other's lives as they studied and shared their learning from this inquiry. Many appropriated a voice for evaluation and self-evaluation as they considered their own and their colleagues' writing in small groups.

Although the fifth graders and sixth graders may seem worlds apart in their writing and the contexts in which that writing occurred, both groups experienced composing as a social process and each member of each classroom made specific, although perhaps unarticulated, decisions about how much of themselves to present to their colleagues. It is this commonality of shared self that I used in making sense of the counterportraits being composed up to this point.

Counterportraits (so far), Context, and the Presentation of Self

For most readers, the children probably remain a blur because so many of them are presented. The official portrait of them intentionally blurs individuals into means, standard deviations, and other statistical representations that perpetuate the *not making adequate progress* status of the school. I encourage readers to: sit with the pieces, reread them, study the themes, and hear their individual voices. Spending time this way enables readers to engage in counterportraiture by doing the demanding work of seeing individuals.

The use of multiple literatures became important in this work as a vehicle for understanding the subtleties and complexity of counterportraiture as intellectual as well as political work. In Chapter 1, I discussed the idea of masks as the ways in which one presents self in a context such as school. In Chapter 2, the focus was on the search for joy (truth) and Chapter 3's focus was on relationships and writing spaces. Now I consider the classroom context and the developing relationships within the classrooms in order to explain the nature of the masks that the children present. I rely somewhat upon Goffman's (1961) work on asylums, but do not mean to assign to these classrooms the negative connotations that the word often conjures up. Schools have many of the attributes of asylums and I will consider some of these relative to the writing that the children have done. For example, kids in schools face "involuntary membership" (Goffman, 1961, p. xiv) in a physical and social setting—they're required by law to be there. A "'total institution' may be defined as a place of residence and work where a large number of like-situated individuals, cut off from the wider society for an appreciable period of time, together lead an enclosed, formally administered life" (Goffman, 1961, p. xii). Although kids at school do not reside there, they do spend many of their waking hours there. They work with "like-situated individuals" and are cut off from wider society for many hours. Their lives in schools are enclosed and formally administered. Further, "Their encompassing or total character is symbolized by the barrier to social intercourse with the outside and (barrier) to departure that is often built right into the physical plant" (p. 4). I know this sounds extreme, but the students' experiences in school have previously included so little of their lives beyond school that I find Goffman's ideas resonant with life in school.

The students' school masks were confined to their understandings of the possibilities of what could occur within the classroom context. Historically, they learned to defer to their teachers for the substance of their school masks. This occurred over their years of being in school because so much of what happens officially in school comes from outside the individual. Coming into an institution, like school, students make what Goffman (1961) calls a "primary adjustment" (p. 189) in which they are (or may choose to be) compliant with expectations. There are "secondary adjustments" (p.189) that look like compliance but are rooted in other intentions and purposes. For example, when the kids joined the student council or band, it appeared that they were engaging in legitimate school-based activity. However, some joined in order to leave the classroom; a few found that band was more painful than the classroom and dropped band because the band teacher was demanding. Juliana was thrilled to be elected as president of the student council. Her tenure lasted less than a month because she found that being president meant an increase in the number of interactions with teachers, and, ultimately, compliance with their ideas. Patia reported that Juliana was too social and bossy, did not complete her regular schoolwork, and eventually was dismissed as president. A secondary adjustment is a way of responding to official demands. Our writing work was a secondary adjustment to the official portrait of deficit and failure. We wrote, but not in the way that was expected officially.

Secondary adjustments are the site of and contribute to an "underlife" (Goffman, 1961, p. 199) in a school. Underlife is "to a social establishment what an underworld is to a city" (p. 199). The underlife in a school is a way of being at the school that is often parallel to the regularities of the institution. The underlife typically flows along unrecognized and unnoticed or considered of such little value or threat that its presence is deemed insignificant by those in power. Thus, it is, on the surface, a good thing that a child joins the band and learns to play an instrument or chooses to be in student council. However, when a student does so for unofficial reasons (getting out of class, being in charge of other students as their president), it is a secondary adjustment.

There are "disruptive secondary adjustments" (p. 199) in which students want to "abandon the organization or radically alter its structure . . . leading to a rupture in the smooth operation of the organization" (Goffman, 1961, p. 199). Bullying on the playground or directly challenging a teacher's decision, reprimand, or the curriculum are disruptive secondary adjustments. Bullying in particular is a dangerous route to take as it leads to suspension. However, the more common "contained secondary adjustments" fit the "institutional structures," don't demand radical change and are not disruptive (Goffman, 1961, p. 200).

When a student responds to texts or school experiences in unexpected ways, regardless of the intellectual integrity of the child's thinking, it may be considered disruptive. Hagood (2002) demonstrates this in her case of Timony, a thoughtful and engaged reader and intellectual whom teachers find annoying because he reads ahead of the class; reads a variety of texts outside of class, and makes connections that teachers find uncomfortable. Hagood (2002) discusses the ways in which "differences in conceptualizations of identity and sub-jectivity, though often subtle, produce different constructions of adolescents as literacy users" (p. 248). The contexts, the materials, the relationships, and the dramas that unfold may contribute to disruptions of official school activity and the recomposing of school masks.

I am using 'mask' to convey the idea of students composing their under-standing of who they can be in school. A mask is an option, understood and operationalized in the social milieu. It always includes issues of power, gender, wealth, cultural and institutional capital, language, and voice, although these issues are rarely named, but are intuited with all the urgency inherent in composing for survival, at the least, and, hopefully, success. In discussing the way that we put ourselves out in public as being constructed, but not as a fabrication, Zizek (2007) said, "Masks are real." These real constructions of self are permeable and flexible, within certain settings, and may even be reconsidered and recomposed under some conditions, such as some of what happened in both classes discussed in this chapter. And we have mask memory, something that we can rely and fall back upon if things unfold in a way that makes the new mask untenable. For the sixth graders, in a less safe situation, this was evident during each visit as I worked on reconnecting and rebuilding trust.

Goffman's (1961) idea of permeability as "the degree to which social standards maintained within the institution and the social standards maintained in the environing society have influenced each other, the consequence being to minimize the differences" (p. 161) applies to the classrooms. For most of the students' school lives, the school has remained *impermeable* to the social, cultural, and linguistic realities of much of the community. The teachers discuss poverty, 'problems' with students learning Spanish as their first language, and the supposed lack of dominant culture family values as issues that are to be overcome through schooling. The goal that emerged for this work was to locate and celebrate the capital (Bourdieu & Passeron, 1990) that children, their families, and their community have, while not ignoring issues that detract from a quality life. The state and federal assessment systems that are currently in place make it impossible for the writing presented thus far to permeate into an arena of legitimacy, leaving the work in the underlife of achievement and the stuff of which counterportraits are composed.

Intuitively, Barbara wanted permeability between the institutions of home and school (Goffman, 1961) when she asked what she could do this school year that would be remembered by the students for the rest of their lives. Such a disruption may make a lasting impression. For the sixth graders, writing their truths in poetry and short narrative pieces were moments of permeability that they approached tentatively and cautiously. The content of their writing was a departure from what typically occurred in school and, even if briefly up until this point, influenced the masks they wore in school. In our work, in both classrooms, we were disrupting "expected activity" (Goffman, 1961, p. 186) and the identities that rested within them. We were working to expose the "discrepancies between the official view of the participants of an organization and the participants' own view" (Goffman, 1961, p. 183). Composing a counterportrait involved changing the students', their teachers', and my own ideas about who we all were, the work in which we might engage together, and how that work can change lives. Schools prescribe activity and doing so "is to prescribe a world; to dodge a prescription can be to dodge an identity" (Goffman, 1961, p. 187); we were working to dodge school identities to explore the possibilities that may exist in increasing permeability. Goffman (1961) discussed "disculturation" (p. 13) as difficulty with life on the outside because of spending so much time in an institution. Disculturation in this study began as difficulty with life in school because of life beyond school. The out-of-school lives of the children were beginning to find some legitimacy in school and, as such, would increasingly come to be viewed by them as strengths to share, rather than deficits or problems to be minimized, hidden, or dismissed. This, then, is a process of composing counterportraits, counter to the official portrait. As the children composed, related, read pieces, took risks, and told truths, they were (not necessarily consciously) talking back to the official portrait and they were composing new (writers') masks and voices to engage in that work.

Chapter 5

Expanding Writing Spaces as Communities of Practice

Mike: What am I afraid of?
Ramona: Yup.
Mike: Nothing.
Ramona: You're not afraid of anything?
Mike: There's nothing to be afraid of. Stuff happens, it happens. And no matter what you do about it, what's there to be afraid of?
Ramona: OK. That's a good quote.
(Fifth grader Ramona interviewing her dad, Mike)

In this chapter, I describe and discuss the students as they engage in biography work, having moved from a brief biography of a colleague in their classrooms to more in-depth work about an adult that was important to them. Both classes continued to have rigid schedules involving 90 minutes of reading instruction during which up to half of each class traveled to another classroom because reading instruction was homogenously grouped. Patia explained that, "All of our time is taken up by this program. There's no time for anything else . . ." Patia felt all the pressures that so many teachers felt in this 'failing' school. The teachers called it a failing school and, for the most part, complied with the curricular demands placed on them. I offer their beliefs about the school as evidence of their appropriation of the official portrait. Consistent with what occurred at many such schools, time for science and social studies was replaced with increased focus on reading and math, two areas that were always tested. During morning trainings that occurred at least once each month before the students arrived, the teachers were told to do certain lessons with their students. Barbara also attended these, but did not feel the pressure to use the lessons presented. When Barbara discussed at lunch why she refused to do with her class certain activities from the morning sessions, Patia agreed with Barbara, but Patia tended to teach the lessons because her colleagues in sixth grade all agreed to do so. Barbara told her fifth grade colleagues that she would not do everything that they were supposed to do because she wanted to do the biography work. Barbara was opening a safe space for counterportraits, using my presence as permission to deviate from prescribed curriculum.

The decisions that Barbara and Patia made about teaching writing influenced the way literacy events (Harste, Woodward, & Burke, 1984) unfolded when I was present in the classroom. The fifth graders had more time to discuss, think, write, and revise, sometimes up to two hours twice a week. The sixth graders engaged in biography work when I was present, but only rarely when I was not. The fifth grade work seemed to be moving forward consistently, while the sixth graders' work was intense when I was present and tangential to their lives in school when I was not. Barbara emailed me during the week about the progress of the fifth graders' writing, sometimes asking questions or requesting that I lead a strategy lesson when I arrived. I learned to arrive at the sixth grade classroom with a lesson planned, typically short and often a form of poetry. The story in this chapter once again splits as the fifth graders systematically pursue their work on one person while the sixth graders engage in successive writing engagements during which they could focus on one or many individuals, including themselves.

Within both of these classrooms, the borders between in-school and out-of-school lives shifted. These borders were, of course, specific to individuals, yet as individuals made choices about what to study, think, and write about, the collective sense of borders in the classroom shifted. As with any community, the shift in borders led to further shifts in individuals, groups within each classroom, and the whole classrooms as writing environments. Following the presentation of the activity that occurred in the classrooms, I'll return to the idea of borders, informed by the literature on communities of practice (Lave and Wenger, 1991), as an integral part of counterportraits that speak in opposition to the official portrait that shadows the lives of these writers and their teachers.

Fifth Graders Interview, Transcribe, and Write

The fifth graders were confident interviewers following their experiences interviewing each other. Barbara worked during that process to have them slow down and reflect upon what they understood a person to be saying and what questions lingered because of what the person said. Consuelo's interview and biography of Luisa are examples of the results when we give the students time to interview and write. All of the students in the class knew that Luisa limped, but through Consuelo's interviewing they learned the story of Luisa's leg, damaged when her mom, pregnant with Luisa, had a severe fall. Luisa lived in a small town in South America and when missionaries appeared, Luisa's father begged them to take her to the US for surgery. The goal of a good interview is to find the stories that we didn't know before and the details of the interesting stories we might already know.

We were getting at the importance of stories (Meyer, 1996) and the ways in which good questions help an interviewer gain access to those. Through email, Barbara and I each agreed to bring an artifact to class to demonstrate how 'things' can lead to information. I brought two rocks. Barbara asked, "Why are these rocks important to you?" I told the story of learning about rocks from a sixth grade teacher that took our entire class to places so we could chip off samples for a rock collection, inspiring my love of geology. I suggested to the children that they have to use what they know about me already "to ask more questions to get more interesting stuff to write." Later, once the students collected interview data, we talked about the ways in which direct quotes can make a biography more interesting and credible.

Barbara led the class in generating a list of interview questions, a sort of buffet of possibilities from which they could draw when they were interviewing someone. Here are some of the questions they generated:

What was your life like when you were little?

Did you suffer when you were a child? How?

How did you come to America?

Why do you like _____ (children filled in: America, motor-cycles, the army, and more)?

What was your first job?

Have you ever been on an adventure? Tell about it.

Tell me about your education?

Why did you join the army? (Ramona wanted this because she knew she'd be studying her dad, a veteran wounded in Iraq.)

Why did you _____ (to ask about anything you wonder about)?

What states have you lived in? Why?

What was your first memory?

What are things you like about your life?

Tell me about the neighborhood you grew up in.

Age, birth date, birth place?

Do you have an artifact (something people can remember you by)? [Their wording suggests an emerging understanding of the idea of an 'artifact']

What did you want to be when you grew up?

What did you enjoy?

How did you meet _____? [mom, grandma, etc.]

What was your first goal? Have you reached it? Do you have new goals?

Have you ever been injured?

Do you have any regrets?

Tell me about your first pet.

Tell me about your family.

Some of the children objected to some of these questions because they weren't relevant to the person they selected to write about. Barbara reminded them that they choose which ones they like. She also suggested that they add more if, while they are interviewing or while they are thinking about the interview, they think of other questions they want to ask.

I purchased six digital voice recorders so the children could record interviews. We spent an afternoon reading the directions, learning about loading the batteries, recording, trying various playback options, and learning to download the files onto the computer so the students could listen to, transcribe, and, we would learn, translate their interviews. On evenings when the students didn't have a recorder, we sent home disposable cameras that Barbara bought so the children could photograph their families, including the person they were studying. Some of the children also found and brought old photographs to be scanned into the final biography pieces. Ramona's father sent photos of him in Iraq; Andres' grandfather sent photos of a helicopter with grandpa seated in the cockpit. There were childhood photos, photos of weddings, babies, pets, relatives on both sides of the US-Mexico border, and homes.

Most families were excited to be recorded and enjoyed listening to themselves, sometimes requesting a second 'take' in order to add details they recalled while listening. On a few, we heard the fifth grade interviewer request, "Speak louder." The files were downloaded and the children worked to do two things: first, they summarized so that they could have facts for the biography; second, they transcribed short sections as possible quotes to include in the final written piece. The work with the interview data took close to two months, working twice weekly, to transcribe and summarize. Isabel, like many of the others, listened to her recordings and wrote a list of follow-up questions for a second interview as colleagues asked her questions that she couldn't answer. We reminded her that yes/no questions did not yield a lot of information.

"I know," she said, "I'll ask 'why?' if she doesn't tell me enough."

Some Fifth Graders' Transcriptions (Excerpts)

Marisol decided to write her father's biography and began by listing many additional questions that she would ask. Some of these were 'artificial' in that she already knew the answers, such as the number of children in her family. Others were more authentic and led to surprises, such as having three dead aunts and her father being shot. Sharing her findings with a small group of fifth grade colleagues brought forth a range of questions, some of which Marisol would ask her father in a subsequent interview; others remain family secrets as she clearly did not want to pursue or make public supplementary information. In transcribing the recordings, I use ellipses (. . .) before the child or adult's name at the left margin to indicate one or more rounds of questions and answers not included due to space constraints or repetition. I use them during the flow of the conversation to indicate a pause of three seconds or longer. I also eliminated repetitions, tags such as "uhhh" or "ummm," unless they appeared relevant. Marisol's first interview lasted six minutes and forty seconds. Readers cannot hear the warmth of her dad's voice, the pride he feels in being interviewed, or the love he has for his daughter, yet these elements are clear on the recording.

Marisol: Who are your heroes?

Gregorio (Marisol's Father): My heroes? My dad was always my hero. But, my heroes have always been the cowboys.

Marisol: Why?

Gregorio: Because I admire how they rope and ride.

Marisol: What are you afraid of? Why?

Gregorio: I'm afraid to be alone 'cause I don't like to be alone by myself. I always like to have people around.

. . . *Marisol:* What are things you like about your life?

Gregorio: Like about my life? I like the family I have. I like where I live. I like the kind of work that I work. I work for the railroad. I like the horses I have.

Marisol: What is your birthplace?

Gregorio: . . . Chihuahua, Mexico.

Marisol: What is your favorite artifact?

Gregorio: Ahh, when we get together with the family.

Marisol: What did you want to be when you grew up?

Gregorio: When I was a kid I always wanted to be a veterinarian.

Marisol: How did you meet my mom?

Gregorio: Through my brother's girlfriend, that introduced us.

Marisol: What was your first goal? Did you make it?

Gregorio: To put enough money together to buy my first car.

. . . *Marisol:* Did you ever do something bad and try to fix it?

Gregorio: I don't recall that I ever did something I ever regretted.

Marisol: What if you didn't fix it, would you regret it?

Gregorio: Like I said, I don't remember or have nothing really bad to worry about it.

Marisol: What states have you gone to?

Gregorio: States? I've made almost all the United States from New York to Ohio, Michigan, South Dakota, Wyoming, Colorado, Kansas, Oklahoma, Louisiana, Arizona, New Mexico and I guess every state in between.

Marisol: What is your favorite song?

Gregorio: My favorite song is a Mexican song Una Pagina Mas (One More Page).

. . . *Marisol:* Did you ever got shot or injured badly?

Gregorio: Yeah, I was shot once in my abdomen.

Marisol: . . . [5 seconds] How is your life now in these days?

Gregorio: It's good. I have a good family and good work and I like what we have.

Marisol: Have any of your family members died?

Gregorio: I had three sisters that died when they were too young, two older than me, one younger than me.

Marisol: Did you ever finish school? What grade?

Gregorio: I didn't finish it. I went thru twelfth grade.

Marisol: Do you have any regrets?

Gregorio: [laughs] Yes, not finishing school.

When Barbara, Marisol, some students, and I listened to Marisol's interview, we pointed out how quickly she was going through the list of questions. I talked about how difficult it is to really listen while you interview, but that when she listened to the recording in class, she might think of some follow-up questions. I wondered if Marisol knew many of the responses before she'd asked the questions in her first round of interviews. Noticing the five-second pause after her father mentioned being shot, I asked, "Is that a story you want to know more about?"

"No," she said quietly.

"That's okay," I said. "Biographers choose what to ask and what to include in their final pieces."

Luisa interviewed her 'grandfather,' her guardian who, with his wife, brought her to the US from Peru for surgery that would involve rebuilding her leg from the knee down. In the US for less than three months when I met her, Luisa learned English quickly and spoke English to her guardians, teachers, and classmates and shifted to Spanish when she was spoken to in Spanish. She left school for six weeks during this research to have her surgery at a hospital in another state, but did return for the end of the year celebration of our accomplishments (see Chapter 9).

Luisa: What are some things of your life that you like?

Nick: I enjoy traveling. I have done quite a bit of traveling in my life and it was all job related because I could travel and work as I traveled. I went to Alaska, Russia (of course I didn't work in Russia), Puerto Rico, Venezuela, Panama, Costa Rica, Peru, and Mexico several times. And I'd like to go to Israel; I'd like to go back to Russia. I'd like to go to China. I've been to England and Spain and France.

Luisa: That's a lot of cities.

Nick: Oh yeah. It's been fun. I really like people. I enjoy talking to them, visiting with them, and knowing their culture. And visiting their homes. When I go someplace, I'd rather go visit people in their homes and see how they live.

Luisa: Grandpa, where were you born?

Nick: I was born in New Mexico. In Gallup.

. . . *Luisa:* What are some of the things you like about your grandchildren [foster children].

Nick: Well, some of my favorite things in the whole world are my grandchildren. I love my children dearly; I love my family dearly. And my grandchildren have just been a real delight in my life. And as you know I'm just a recent grandpa. I've only been a grandpa for a little over a year. I started with you, Luisa, and then the other three kids from Columbia. I just love being around you kids, playing with you, and taking you places. I enjoy talking to you and trying to teach you things. And encouraging you to be what you can be because you're now in a country where you can do so many things and I want you to take advantage of them, educationally.

Andres's grandfather is a veteran of the Vietnam War, but Andres had not previously known about some of the things that happened to his grandfather. He also learned about his grandfather's childhood, an uncle Andres never got to meet, and his grandfather's war injury. Barbara and I realized that some of the details that the children knew or learned were not part of the recordings.

Andres: What was your life like when you were a child?

Robert (Andres's Grandfather): I was a very happy little child. We had a lot of things to do when I was a child and we played a lot outside and did a lot of things. I was very happy.

Andres: Did you suffer when you were little?

Robert: No, I never suffered when I was little. We were a very close family and we kept busy and we didn't suffer. We had everything we wanted.

Andres: How did you come to America?

Robert: I was born here in America.

. . . *Andres:* What was your first job?

Robert: My first job was as a dishwasher in a restaurant. It was very hard. I was fifteen years old when I got my first job and I worked in that restaurant for about three years.

Andres: Have you ever been on an adventure?

Robert: I guess the only adventure I been on was when I joined the army.

Andres: Tell me about it. [This is a thoughtful follow-up to the question.]

Robert: Well, the adventure was I went to Vietnam and there was a war at that time and I was a helicopter crew chief. We used to fly in our helicopters and that was the adventure and every time when we went out, it was an adventure.

Andres: Tell me about your education.

Robert: Well I graduated high school. And after high school, I joined the army. After I got out . . . while I was in the army I learned to be a mechanic on helicopters and after the army I learned to make kitchen cabinets at [a local community college]. And that's about all in my education.

Andres: Why did you join the army?

Robert: Well, I joined the army 'cause I wanted to do something different. And I was already nineteen years old and a lot of my friends were in the army so I joined the army.

. . . *Andres:* What are things that you like about your life?

Robert: I like that I'm healthy and I like that I'm retired. I can still do a lot of things. I enjoy spending time with my family.

Andres: Tell me about the town you grew up in.

Robert: I grew up in a little town in northern New Mexico, near the — River, maybe 400 people at the time. We used to go fishing; we had horses, we had cows, we had chickens, we had pigs. Everybody knew everybody and there was a lot of respect for each other.

. . . *Andres:* How did you meet your wife?

Robert: I used to go to school with her brother and that's how we met. I went to go visit her brother and I met my wife.

. . . *Andres:* Have you ever been injured?

Robert: Yes, I was injured in Vietnam in a helicopter accident. And basically recovered from that; it was a shoulder injury and that's about it. I'm doing well now.

. . . *Andres:* Tell me about your family.

Robert: Well I have a very good family. I have my wife; I have three kids; I had three boys and one of them passed away when he was fifteen.

Andres eventually did some follow-up work without the recorder, finding answers to some of his lingering questions and putting that information into his final product (see Appendix 2).

Ramona's father is also a veteran, but of the war in Iraq. He returned home injured, with medals, and happy to be reunited with his family. He started the interview with quick answers and Ramona often asked him to repeat because she couldn't hear him; even then his voice is, at times, muffled on the recording. However, as she continued, he became somewhat more forthcoming about his experiences within and beyond the army. Although the content of some of this interview has, as a subtext, the reality of war with all of its horror, Ramona's dad gradually moved into speaking softly and warmly, protecting his daughter from too many details. He joked about IED's (improvised explosive devices), but it was clear when he visited the classroom that he was in pain when he walked. The other students' interest in Ramona's dad increased with each story she told, eventually resulting in her inviting him to the classroom. He came with MREs (Meal, Ready to Eat) for each child. Politics was moved aside, as we did not discuss the merits of the war; we focused on a daughter who had her father as her hero. Ramona designed questions to elicit some of what she knew and to find out more about her dad.

Ramona: Where and when were you born?
Mike (Ramona's Father): Long Beach, 19 [inaudible]
Ramona: 19 what?
Mike: 1964. [He laughs]. It's personal. [Ramona laughs]
. . . *[inaudible responses] Ramona:* Why did you join the army?
Mike: [inaudible] To do my part for my country and to protect my family.
Ramona: What awards did you get and how?
Mike: Iraqi Freedom because I was in Iraq, National Defense because everyone gets one of those, Army Achievement Medal, Bronze Star, . . .
Ramona: How'd you get the bronze star? What'd you do?
Mike: [inaudible] thirty-two guys . . . [inaudible]
Ramona: That all?
Mike: I identified over 500 Iraqi terrorists like [name of terrorist] and I arrested thirty two. I also took down the number three guy of al Qaida in Iraq and I took down [inaudible].
Ramona: What was your first job?
Mike: Truck stop.
Ramona: Why did you want children?
Mike: Why not?
Ramona: OK, ummm, do you regret anything?
Mike: Yeah, not staying longer in Iraq and taking out more guys.
Ramona: And your injuries, tell me about them.
Mike: OK, it's gonna be a long tape. [Ramona laughs].
Ramona: OK.
Mike: Umm, right knee is messed up, left knee is [inaudible] messed up, and back is messed up.
Ramona: Why are they messed up? What happened?
Mike: An IED went boom boom [Ramona laughs] and knocked me on my butt [Ramona laughs].
Ramona: And that makes all your . . .
Mike: I ruptured one of my disks, and [inaudible] four other disks, and caused me to lose a couple of things in my right knee, in front of it. OK?
Ramona: OK. Have you always wanted to be in the army?
Mike: Yeah.
Ramona: Ever since you were little?
Mike: Yeah.
Ramona: You never said, "I wanna be a fireman!"
Mike: No.
Ramona: OK.
Mike: I [inaudible] got to shoot people. [Ramona laughs]

Ramona: OK. How did you meet my mom?

Mike: I played little league with her brother. My mom and her mom were best friends. And I played baseball for you grandpa.

Ramona: OK.

Mike: And then I coached with your grandpa.

. . . *Ramona:* OK. Why is Milo your favorite pet?

Mike: Because he listens and he ain't stupid.

Ramona: Do you have any heroes, like people you look up to?

Mike: Yeah, everybody that puts on a uniform and goes in Iraq, everybody that went to Vietnam, World War II, World War I, everybody that's ever put on a uniform and went to a conflict.

Ramona: What is the best thing that ever happened to you?

Mike: What do you mean? Like outside of the kids, marriage and that kind of good stuff? Getting the Bronze Star. [Ramona would eventually find a photo of the Star on the Internet to include in her biography.]

Ramona: [her question was inaudible]

Mike: I'd have to kill you. [Ramona laughs]

Ramona: Like if I asked you anything else you'd have to kill me?

Mike: Right, you can't ask that question. If I tell you, I gotta kill you.

Ramona: What's something important in your life besides Army and family?

Mike: Well, that's it.

Ramona: Really? That's all you care about is Army and family?

Mike: Umm hmm [yes].

Ramona: You don't care about *Family Guy* [a TV show, she laughs]?

Mike: Less than Iraqis.

Ramona: That's enough.

Mike: Actually, it's not. I could be doing that on the civilian side when I get done, like teaching candidates to catch Iraqis.

. . . *Ramona:* What is your hobby?

Mike: Softball, baseball.

Ramona: What are you afraid of?

The interview ends with the quote at the beginning of this chapter. Ramona used that quote and others from her dad as she wrote the biography of her father. Like many of the children, Ramona heard that the most important thing in her father's life was his family. This was a theme that came up again and again across interviews. This intense love and dedication are not part of their official portrait and relying upon that love as a foundation for school literacy events is a cornerstone of counterportraiture.

Estevan and Consuelo both interviewed parents that were originally in the US without official papers of permission. They interviewed in Spanish, although Consuelo's mom wanted to try it in English, and then changed her mind once they started. The parents' wishes and hopes are articulated in the following child-translated excerpts from their interviews.

Estevan: When were you born?

Javier: I was born in Pena Blanca, [Mexico] March 29, 1962.

Estevan: Where did you go to school and did you graduate?

Javier: In Pena Blanca [through] secondaria [grade levels similar to middle school in the US].

Estevan: When did you come to the United States?

Javier: I've been here 17 years but before that [inaudible].

Estevan: How did you get here?

Javier: I came with my brother in a van. It had a top so the immigration couldn't see us.

. . . *Estevan:* When you came to the US, what did you do?

Javier: My job was to lay carpet.

Estevan: When did you have your first child?

Javier: It was you, November 13, 1995.

Estevan: It's the 12th

Javier: It's the 12th, not the 13th. [Both laugh.] The day that you were born, I was very happy.

Estevan: Why were you so happy when I was born?

Javier: Because you were born in America and because the first child was a boy, too.

Estevan: After I was born, what did you want for me?

Javier: My dream is for you is to do well in school and become a doctor.

Estevan: What about your family?

Javier: I want everybody in the family to never be without food.

Estevan: Is that all your work jobs?

Javier: I've always done carpet, laid carpet.

. . . *Estevan:* After he [your second son] was born, how did you feel?

Javier: I was happy. I have two sons and a wife.

. . . *Estevan:* Are you still doing carpet?

Javier: Yes, I'm gonna die doing carpet because that's the only thing I know how to do. That's the only thing I know how to do.

Consuelo [in English]: Did you suffer when you were a child?

Leticia (Consuelo's Mom, in Spanish): You have to tell me in Spanish.

Consuelo [remainder of the interview was translated from Spanish by Consuelo]: Did you suffer when you were a child?

Leticia: Well, I don't remember.

Consuelo: How did you come to America?

Leticia: I came as a mojada [literally, 'wetback', but not with the negative connotation as when said in English; here it means she crossed illegally], with no papers.

Consuelo: What do you like?

Leticia: I don't understand, what do you mean? Here? I like it better here than Mexico.

Consuelo: Why?

Leticia: There's more opportunity . . . they help you more here than they do in
 Mexico.
Consuelo: Did you have any adventures?
Leticia: When I crossed over, when I was a mojada was an adventure for me
 . . . on the road there were a lot of immigrants.
Consuelo: And did you come walking?
Leticia: Yes. I walked for three days.
Consuelo: You didn't sleep?
Leticia: No.
Consuelo: And when you got here, what did you think?
Leticia: Thanks to God I got here OK.
Consuelo: Tell me your education.
Leticia: I only went to primaria [primary grades in US]. Secondaria at night.
 . . . *Consuelo:* What's your first memory?
Leticia: Of what?
Consuelo: The thing that you remember.
Leticia: My grandmother. Because I lived with her for nine years.
Consuelo: Do you have an artifact?
Leticia: Everything I remember from when I was little with my grandmother.

The fifth graders used the recordings to take notes on the person they were
studying. They listened to downloaded files on one of the eight classroom
computers or on the voice recorder using headsets for privacy and noise
control in the classroom, played them again and again, and worked to
transform oral information to written data. Figures 5.1–5.3 are examples of
their early note taking.

 A few of the children were concerned about finishing, expressing a desire to
be done or belief that they were done. The students learned to produce
completed pieces in short periods of time because they were not previously
given long periods of time to work on pieces. They didn't invest significant
energy into written work at school because during their school careers the
demand was more for mass output or speedy output (or both), rather than a
slowly crafted piece for which they felt genuine concern for their topic and
their audience. I suggested that Barbara invite some of the children that were
'done' to become part of a whole-class critique as a way of teaching the students
that they would have sufficient time to craft a piece, reflect upon it, study it
with colleagues, revise, and complete something that they and the person they
were writing about would be proud of. In an email, Barbara described the
process, which occurred on a day when I was not present:

> One of the boys was the first to bring his biography to me. "I'm done," he
> remarked as he handed me his paper . . . . It was important for him to see
> for himself that this copy was just the beginning. There were many more
> ideas to explore and write about on his father's biography. Would a class

Figure 5.1
Andres' notes on a classmate.

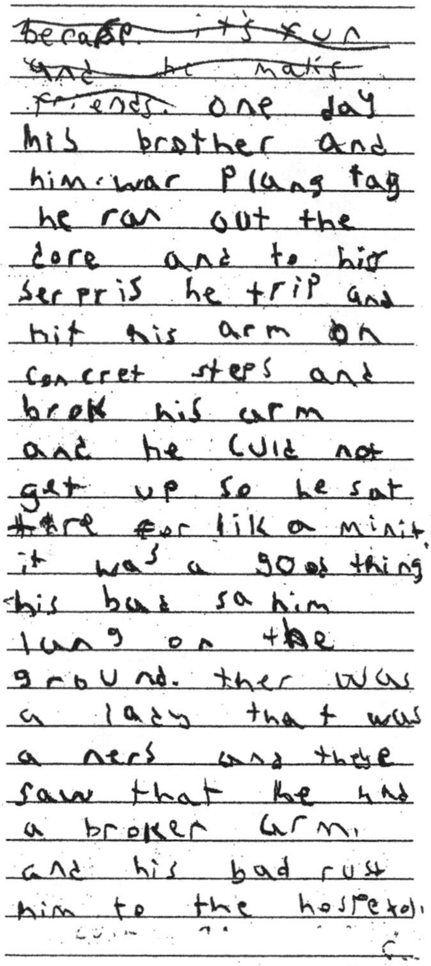

~~because it's fun and he makes friends.~~ one day his brother and him war plang tag he ran out the dore and to his serpris he trip and hit his arm on concret steps and brok his arm and he culd not get up so he sat thare for lik a minit. it was a good thing his bad sa him lung on the ground. ther was a lady that was a ners and they saw that he had a broken arm. and his bad rust him to the hospetol.

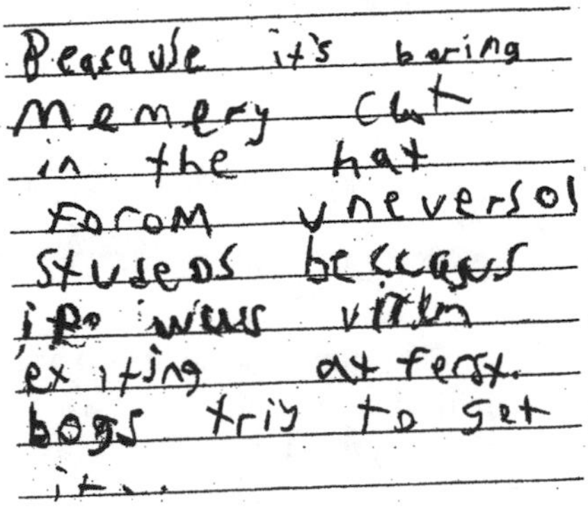

Beacause it's boring memery chat in the hat forom universol studeos because ito wass vitim exiting at ferst. boys triy to get it..

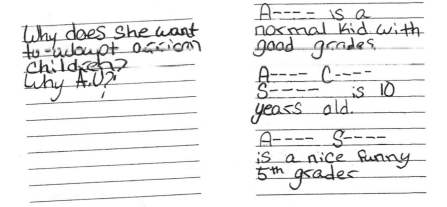

Figure 5.2 Ramona's notes on a classmate.

critique hurt his feelings? He was actually honored to have his paper up on the overhead with a copy in every student's hands. Before we looked at the piece, we discussed how personal writing is, how we need to be sure to be constructive with our remarks and not destructive. We needed to look for 'likes' and words that struck us in some form. We needed to ask questions like, "What did we want to know more about?" Immediately after reading the piece, hands went up all over the room. There were a few likes, but mostly, there were many questions. The students' questions were written on the overhead. [The boy whose piece we critiqued] proudly answered what questions he could, and then requested to check out a recorder again. "I need to do more interviewing!" he said. That day, he went home with a recorder, showed his dad the overhead with all of the questions, and together spent the evening recording a stronger interview, full of personal stories. He returned to school, excited and motivated . . .

When I next saw this young writer, he said, "Dr. Meyer, I wrote ten pages!" I asked what happened. He explained, "After my father saw the list of questions, he told me, 'We gotta talk a lot more.'" Working twice a week, the students took almost two months to craft their biographies. Once they understood that they would be given time for writing, time to engage in thoughtful interaction with colleagues about their progress, and time for multiple drafts, they began to assume a stance towards their writing that was reminiscent of real authors. They discussed problems with their work, challenges, issues of conventions and content, and the importance of the placement of exact quotes.

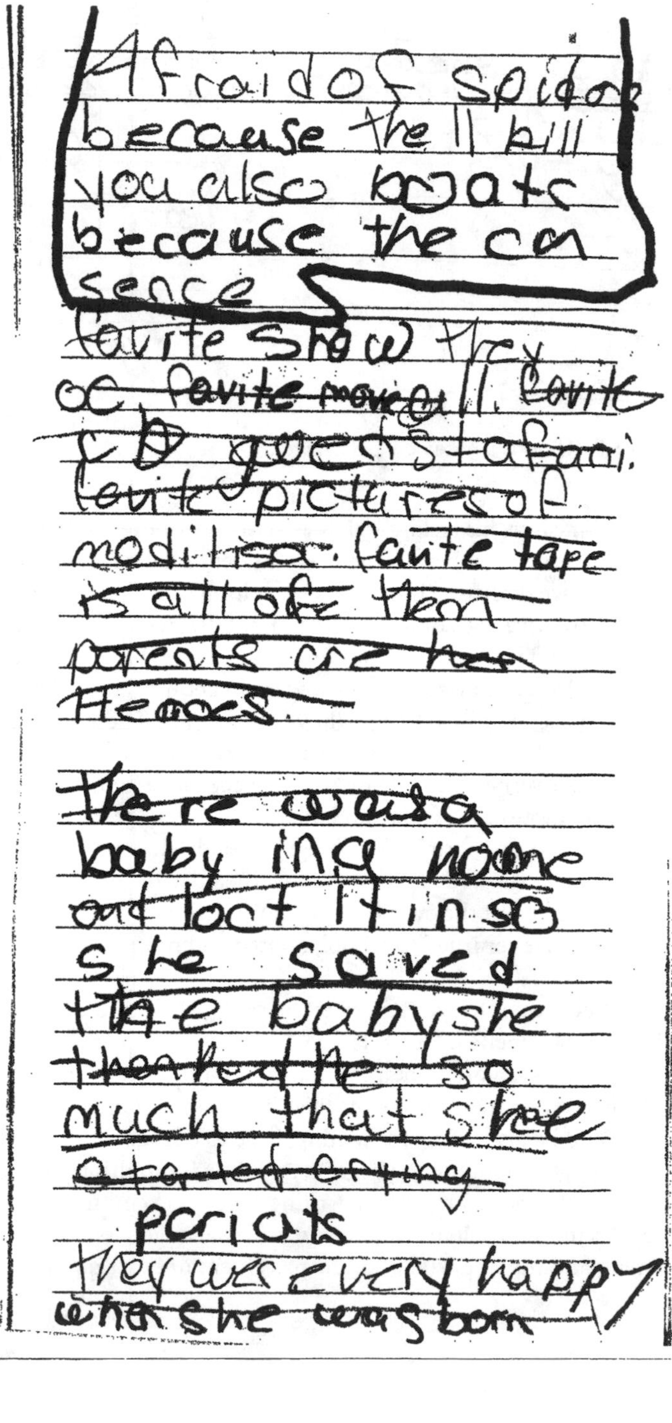

Figure 5.3
Debi's
notes on a
classmate.

And in the Sixth Grade . . .

I was teaching a university course during the spring of the year of this study and discussed the sixth graders' writing quite frequently. Each time the sixth graders wrote, I asked if I had their permission to read their work to the students that I was teaching. I read their *Where I'm From* poems and their *I used to, but now* pieces, including the longer pieces that were generated from them. In early February, I arrived at the sixth grade class with a seasonal (Valentine's Day) lesson in mind: we'd write love stories. I knew they'd hoot and laugh at this, which they did, but then I explained that they would get to write about people that they knew that seemed to be in love and also write about what it meant to be in love. I suggested that it would be someone in their family because they knew those people well. There was much resistance to the idea, but I pushed saying, "Well, some of you are going out with someone. Why not write about that?" I knew that this reference to their love lives would also be met with resistance. I'd learned that going out meant that they agreed that they were going out, but they didn't necessarily go anywhere. They might hang out together on the playground, which could result in some serious teasing for the more vulnerable students, or pass notes to each other before and after school. A few called each other in the evenings or on weekends.

"Noooo," came the resounding cries. "We can't do that. We can't write about that?"

"Why not?" I asked.

No one could articulate a reason. "Well, then I guess you could write about it," I said, knowing I was pushing the limits of our very limited relationship.

Silence. Again.

"Well, what about this, then. You could write a love story, true or made up, but not about anyone in this class unless you're writing about yourself."

"Nooooo."

"Orrrrr," I tried again, "you could write a letter to the teachers who have been hearing your poetry in the class I'm teaching. What do you want a teacher to know about teaching, about life, about making school a good place, or anything else you want them to know."

"We can choose?" asked Juliana.

"Yes, you decide which to write and then write it. A love story or a letter to a teacher." I knew we were not focusing on biographies, but at this point the goal became the production of any truthful writing in which they invested energy.

I present the love letters first because they are evidence of the non-biography biographic tendencies (i.e. not traditional expository text) that the students have in their writing. Telling a love story involves reflection, tact, honesty, and voice, all of which are present in the narratives that follow.

Vianca wrote:

> My sister was always so lonely. Then one day she went to a party. She knew some friends [there]. Then she knew a guy, that guy had a brother. My

sister's boyfriend's brother did not like my sister. My sister didn't like him either. Then the days past and my sister and the brother were boyfriend [and girlfriend]. Now they are almost going to get married.

Mercedes wrote:

When I first saw him, I used to think he was a boy who thinks all bad, but we started to talk to each other. Then I went out with him for about three weeks, then we broke up because he supposedly liked another girl. Then four months passed and right now I'm going out with him. We first met because of my friend G— because they are cousins. We saw each other in the gym and then we started to talk to each other on the phone. I was really confused because I didn't know what to say.

After reading Mercedes' piece, I loaned her *Romiette and Julio* (Draper, 1999) and she read it over one weekend.
Ricardo wrote:

There was a time when I was in 3rd or 4th grade when my mom and dad were getting along just fine. I was happy and they were happy. After a while, they started arguing and fighting. I thought it was no big deal. But then one day when it was just about ready for my dad to go to work, they had another fight. My mom was peeling green chili so we could eat tomorrow. At the time, my mom had been mad at my sister about something that I don't even remember. My dad had been letting my sister in the house, and my mom didn't like it. Just when my dad was leaving, my mom started yelling, cussing, and throwing chili at him. When he left, there was chili on the walls and on the floor. I started to cry because I never saw my parents fight like that before. The next day, my mom woke me up early in the morning. She told me to get dressed quickly. We left the house and went to an Inn. We got a small room to spend the night in. The Inn had a swimming pool so my mom told me, "Let's go to Wal-Mart." We bought some food and I bought some swim trunks. We went back to the Inn so I could swim. I remember we stayed up late watching "Tales from the Crypt." I thought my parents were getting a divorce. But after a while I didn't think so because my mom seemed really happy. The next day we went back to the house to find my dad asleep in the shed since my mom had locked the house. My mom and dad said sorry and their love and marriage continued.

Esperanza wrote:

Dear Dr. Meyer,

This is a love story. My mom and dad are "married" [she used quotation marks]. One day that my dad was "drinking," my mom got very mad. My dad used to "drink" a lot. One day mom told my dad that it was over. My dad realized that he was destroying our family. He went to get help. He went to this place that helps them stop "drinking." Three weeks later he came to the house and they fixed that and now we are very happy. Now he doesn't "drink." Like they say, there's a way to stop. But for death, there's no way to stop. Now we are a happy family with two boys and two girls and my mom and dad. I share this with you because I have trust in you. So please be with like you always have been good. [sic]

The letters to teachers reveal some of the students' understanding of what good teaching is as well as how they've appropriated the language they hear about teachers, both in and out of school.
Juliana wrote:

Dear New Teacher,

What you need to know to be a teacher is how to support kids. Sometimes they cry or talk back to you. You could learn how to be a nice teacher. Give them recess. Let them have time for their work and time for themselves. Don't be a mean teacher. Be a nice one and children will listen to you. You need to be patient with them. If they are mean sometimes, just ignore them, and if you can't, just take them to the office or take recess from them. Just be a little strict.

Isaac wrote:

To new teacher. Let me tell you what us kids want of a teacher. A teacher who talks a lot about them self. Who lets you hear music in class. So I can bring my mp3. Our teacher, Ms —, is pretty cool. She lets us hear music. I brought my mp3 once but I did not take it out of my backpack. My friend, G—, let me use his. If Dr. Meyer gives this to you, follow them and you will have a good year. But still you have to be strict. Keep you eyes open. Girls pass notes.

Jesus, who resisted his teacher's efforts to have him learn and behave in class, wrote:

If you teach kinder, you need to be nice and fun. If you teach sixth, you don't have to be mean. You just have to be strict. For me, fifth was the best. My teacher was funny, nice and strict. We did lots of projects. She helped me understand math more. She even gave us a big field trip at the end of the year. We went to Santa Fe for one night. We saw the capitol. We also went swimming and saw three museums. That's a year I wont forget. To be a good teacher, you need to have a little bit of kid in you. There will be good kids and bad kids. You just need to know how to handle it. I kind of consider myself more on the bad side because I like to make jokes and be with my friends. Man, time has flew by. Oh yeah, try not to have too many subs. Kids are crazy with subs. Good luck becoming a teacher.

Sincerely,

Jesus

Verdad wrote:

Dear New Teacher,

Well first of all my name is Verdad [last name] but they call me Ver. Well if you want to be a good teacher you need to really learn a lot of stuff. You need to go to college for a long time. They need to teach you math, language arts, and all of those things. You need to do good in college because if you don't, they don't give you the scholarship to be a teacher. By the way, what grade do you want to teach? If I was a teacher, I would like to teach 6th grade. I want to teach 6th grade because I think by now they are intelligent. I prefer kindergarten. They know how to behave, not like 6th graders.

Corazon wrote:

Dear Future Teacher

I think that being a teacher must be so hard. You must have trouble by understanding and taking care of other children's problems. And you must be really really. I mean really patient. Once me and my cousin R— were babysitting for the [family name] and I really got frustrated and started yelling at one of the kids. After that, I really felt bad. I mean they pay me and all I do is yell at one of their children. Well, any way, back to being a teacher, honestly, I would enjoy being a teacher but they really don't pay teachers that much money. I want and am wishing I would be part of the CSI even though I know it must be a pretty hard job. I am going to fight for it. But if that doesn't go well, I would also like to be a lawyer, even though I really want to be part of the CSI. Being a lawyer is most likely what a girl like me would do for a living. Being a teacher would be like a second job to me like for example being a substitute at many different schools. I consider myself very mean or strict so they'll probably hate me. Bye, it's time to go home but I think I kind of would like being a teacher.

Hope you can accomplish your dream,

Corazon

The sixth graders read some of their pieces to each other and listened to each other. Some smiled and others offered relevant (even kind) remarks. We'd negotiated the topics of the day's writing and they invested energy and thoughtfulness in their pieces. They considered the audiences and were forthcoming with their beliefs and truths.

The stories that the fifth grade and the sixth graders heard, recorded, and wrote were signifiers of many more details that were not told or written. Some, indeed most, of the kids wrote about something that was quite complex, for example an uncle that was murdered, a mother crossing the border illegally, or a brother in a gang. But, the piece that was produced was almost a summary, a telegram with only the barest of facts. The children were told by their teachers throughout their schooling that details are important and some may have even had a few lessons on including details or being descriptive. As readers, we only see the tips of figurative icebergs, with the substance of the story often lying below the surface or between the lines, hidden in the subtexts that didn't get written. Yet, for the most part, the classroom audiences knew the details. They'd heard each other's interviews, read transcriptions, and discussed many details orally. A child might ask, "When did he get shot," and the details would pour forth, details about nights in the hospital, recovery time, and how one gun was exchanged for another. The children in this book lived their lives steeped in these details and shared the details orally, but were only beginning to understand the importance of putting them onto the page.

At first, I thought that they were struggling with making the familiar strange, the way that good anthropologists or authors do. But in reality, they knew the familiar well and typically liked to talk about it, reliving the details of events. It was in the move to writing that they struggled and that struggle was one imposed by their teachers and me. We wanted them to compose the details in writing so that readers far from the source would see in their minds the events composed for the page.

When the students presented their work to future teachers (Chapter 9), they were asked many questions. Consuelo said to me, after her reading of her book about her mom, "They asked a lot of questions." "How come?" I asked. She smiled and said, "We needed to put in more details." This was a lesson learned late in the year. Yet when she read her piece to her mom, they both knew the subtexts. I glanced over as they read her book together and talked in Spanish after each page, both crying and moving closer and closer together to create a private space in which to celebrate both Consuelo's and her mom's accomplishments. "My book made my mother cry," Consuelo told me later in the evening. "I saw that," I answered. "You're a good writer." "I know," she said.

One genre that thrives on icebergs—tips of meaning that suggest worlds deep below—is poetry and that is where the sixth graders thrived. They liked the conciseness and the permission to leave out details that is inherent in the genre. There are many icebergs in this book, pieces written with multiple stories beneath the surface. Sadly, the struggle to bring the deeper parts to the surfaces of sheets of paper or computer screens was not always successful. However, I'm not convinced that this means that we failed at developing thoughtful writers. Small changes on the surface, evidenced throughout the year of the children's writing, suggest legitimate and authentic growth. And sometimes patterns, such as *Where I'm From* (in Christensen, 2000), were vehicles for bringing more to the surface. These vehicles served as tools with which the kids could dig into their depths and find something that they realized as familiar to them but important to the stuff of who they were as individuals and writers. We saw the changes in their discussions, first, as those grew deeper and lasted longer. The discussions, evidence of increased safety and reflection, although quite different across the two classrooms, suggested a shift in what was happening in school.

Communities, Borders, and Counterportraits

As the work on biographies progressed, the fifth and sixth graders found that their out-of-school lives were increasingly legitimate within the school setting. The everyday occurrences of their families were not only welcomed in the classroom, these events, personalities, and achievements became part of the "official curriculum" (Dyson, 1997) of the classroom. The borders between two previously well-defined, impermeable, and separate worlds were becoming permeable (Goffman, 1961). Gee (2000–2001) refers to the home as the primary discourse and school as the secondary. Students, he argues, perform with increased proficiency in school when the primary and secondary discourses are similar because language, expectations, and relationships are more consistent and familiar. The biography projects introduced primary discourse as a focus for study within secondary discourse. The use of primary research in which the students collected data, interviewed, and photographed their primary discourse helped address Barbara's desire to have her students write more substantial and memorable pieces. The intensity of both groups of students' engagement as writers and thinkers and their willingness to sustain the work over a long period of time is largely due to two factors: the teachers' willingness to provide the students with the time to write and the topics about which the students were writing. The borders between acceptable and unacceptable content, conversations, and process shifted. The practice of writing in the classrooms shifted and the composing of counterportraits—as "failing students" wrote passionate and articulate pieces—gained the status of legitimate classroom practice.

Lave and Wenger (1991), in their discussion of communities of practice, suggest, "the important point concerning learning is one of access to practice as resource for learning, rather than to instruction" (p. 85). It is the very nature of practice that is at the heart of a community of practice. They continue, defining a community of practice as "a set of relations among persons, activity, and world, over time and in relation with other tangential and overlapping communities of practice" (p. 98). In the fifth and sixth grades, the "overlap" changed for the writers in both classrooms because the nature of *practice* of writing changed. In the contexts of their lives as writers, *practice* became more akin to the way the word is used in medicine or law, as something in which professionals engage while learning for the duration of their professional lives. Previously, school was a place that controlled not only the broad categories of what constitutes *important things to know*, but also the very content within those categories and the processes by which they must be mastered. The biography work in which they engaged changed the practice and its inherent borders because of the teachers' willingness to welcome different content, the students' and the families' willingness to bring it into the classroom, and changes in the writing process as it occurred during biography work. Smith and Whitmore (2006) suggest that:

> We all move between communities as we go throughout our daily activities. Which communities we are members of contributes to the formation of our identities. How we participate in each community depends on our status. Our identities and our status in communities define what and how we learn and who we become. (p. 166)

The work of the writers in this book and their teachers contributed to the shifting nature of the community of practice within the classroom. The work changed what writing was, what a writer could do, how a writer could do it, and who each writer could be, at least for these moments in time and place.

Practice in the school context sets parameters for what can occur legitimately—or even be invented—within the classroom. Lave and Wenger (1991) state "in shaping the relation of masters to apprentices, the issue of conferring legitimacy is more important than the issue of providing teaching" (p. 92). In many school settings, legitimacy remains defined by Mehan's (1982) discussion of recitation scripts in which a teacher initiates an interaction, students respond, and the teacher evaluates the response (IRE). In such settings, school-based curricular legitimacy may simply mean that students show the teachers what is expected or desired by the teacher. Students may even work to perpetuate these superficial structures, a communicative process that Bloome (1983) refers to as "procedural display." Legitimacy is a place of tension as some students might resist, others comply, others withdraw, and others search for ways to strike out at the school, each other, their classroom, or their teachers.

Traditional school practice is considered legitimate unless it is disrupted or changed in some way. The biography work was instrumental in disrupting the typical practice, thus redefining legitimate practice. The children had never written in school as they did during this research. Lave and Wenger also write that "communities of practice are engaged in the generative process of producing their own future" (pp. 57–58). The school, as a community of practice, may contribute to the limiting or opening of that future. This is, of course, further complicated by the reality that children have different teachers each year with different views of the child, writing, curriculum, and the community. Each student in this study, internalizing their understanding of the school culture, thus invents a tentative school subjectivity to which they hold firm or renegotiate as a function of their interactions within and beyond the school context and their understanding of legitimate participation in those settings. It is within this tentativeness that I sought to work with the children and their teachers to reconsider their lives as writers and thinkers.

We worked together to change writing, an *everyday* activity (see use of 'everyday' below), as a way of changing the nature of school, the relationships that occur there, and the possibilities of what one can do with writing. We were recrafting legitimacy and legitimate work in school as a way of composing counterportraits. This increasingly complex view of communities of practice is consistent with Holland et al.'s (1998) explanation of "figured worlds":

> By 'figured world,' then, we mean a socially and culturally constructed realm of interpretation in which particular characters and actors are recognized, significance is assigned to certain acts, and particular outcomes are valued over others .... A figured world is formed and re-formed in relation to the **everyday** activities and events that ordain happenings within it.
>
> (pp. 52–53, emphasis added)

Within the figured world of school, subjectivities (Holland et al.'s "identities") are fluid, changing, political, and reflective of ongoing and ever-changing relationships between students and teachers within the classroom and others beyond it. The children lived the newly legitimated activity, not discussing much about it until we worked on evaluations at the end of the year; the teachers felt a shift in their views of their students—all of this is the stuff of counterportraits. Counterportraits grow from both the evidence and shifts in thinking that question and challenge the official portrait. These are concomitant shifts in the students as writers, their communities of writers, their teachers' thinking, and even their families' understanding of what occurs in school.

Legitimizing a Context for Counterportraiture

Within the present political contexts in which schools strive to survive, it becomes important to consider the subjectivities of the teachers as well as the students. At MVE, the pressure to 'make' adequate yearly progress was constant because the school never achieved this status. It is a status constructed far from the school, yet influencing the lives of the teachers and children that attend each day. The pressures to comply with rigid and often scripted programs that were composed with only official knowledge of the students (low test scores, English language learners, economically poor), coerced teachers (and the students and their families) into "fictionalized" (Walkerdine, 1990) subjectivities. I refer to these subjectivities as fictionalized because they are rooted in others' beliefs about the children's aptitude and achievement and do not consider the facts about the children presented here. The biography project was an opportunity to engage in the reflection that Grumet (1988) calls for:

> if the world we give our children is different from the one we envisioned for them, then we need to discover the moments when we, weary, distracted, and conflicted, gave in, let the curtain fall back across the window, and settled for a little less light.
>
> (p. xv)

Grumet also wonders about the nurturing role that women supposedly would bring to schools:

> The promise that women would bring maternal nurturance into the schools was sheer sentimentality, as it denied both the aspirations of the common school movement and the motives of these women who came to its classrooms in order to escape the horrifying isolation of domestic exile.
>
> (p. 56)

She continues:

> even as we celebrated their maternal gifts, we have required women to draw children out of the intimacy and knowledge of the family into the categorical and public world. We have burdened the teaching profession with contradictions and betrayals that have alienated teachers from our own experience, for our bodies, our memories, our dreams, from each other, from children, and from our sisters who are mothers to those children.
>
> (p. 57)

The community of practice that emerged, at this point in the study, was one that legitimized some of what Grumet says women have lost. We began to allow the light back in, drew back the curtain to show what was outside the window (even if it wasn't that pretty), and sought to end the isolation that not only women feel in their classrooms, but children feel as they are cut off from their home lives, often learning that their homes are not considered to be worth as much as what school has to offer. The biography work acknowledged, accepted, and welcomed intimacy and knowledge of self and family as strengths. We began working, though not conscious of it at this point, to end the self-betrayal that teachers and students feel in school. These border shifts became more intense as the work progressed and the counterportraits that the young writers composed of themselves, their families, and their community were further articulated. The border shifts led to changes in the masks that the students wore in school (particularly during our writing sessions) and the thoughts, ideas, and experiences they were willing to commit to the page. This was a continuation of the recomposing of the portraits they held within themselves and the portraits they presented in school. This recomposing, initiating from within both the writers and the changing parameters of legitimacy within the classroom, is essentially a grassroots movement that ignited further changes within the teachers and students and, like many grassroots movements, it may eventually reach more official forums.

Chapter 6

Writing Changes Writers
The Impact of Inertia

> Numerous critically conscious language and literacy studies include descriptions of the race/ethnicity and language/s of participants, but the majority are students of Color from poorly resourced communities and schools. The participants' ability to translate and transcend the ideological hegemony that permeates their communities and schools is seldom examined.
>
> (Willis, Montavon, Hall, Hunter, Burke & Herrera, 2008, p. 84)

At times during our work together, the students, teachers, or I commented on our work as "life-changing" (Barbara's words), realizing that a writer has a "brain with words" (Esperanza's words) or "how to get all my thoughts and writing them" (Juliana). We were *translating* and *transcending the ideological hegemony*, but not consistently participating in the political discussions inherent in such wording. We acted more intuitively, most of the time, because, I conjecture, things at the school seem to move so fast. The constant thrusting of curriculum, test preparation, interventions, professional development, alternative programs, and more upon teachers and children left us struggling to focus on and plan the writing work at hand. It wasn't until the year was over and I had time to analyze the data in greater depth that the political work we'd done—counterportraiture—became clear.

In this chapter I draw upon the concept of 'inertia' that physicists use in describing an object in motion as staying in motion unless acted upon by another force, such as gravity, friction, or an impact from another object. In a school setting, the 'motion' is the set of beliefs in operation. These beliefs are a sociocultural construct rooted in the official portrait of the school, which in the case of Mesa Vista Elementary includes such terms as *at risk, failing* and *not making adequate yearly progress.* These were inertial forces at MVE, part of the ethos of the school, appropriated by those at the school, and evident in the teachers' and students' discussions about the school. These discussions almost always originated in and seemed like a response to the litany of deficits about the school, community, children, and even the teachers. Interrupting inertia occurred with the students as they assumed the responsibilities in becoming writers with genuine purposes and goals. It occurred in the teachers' minds as they supported and learned from the students' writing activity. And it occurred in the minds of the principal and her colleagues when she showed them some of the students' work at a principals' gathering. The interruption of the inertia intensifies further when the children are invited to present completed pieces in other official forums. These are all tiny nudges against a huge object and force, tiny nudges felt within individual truth tellers much more powerfully than within the school, district, or state.

Each week the children's writing took new directions, twists, and turns that we explored like scientists, asking questions, challenging ideas, and pushing towards new understandings of what was written, how it was written, and who wrote it. As the community of practice changed, as masks morphed into different iterations of truthfulness, the writing and discussions about writing became more lofty, thoughtful, questioning, and tentative. The sixth graders' stories of themselves and their family members, told in their poetry and biographic in nature, took another turn when I invited Consuelo and Andres to visit the sixth grade with me. Some news from the university also changed the work.

Good News

After reading a few weeks worth of sixth grade poetry with my class of preservice teachers and also sharing with them the biographies-in-progress that the fifth graders were writing, one of the university students asked if our college class could meet these writers. Following some discussion with Barbara and Patia about a field trip to the university and further discussion with the college's undergraduate committee, a conference was planned. The undergraduate committee sponsored annual conferences focusing on timely professional issues. The conference in spring 2007 focused on children's well-being and the fifth and sixth graders were invited to present their writing. Since the students would be in Albuquerque, I arranged for them to have lunch on campus and then meet and work with the Albuquerque slam poets, a group of nationally award winning slam poets.

The fifth graders were thrilled at the prospect of having a real audience for their work. Many of them, although not yet near completion of their writing, could imagine what their final products would look like and also could see themselves reading their work to future teachers. The sixth graders panicked, literally screaming, "I won't go!" and "I can't read this to other people." I reminded them that some of these students had already heard their work in my class and that they (the sixth graders) had written very honest letters to the future teachers. I told them that there would be about 100 college students in the room, but that they could read to smaller groups if that was easier. Once again, I gave one of my brief, impassioned, and not-responded-to speeches to the sixth graders.

"Your writing is so important," I began. "You've worked hard on it and you tell the truth. You want teachers that will listen to kids' truths and now is your chance to show them what some kids' truths sound like. Your work shocks these future teachers because they thought they knew what teaching was going to be like when they went to school. They don't know kids that have family members that are sick, in gangs, involved with drugs, or don't have gas for heat in their homes. That's important for them to know."

Silence. Burning silence.

"Think about it," I add. "If you really don't want to go, you don't have to." Then I explained about slam poetry being like rap music and that they were going to love these poets' work. "Just think about it," I implore. Patia urged the class to go, too. I wanted the sixth graders to learn about what the fifth graders were doing and Consuelo and Andres provided that information.

Sixth Graders Consider Expository Biography

Consuelo and Andres stood at the front of the sixth grade class as I explained to the sixth graders that the fifth graders were writing about themselves and important people in their lives, too. The fifth graders weren't writing poems because their teacher wanted them to write true stories about the people they were studying. Patia said, "You'll write these kinds of stories, too, for the trip to the university."

"Or you can read your poetry," I added.

"Yes," Patia said. "Your poetry is fine, but you should do a story, too." Patia said at lunch that her class would write using the more traditional expository form of biography. I agreed that these would be very interesting based on the poetry we'd seen thus far. Barbara and I offered to share the digital voice recorders and cameras with the sixth graders.

Consuelo played an excerpt from her recording that is transcribed and translated in Chapter 5. The sixth graders were riveted.

"She learned a lot, didn't she?" I ask.

The sixth graders began asking Consuelo questions in Spanish because the recording was in Spanish. After their questions and her responses subsided, I explained that Consuelo had written three different leads for her story about her mother. Consuelo read one (in English):

> My mom was born on March 7, 1969 in a crowded house and poor family in a place known as Juan Aldama, Zacatecas. She had 5 sisters (including her) and 4 brothers. She had fun in her childhood because she would climb into the Mesquites (a huge tree), but after a while she would lose her fun because her mother would come after her and take her down.

Some of the sixth graders knew this city and one had a relative there, information that spurred discussion in Spanish, even though Consuelo had translated her mom's information into English.

Consuelo read some of the questions that she'd asked her mother, looking at the list she'd generated with her colleagues in English and translating them for the sixth graders, something that she did not need to do, but did. Consuelo added that her mom was learning English but requested that she be interviewed in Spanish.

"You can interview your person in any language that you need to," I offered, "but, most of the future teachers only speak English. Why is that?"

"They're all white," came a voice from the back of the room.

"Most of them are. But some are not, but they didn't learn Spanish at home the way you did. So, if you want all of the future teachers to understand your work, it needs to be in English when you present it."

I asked Consuelo to read one more part of her work so that the sixth graders could hear how she dealt with a Spanish word that she chose to keep in Spanish. Consuelo read:

> When my mom passed by *mojado* (illegal immigrant) it was a hard and fascinating adventure. It was a risk in her life because you don't know if you'll get here safe or you get stuck in the middle of nowhere like any other immigrant. My mom had to walk for three days without sleeping. The first thing she thought when she got here was to thank God that she got here safely.

We never had a mini-lesson on the use of parenthesis, but Consuelo explained how and why she used them. The word *mojado* actually means 'wetback' and, in Spanish, refers to the way that someone's back gets wet when walking or swimming across the Rio Grande River to enter the US. Consuelo's parenthetical English comment explained the status of a *mojado* rather than use the literal translation.

Andres read drafts of his first two pages, which were quite close to their final versions:

It's Just the Beginning

Robert D— was born June 2, 1948. He was hurt in the Vietnam War when he was 19. He was in a helicopter accident. He was cleaning the fans when his friends were filtering the helicopter and one of his friends punched the wrong button and the helicopter exploded on him. (p. 5)

His legs caught fire and his friends rolled him in dirt. When the fire went out, they rushed him to the hospital. His legs were fine but his shoulder was not. Now he has scars but he recovered from the accident. (p. 6)

Andres explained that the first line he read was the title of the chapter. The page numbers are the pages from his book about his grandfather.

Again, the sixth graders began to tell stories of their families' veterans, connecting to Andres and his work. We thanked the fifth graders and they returned to their classroom. I asked the sixth graders to write for ten minutes about the person whose biography they might write. They were quiet. I noticed that Verdad was absent and I regretted that because her story about her uncle is so important. Jesus was in the principal's office for fighting. I asked someone in the class to tell them what we did today. Here, then, are the first thoughts of some of the sixth graders as they think systematically about someone whose biography they might write.

Carlos's piece is both humorous and serious, having a grandmother in the hospital but also being playful while there.

> The last time I went to visit my grandma at the hospital, I was bugging her and she stabbed me with her fork. She stabbed me because I was bugging her.

Vianca is honest as she writes about her grandmother being both nice and mean.

> My grandmother is a Mexican. She never lies about it. She's sometimes nice or mean. She has feelings.

Lorenzo's family owns some horses and his admiration for his brother is evident.

> I want to talk about my big brother. He's funny and tall and he always makes me laugh. He likes to rope and ride horses. He always tells me that he wants to compete and become a champion.

Miguel senses the importance of the work:

> I would like to talk about my uncle or my dad or mom. I would like to talk about them because they are very special to me because they are always talking to me and telling me how their day went and how they feel.

Mercedes eventually decides to interview her mother, but initially considers interviewing her sister:

> Someone who is special to me is my sister because I could trust her and I could talk to her when I'm scared. My sister is a special person because she is the only sister I have. One day I went to the mountains and I went with my sister to walk and we got mad at each other and we went our separate ways. My sister got faster at the camping area [arrived there first] and I wasn't there so my sister went to look for me.

Isaac discusses his relationship with his mom:

> I'm going to interview my mom. She is very cool. She likes sports. Every time I come outside, she joins me. She knows lots about science. In

summertime, she likes to go to the mountains. Last summer we went four times. I bet when we have no school she is going to ask me. She only asks me because my sister gave up right away. Last time my big sister came back right away. She came back because she had a date.

Ricardo, the gentle and very big boy, offers an intuitive understanding of gangster life and worries his nephew's choices:

Sometimes I think I know my nephew very well. Sometimes I feel like I don't know him at all. I know he can do great things. But sometimes I worry he will make a wrong decision. I know he is really smart, but sometimes he won't try as hard as he really can. He's like me in a lot of ways, but he is different too. Sometimes he speaks before he thinks and says the wrong things. Sometimes I think he is trying to act like a gangster. He is nine but I think he has the mind of a 15 year old. He watches rated R movies, plays rated M for Mature games like Scarface, and Grand Theft Auto. At times, I think these games and movies are influencing him in the wrong way. He's already been telling me that Scarface Alert Tony Montana is cool.

Ricardo

Esperanza cried when she wrote, gently folding her head into her arms and resting them on her desk, quietly sobbing. She selected someone she loves and misses and doing so is emotional work. I suggested to the class that when we write something really important that it is emotional work. "It's okay to cry because it means you are being honest and telling your truths," I said. "Esperanza is doing important work. We should admire her." She also let her innermost voice leak onto the page, along with her tears. Her honesty in subsequent pieces and her truthfulness to the emotions she felt about those about whom she wrote affected others in the class. Esperanza, by her crying and the sharing of her writing, helped shift the community of practice further into the new territory (space) of truthfulness.

I want to interview my dad and mom about my grandma who died. My grandma died. She was so special for us. My mom says my grandma was just like me because I help every people in home [sic] who has a problem, helping cooking, homework, cleaning. My grandma died because she had cancer and they found it very late. One day we went to visit her. We went to get corn from the corn crop. Next time I will write a lot.

Esperanza

Juliana, who wrote earlier about her father's drinking, wrote a letter to me about her family.

Dear Dr. Meyer,

This is something really personal but I am going to tell you because I feel that you are a person I could trust and not just me a lot of persons or students. Mr. Meyer, my uncle is an alcoholic, 100 percent of his time all he does is drink. I care because my aunty is always saying that it is my dad's fault because he is always drinking. Yes I know my dad is one too, but he doesn't drink that much anymore. The reason my dad doesn't drink a lot anymore is because my other uncle got really sick and he even had to go to the hospital. Right now my aunty and uncle, their brother and sister, they owe 1000 dollars in the hospital. My mom says that those accounts don't get never paid. I don't know. That is too much money for me to pay. I am glad my dad doesn't drink that much any more. I mean a lot more than he does now.

I asked the sixth graders to share their pieces and many did. Some asked a friend or me to read for them; others read their own. No one stood up and some faced their papers with such intensity that their voices were sucked up by the page. I suggested that they could start their interviews soon. I would show them how to use the digital voice recorders at our next meeting.

Our time was running out, but I'd brought some poems to share with the sixth graders. I distributed and read some of them. These pieces were from a collection of "stories and poems by American Indian teens and young adults" (from the title, Ochoa, Franco, & Gourdine, 2003). I only read pieces by children, focusing on issues of family and self, and about the same age as the sixth graders. We'd return to these during my next visit.

Featured Fifth Grade Writer

I will feature fifth grade writers beginning in this chapter and continue doing so for the next few chapters. My intention is to demonstrate the investment of time and energy by both the children and Barbara into a single piece of writing. This investment was part of the substantive force needed to change the NCLB inertia that was propelling the school's academic activity during the year we did this work.

While the sixth graders explored various poetic devices and began some biographic work, Barbara kept the fifth graders focused on the biographic process that was emerging: creating tools for gathering data, analyzing data, writing multiple drafts, organizing those drafts, meeting with writing support group, editing, revising, and designing their final piece. Each student writer personalized the progression of this work with input from Barbara, Roberta (the bilingual writing teacher that arrived in March), and me. The focus on individual writers will afford some insight into those writers, but also into the composing processes that the students either invented or appropriated from strategy lessons that were delivered to the whole group, small groups, or individually (by Barbara, me, or another student).

Marisol is a 'regular' student at MVE, meaning she is bilingual, speaks Spanish at home. Spanish was her first language, and she's not in any special programs such as English language learner, gifted, or special education. She's tall for a fifth grader, loves to laugh and converse with friends, and tries to please Barbara. The biography project was the first time that Marisol could remember wanting to write, wanting to spend long periods of time engaged in her writing, and willingly composing and recomposing multiple drafts.

Marisol's biography of E—, a fifth grade colleague in the class, was presented in Chapter 4. That work helped Barbara and me realize the importance of questions in the collection of data. By asking about funny stories, things that he did that changed people's lives, and important people in his life, Marisol composed a short but telling piece about E—. As she read the completed piece to the class, their responses of laughter, moans of "oh nooo," and empathy for E—'s loss demonstrated the power of quality data when it was carefully crafted. Barbara and I worked to point these things out to the students as they composed and read that first round of biographies.

Marisol began her larger work the way many in the class did, as Barbara suggested, by listing what she knew about her father (Figure 6.1 shows page 1 of her two page list). *Moreno* translates as *dark* or *brown* and may be referring to the color of his skin. On her second page, she continued, "loves the food my mom makes; buys stuff for us; likes the work; he has four children one wife."

Marisol selected interview questions for her dad from the list the class had generated and she composed more questions after her first interview. Some of Marisol's questions were presented in Chapter 5. She sat summarizing and transcribing for hours when the students were given time to work on their biographies. Although this process is easily written in the previous sentence, it is a complex one involving multiple decisions as Marisol considered which of her father's words to transcribe verbatim and which to summarize. She listened repeatedly to the same section of the recording before moving to the next. Figure 6.2 is one of the seven pages of notes and quotes that Marisol wrote.

One of the strategy lessons that we did with the children was a discussion of sequencing. "Once you have all this information, how do you know what order to put it in?" Barbara asked the children. The wonderful part of this question is that Barbara and I didn't know the full range of answers. Chronological order was the obvious response, which was volunteered by one child as she suggested that we start with birth and go up until the most recent things we know. Other students wanted to begin with a really interesting story about their focus person; still others wanted to start with how they arrived in the US from Mexico. The question of sequence arose for Marisol when she realized she had a huge amount of data and wasn't sure what to do with it. She had the running text of data shown in Figure 6.2, but the seemingly insurmountable task of organizing it appeared to freeze her progress.

He is nice

His ~~the~~ greatest dad ever

He likes horses

Works a lot

has lots of friends

tall

black hair

brown eyes

moreno

born in Mexico

loves my dog's Sucko, Peluche,

and blacky, and my other dogs

who died

loves his family

and loves my little puppy Nena

who lives inside

loves his family

Figure 6.1 Marisol's list of what she knows about her dad.

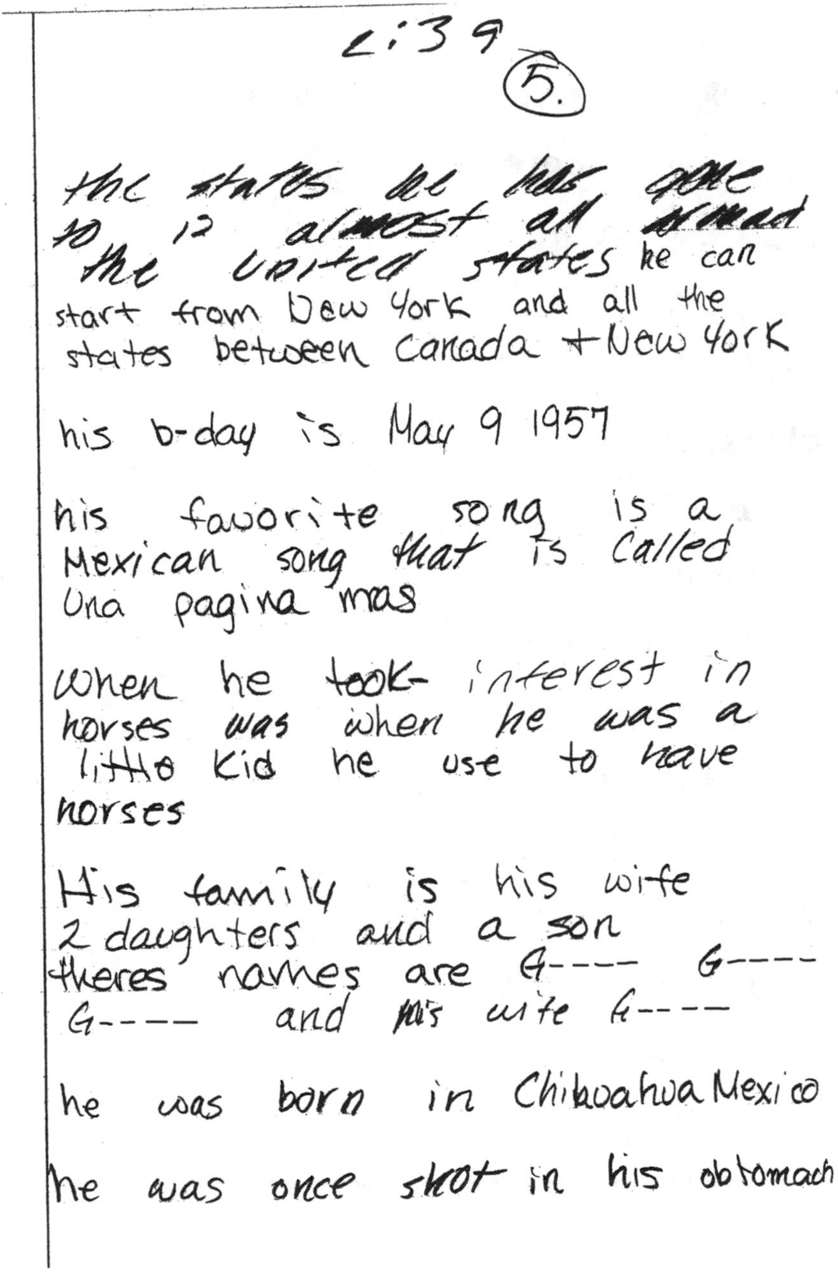

L:39

5.

the states he has gone
to is almost all around
'the' United states he can
start from New York and all the
states between Canada + New York

his b-day is May 9 1957

his favorite song is a
Mexican song that is called
Una pagina mas

when he took interest in
horses was when he was a
little kid he use to have
horses

His family is his wife
2 daughters and a son
theres names are G---- G----
G---- and his wife G----

he was born in Chihuahua Mexico

he was once shot in his ob tomach

Figure 6.2 Page 5 of Marisol's data.

"Look at all this," she said to me, her big eyes wide and round with intimidation caused by the data she'd worked so hard to commit to paper.

"Well, you do it a piece at a time," I began.

"What do you mean?"

We made photocopies of her notes and she cut those up into strips that she spread out on a table, reading and rereading them in order to establish the order in which she wanted them. She wound up with 48 strips of paper, which she moved multiple times before having them in the order she liked. Figure 6.3 shows some of these strips and the numbers that she placed in the left margins after she made decisions about the order in which they should appear. She scribbled out a few numbers when she realized that she wanted a strip in a different place.

Marisol spent the next few days of biography work time typing the work she'd handwritten and sequenced. When a strip needed work, she turned her full attention to it, sometimes muttering softly, "That doesn't make sense that way," or some other self-monitoring language. At that point, she'd ponder the segment, make changes, read it again, and then move to the next strip. Marisol and other fifth graders kept the eight computers in the room busy all the time; sometimes Barbara sent small groups to one of the two computer labs in the school.

Each day, the students printed out what they'd worked on for two reasons: first, in order to meet with colleagues in writing groups and second, in case they didn't save it correctly or in a place they could locate. Barbara and I tried to monitor the saving of work, but a few of the children lost it. The hard copies could then be used to retype, something Barbara or I did so that the author wouldn't feel like they were starting over. We decided that PowerPoint was the most practical program to use to publish final pieces because the children had learned to use it during their computer class. The slides of a PowerPoint set practical limits on the amount of text and image that could fit on a page, building in some of the aesthetic qualities we hoped for in completed pieces. Figure 6.4 shows Marisol's sustained typed piece with lines and numbers to denote which chunks she would place into different slides of her PowerPoint.

I created a storyboard (Appendix 3) that the students could use to plan out the pages of their books. Figure 6.5 shows the first page of Marisol's storyboard sheet with notes about images and numbers corresponding to chunks of text in Figure 6.4.

Although Barbara and I worried about the difficulty of typing such long pieces, the students divided the work by typing some, editing, discussing, revising, and pondering the sequence of their pieces. Once they cut chunks from their word processing documents and pasted them into PowerPoint, they sometimes changed the sequence of the slides. They spent two hours on one day when I was not present and another two to three hours when I was at the school, working on their biographies. They scanned photos, found public domain images on the World Wide Web, and even incorporated sounds and

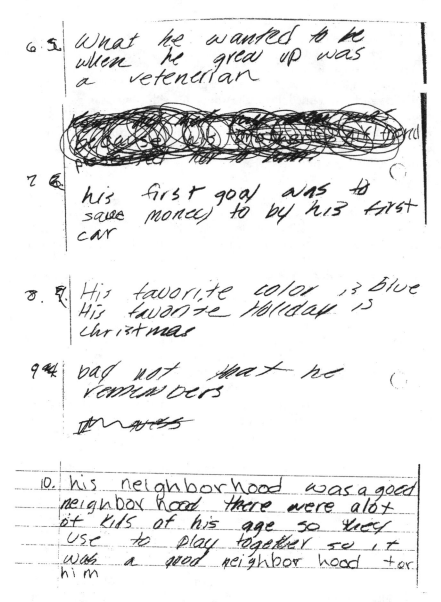

6 5. What he wanted to be when he grew up was a vetenerian

7 6. his first goal was to save money to by his first car

8. 7. His favorite color is blue His favorite holiday is christmas

9 8. bay not that he remembers

10. his neighborhood was a good neighborhood there were alot of kids of his age so they use to play together so it was a good neighborhood for him

Figure 6.3 Some of Marisol's 48 data strips, numbered after she decided their placement in the sequence of her biography.

The Life of a Mexican Child

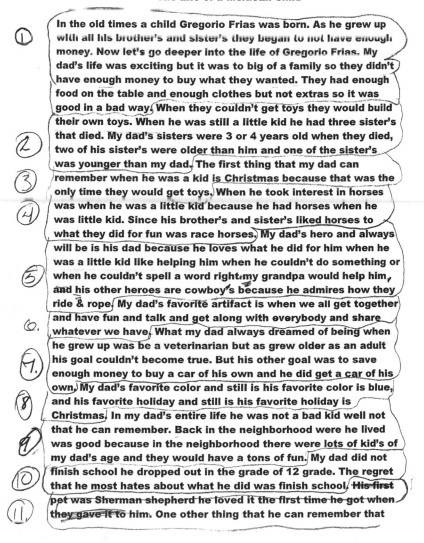

In the old times a child Gregorio Frias was born. As he grew up with all his brother's and sister's they began to not have enough money. Now let's go deeper into the life of Gregorio Frias. My dad's life was exciting but it was to big of a family so they didn't have enough money to buy what they wanted. They had enough food on the table and enough clothes but not extras so it was good in a bad way. When they couldn't get toys they would build their own toys. When he was still a little kid he had three sister's that died. My dad's sisters were 3 or 4 years old when they died, two of his sister's were older than him and one of the sister's was younger than my dad. The first thing that my dad can remember when he was a kid is Christmas because that was the only time they would get toys. When he took interest in horses was when he was a little kid because he had horses when he was little kid. Since his brother's and sister's liked horses to what they did for fun was race horses. My dad's hero and always will be is his dad because he loves what he did for him when he was a little kid like helping him when he couldn't do something or when he couldn't spell a word right, my grandpa would help him, and his other heroes are cowboy's because he admires how they ride & rope. My dad's favorite artifact is when we all get together and have fun and talk and get along with everybody and share whatever we have. What my dad always dreamed of being when he grew up was be a veterinarian but as grew older as an adult his goal couldn't become true. But his other goal was to save enough money to buy a car of his own and he did get a car of his own. My dad's favorite color and still is his favorite color is blue, and his favorite holiday and still is his favorite holiday is Christmas. In my dad's entire life he was not a bad kid well not that he can remember. Back in the neighborhood were he lived was good because in the neighborhood there were lots of kid's of my dad's age and they would have a tons of fun. My dad did not finish school he dropped out in the grade of 12 grade. The regret that he most hates about what he did was finish school. His first pet was Sherman shepherd he loved it the first time he got when they gave it to him. One other thing that he can remember that

Figure 6.4   One page of Marisol's typed piece with numbers denoting chunks for pages.

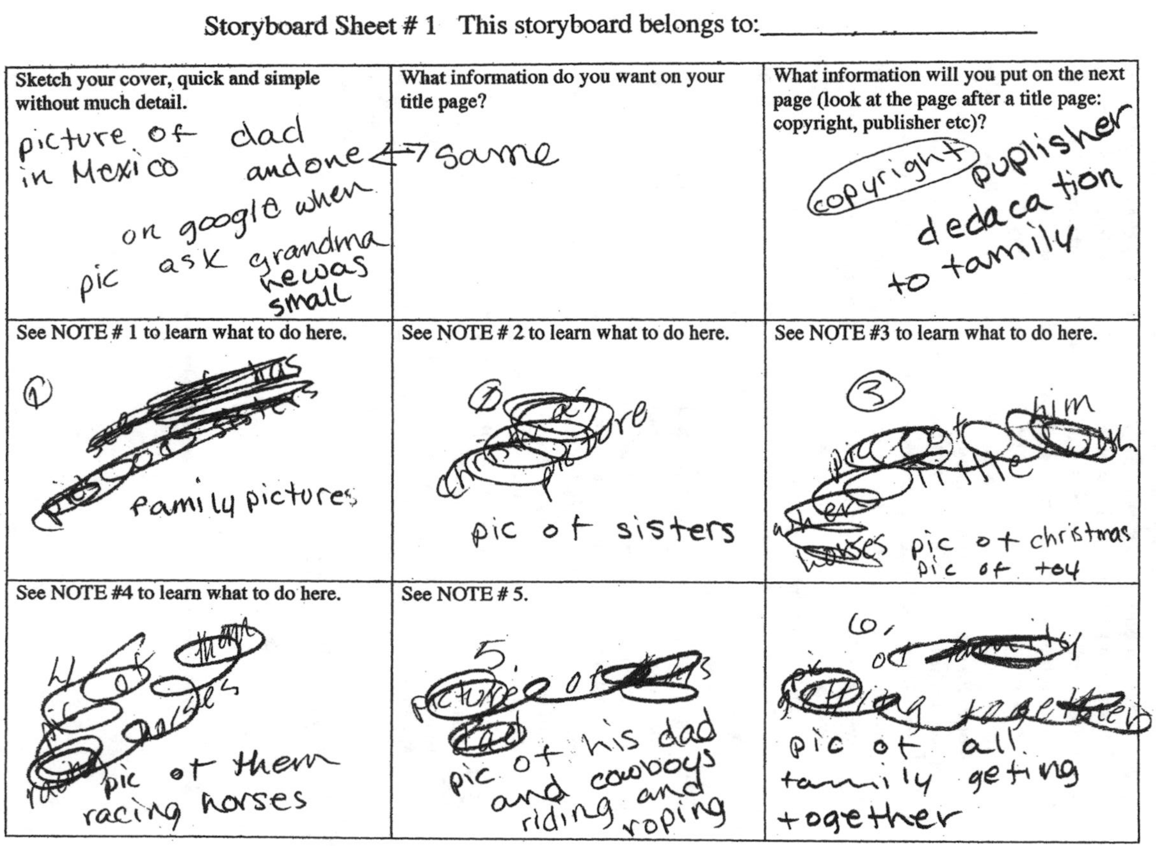

Storyboard Sheet # 1 This storyboard belongs to: _____

Sketch your cover, quick and simple without much detail.	What information do you want on your title page?	What information will you put on the next page (look at the page after a title page: copyright, publisher etc)?
picture of dad in Mexico and one when he was small on google ask grandma	source	copyright publisher dedication to family
See NOTE # 1 to learn what to do here. family pictures	See NOTE # 2 to learn what to do here. pic of sisters	See NOTE #3 to learn what to do here. pic of christmas pic of toy
See NOTE #4 to learn what to do here. pic of them racing horses	See NOTE # 5. picture of his dad pic of cowboys and riding roping	pic of all family getting together

Figure 6.5
Marisol's storyboard with her notes.

music into the PowerPoints. We knew the printed versions of these would work well as books and the digital versions allowed the children to think about, make decisions, and incorporate other media (Halliday's [1978] "mode") into their work.

When Barbara and I noticed Marisol's title, we asked the children about titles of the biographies that rested on the ledge of the markerboard. They found some of the titles boring and others more enticing and interesting. We asked them to list at least three titles for their piece and explained that they didn't need to select one yet. Further, they could add to this list at any time. Marisol took out a piece of paper and wrote:

Dad

My hero known at my house

The life of a Mexican child

The children were put into groups to discuss their titles and evaluate them using some of the criteria that arose during our earlier discussions. The conversations lasted about ten minutes and then they went back to their work. Marisol kept her original title, receiving affirmation for it from her colleagues. They explained that "Dad" was too simple and didn't grab a reader's attention. Ramona's use of "hero" led Marisol's group to a discussion of the use of that word. They all liked it and interrogated their own work for evidence of a hero.

The writing groups worked fairly independently, although Barbara or I (and later Roberta) joined them to constantly demonstrate (and struggle with) being reflective about pieces of writing. I watched one group work with Marisol's draft. She'd printed out a few of her slides, those containing chunks of text from Figure 6.4.

"Read it to us," Consuelo requested.

Marisol read, "My dad did not finish high school he dropped out in the grade of 12. The regret that he most hates about what he did was finish high school." This was a difficult slide with which to work because of the run-on sentence and the awkward construction of the second sentence. Marisol read it again at the request of a group member.

"She read this part like two sentences, but it's written as one," I said, pointing to the first sentence. Marisol studied it and placed a period after "school." Then she put three short lines under "he," one of the editorial marks they'd used the entire school year, indicating that it needs an upper case 'H' when she returns to the computer.

"Read the second sentence again," I asked.

Early in the school year, asking a child to reread a piece of her writing indicated that she had made a mistake. Barbara recognized this, but wasn't sure how to adjust it so the children would understand that writers do this kind of work, crafting and recrafting sentences as they write pieces. Having children brainstorm different titles or compose a number of leads or endings for a piece, gradually changed into part of the work, not as joy in most cases, but as something considered worth doing by most of the children, especially when they had the time. Wordsmithing became a group effort. Marisol decided that her slide sounded best this way, "My dad did not finish high school. He dropped out in 12th grade. The regret that he most hates is not finishing school." It's not perfect, but it certainly is clear and sounds like Marisol.

We were well into March as Marisol and the other fifth graders continued to work on their pieces. Barbara asked me one morning, "Are the pieces supposed to be perfect? I want them perfect?"

"What's perfect?" I asked.

"You know, no spelling errors, and umm . . ."

"all the conventions are conventional." I finished for her.

"Yes. They need to revise until they're perfect."

"But that's not revising," I offered. "It's editing. I have a copyeditor that catches some of the final mistakes in my writing. Why don't we just edit for the kids?"

"But how will they learn what's wrong?" Barbara asked.

"We tell them, or show them, or maybe just choose one or two to teach them about."

"We've had this conversation before," Barbara smiles. We had. The push for perfection in final pieces (a common form of inertia in school) has led many children to reduce the length of their pieces and the risks they're willing to take as writers (Murray, 2004). If we were going to read and copyedit all the biographies, I suggested we develop an editorial checklist (Appendix 4) that the students could use with a colleague, perhaps leaving us less to address.

Working for Hours

On many mornings when I was present, the work began after the fifth graders ate breakfast and wrote "what's on your mind" pieces, which they often shared. These were good warm-ups for our work because they often wrote about wanting to work once more on their biographies. As lunchtime approached one morning, Barbara said, "They've worked for over two hours and didn't ask for recess or anything!" It was time to clean up for lunch, with just about five minutes of work time remaining.

"We have five minutes left," I began, and the children moaned a collective, "Oh nooo."

"Let's do this. You worked for so long today and we want to know how it went because we didn't get to talk with everyone in the class. So, on a piece of paper, finish these four sentences, or just do one or two or three of them. It's up to you." I wrote on the board:

I feel good about _____

I want (or hope) _____

A question

I want you to know _____.

I explained again that they could choose any or all of these and write to Barbara and me about the morning. If they had a question for us, that's what the third item was about. Their responses demonstrated their growing thoughtful natures about their writing and themselves as writers. They were monitoring what they needed, what they wanted to know, what they'd like to do, and things they wanted to find out. They spent the morning writing, but for these last few minutes they used language to discuss their work as language users, being metalinguistic.

Debi wrote:

> I feel good about changing my story and adding more detail to it and crossed out some stuff that does not go with it. [A huge accomplishment for her as she typically was 'done' at the first pass.]

> I want to write and add more details to my biography and make some more corrections on my biography on my mom. I still need to record me and my mom.

Consuelo wrote:

> I feel good about . . . I am going to start my rough draft and finished taking notes on my interview.

> I (hope) (want) to finish my biography by next week.

> How should I organize my story? [She'd seen Marisol and wanted to cut and sort as well.]

> I am getting to know more and more information about mom than what I used to know. I think this biography thing is a good idea.

Andres wrote:

> I feel good about being almost done with typing.

> I hope to get on with revising.

> Do you like yams? [He was joking.]

Ramona wrote:

> I feel good about . . . finishing typing my biography and that I did the biography on my dad.

> I want to . . . add pictures to my biography.

> I want you to know I learned more about my dad.

Estevan wrote:

> I finished typing and scanning.
>
> [I want to] publish my biography.
>
> How long will it take to publish it?

Marisol wrote:

> I feel good about writing nonstop which was real hard and I feel good about that my dad answered all 50 questions and that I am already on my rough draft.
>
> I hope that I get done pretty soon because I want to show people how important and special my dad is to me.
>
> When are we gonna read our bio. to the class?
>
> It is going excellent on the rough draft. I'm already on the second folder. [Not sure what she means.]

Luisa wrote:

> I feel good about adding more information on my biography.
>
> I want to read to the class.
>
> Somebody help me on the ending.
>
> I want you guys to know that if I could get the recorder again because my grandpa has more information.

Counterportraiture, Working in the Plural Form, and Inertia

A sample of one student, such as Marisol, does not constitute a counter-portrait of a classroom or a school, rather it may even appear to some to be an aberration. We know the importance and usefulness of case studies (Stake, 1995; Merriam, 1998); the presentation of individual students in this and the next few chapters is intended to demonstrate the uniqueness of each child's power as a writer. While an official portrait is presented as the true story of a school, represented by demographic and test data, counterportraits are collections of stories (plural). The official portrait (singular) of MVE presents a failing school by presenting the school's story in one way, but counter-portraits are intended to complicate and challenge the official portrait by presenting substantive contrary data and analyses. The intention is to impact the powerful inertial forces that perpetuate images of failure under the guise of "leaving no child behind" (see, for example, Berliner & Biddle, 1995 or Bracey, 2003).

When a teacher at a school officially portrayed as a 'failing school' notices a child that is performing strongly, she might refer that child to a 'gifted' program or tell her parents that the child should go to college. But our work was not about such aberrations, rather it came to focus on influencing, challenging, or changing children's views of themselves as writers involved in important work. We were not about one child 'making it' or 'making it out,' as much as we were focused on the recognition, by the children, that they have hearts, souls, minds, experiences, and relationships that matter both in and out of school. Barbara supported this idea fully, as did Roberta. It was a little more difficult for Patia, but she was willing to discuss it at our lunch meetings.

Consider, for the sake of comparison, students at middle and upper middle class (socioeconomic status) schools where almost all students are expected to perform in a way that will lead them to college (Lareau, 1989) and aberrations are those students that do not perform well. Although I do not subscribe to simplistic dichotomies, it seems there are two directions to consider in the professional literature when studying the differences between economically secure families and their children and economically insecure families and their children. One direction is that students' heredity (nature) predisposes them to have low intelligence quotients and, therefore, perform poorly in school (Hernstein & Murray, 1996) and, for the most part, remain in poverty because only intelligence leads to success. The other direction favors consideration of the impact of environment (nurture) and critiques the ways in which typically white institutions perpetuate themselves and the power they have. The first direction seems to offer little hope of changing portraits while the second creates opportunities aimed at change. Yet that second direction is tempered by an environment (larger social, economic, and cultural conditions) that is racist (McIntosh, 1990). Marisol has family in and from Mexico, has rich, dark skin, and learned Spanish before English. Both parts of the dichotomy disfavor her success in school and society. One part of the dichotomy provides genetic reasons for her failure; the other provides sociocultural ones. The latter helps us understand and, to some degree, unpack racism, but has not penetrated the broader dominant society. I offer the present work as one of many emerging beacons of hope and action (Edelsky, 1999) that are part of reframing literacy research (Lewis, Enciso, & Moje, 2007) with the ultimate goal of such work as part of an advocacy agenda (Cherland & Harper, 2007) for enhancing the quality of life.

One of the purposes of this study is to consider counterportraits and their composition within communities of practice. The community of practice of the middle class school has an ethos, a system of beliefs, or a Discourse (Gee, 2006) in which ways of being are consistent with dominant culture views of success and how to earn it. Discourses exist because of power, language, histories, beliefs, positions, and positioning. Part of the power of a Discourse has to do with its numbers as well as its accumulated wealth. *Numbers* here does not mean the amount of people in a group, but more accurately refers to the ways in which powerful groups control others by manipulating data. Numbers such as test scores, positioned as accurate measures of learning or intelligence, have power. The number of students and teachers being forced to use basal reading programs that are inappropriate for many reasons (Goodman, Shannon, Freeman, & Murphy, 1987) are held captive by the profits to be made at their expense.

In a counterportrait, numbers also matter, but in a different way. They first serve to challenge the official portrait, as, for example, when Marisol had 42 chunks in the biography she was writing about her father. Marisol changed, her view of her family changed, and her family's view of her as a student, thinker, and writer changed (discussed further in Chapter 9 when families saw their children's presentations). This counterportrait begins as a local construction and cannot be imposed from the outside. It's locally grown, something that happened intuitively as we learned with the children and designed, with them (to differing degrees across the classrooms), what they needed next.

Counterportraits are rooted in the desire to do something that, as Barbara put it, the students would remember their entire lives (an internal shift). Also, they have the potential to change how others perceived the students. The principal of MVE brought some of the completed biographies to a district level meeting and her colleagues and superiors were quite surprised at the content and level of sophistication of the children's work. These surprises, as they grow not simply in quantity but in presence and power (by beginning to 'count'), may accumulate to spread the counterportraits, for example as other principals ask how teachers at their schools might engage students this way. Marisol's work may not disrupt the status quo of the official portrait, nor will students' writing about grandparents, gang deaths, and the other realities of the students' lives, until their work accumulates the kind of wealth that is generated by families being amazed at their children's accomplishments, and talking about them, principals talking, and legislators and the larger public acknowledging their work as significant. Such acknowledgment is a threat to some of the regularities (Sarason, 1972) of mainstream dominant classrooms and publishers of curriculum materials and tests used therein. Those are strong forces already in motion (inertia) that work against counterportraits gaining mainstream or official wealth or even recognition. Still, our work pushes against the mainstream, contributing to the forces counter to the present inertia in many schools, legislatures, newspapers, and curriculum publishers.

The students legitimized their own linguistic, cultural, and social worth as members of a community of practice in which they had voice and their lives mattered. This was a local beginning and it was being brought to fruition by Marisol and her fifth and sixth grade colleagues. Barbara used her local power, within her classroom, to change what school could be, the nature of her relationships with her students, and the ways in which they used written language and digital media. Teaching, in this counterportrait, became a creative and collaborative (John-Steiner, 2000) act. The students and their teachers and a researcher, working within the institution, built a grassroots movement to change writing. In Goffman's (1959) terms, they created an underlife that was not part of the official institution, yet thrived within its periphery for a few hours one or two days a week, a political act.

Within the regularities (Sarason, 1972) of the school day, investing time this way involved overcoming the inertia that existed at the school. This was inertia that kept things going the way they have been going, initiated by the district or state (with a strong dose of federal legislation and dollars) and ridden by the teachers and their students. As with any physical act of inertia, forces exist to keep things in motion as they are. To carry the metaphor just a bit farther, our work is part of the friction that might lead to slowing down or torque that may lead to a change in direction in which the mainstream is headed. It is inertia that keeps some teachers believing that they must do as they are told because they've always done what they were told. Inertia keeps the official portrait sound, strong, and as the central driving curricular force; it keeps the children at MVE at risk of school failure. Inertia keeps children believing that they: are failures because their school did not make adequate yearly progress, have nothing important to write about, and can't bring their truths to school. Any counterforce is a potential threat to the status quo that benefits some, typically at the expense of others. The students and teachers did not set out to address this inertia, but our work changed them and those changes create ripples (viewed by some as threats, I am sure). They are the ripples of hope and may work to diminish the power or direction of the official portrait and inspire many more counterportraits as sources of friction or torque.

The power of the students' writing as we worked together over time initiated inertia that pushed for a new direction, one that was local in some ways (it is Marisol's father and no one else's), yet universal in others (everyone has or had a father of some sort). I can only conjecture (and minimally, at that) about the ways in which these young writers' intellectual wealth as thinkers, talkers, and writers will influence what happens in their futures. Their writing is evidence that such wealth is being built—it is in motion—and that future teachers, friends, lovers, family members, employers, and our governing structures may, in some ways, get to contend with it.

Chapter 7

Heroes, Dark Secrets, Otter Pops, and Struggles

> Against the failings of the political, rational-progressive, mythical, and revolutionary Utopias, a pedagogical Utopian perspective needs to be created that can still be relevant to the present situation of the child living in a postmodern world. This postmodern reality of the child needs to be related in a lifelike way to life in society with its culture, its social, political, economical contents and problems, and with its philosophies of life.
>
> (Miedema, 1992, p. 35)

Miedema offers an optimistic view of pedagogy in a complicated world and it is his positive view, his hopefulness, that led me to open with his words. In this chapter, hope may not come forward as the central point of what unfolds in the weeks described herein, but I view hope the way that Edelsky (1999) discussed it, as a necessary successor of intense critique and a crucial precursor to future actions. Hope is struggle's companion if we, as teachers, children, and researchers, are to use struggle as a vehicle for a greater good.

The fifth and sixth grade classrooms continued their very different work over the course of the weeks leading up to the presentation at the university. The fifth graders continued to work on the longer biographical pieces of someone important to them and the sixth graders continued to explore through poetry and some beginnings of more traditional biographical writing. In this chapter, I suggest that *struggle* is one common thread between two very different teachers, two very different classroom worlds, and many different journeys of growth as writers and people. First, I describe some activity in both classrooms, before returning to and elaborating on *struggle* as a theme of counterportraits.

In the Fifth Grade

Barbara began each writing session with a status of the class (Atwell, 1998) because, as she explained, "I need to know what everyone is doing because I'm not sure how to organize this when everyone is doing something different." As she went around the room children called out, "Type," if they were going to work on the computer inputting their sequenced data. Other responses coming from around the room, included "Put in order and type . . . spell check and edit . . . finish last paragraphs . . . listen to recording of interview . . . scan photos . . . work on new rough draft because I'm doing dad and not grandma . . . I don't know." The last response raised the most concern because one student had little data, very short interviews, and didn't have much to do because of that. Barbara asked that student to be in a writing group with two others that were working on drafts, but needed some feedback on content. Students in these small groups sometimes raised issues that we overheard or they brought to Barbara or me, and we, in turn, developed strategy lessons. Before the children were let loose to work, Barbara said, "The classroom has to be like a newspaper office, where everyone is busy writing, scanning, and typing."

When the topic of endings for their biographies came up in small groups, Barbara wanted the class to engage more thoughtfully in discussions of how to wrap things up. It was close to April and the writing was progressing, but Barbara had never before allowed children to work this long on a project. She wanted to move towards a product. She placed the children into five groups and let them study endings of the biographies from the library. Then she asked them to write, on poster board, the characteristics of a good ending. One group held the two by three foot piece of poster board horizontally and wrote "Good Ending!" at the top in a combination of red and blue markers that made the letters look a little like candy canes. Then they listed and numbered seven qualities of a good ending:

1   your ending should wrap up your story;
2   gives feelings, good or bad;
3   honors person;
4   meaningful quote from the person;
5   change in person's life;
6   talk about person's achievements; and
7   talks about what was happening in the world.

A different group made two columns, one labeled "Good End" and the other "Bad End" using many of the same qualities that the other group wrote. One group made a rubric with a three, two, and one at the top of columns on the chart. Under three, they wrote, "Sentence that ties back into the lead and wraps up the story." Under two, they wrote, "That was the person's life; story just ends." Under one, they wrote, "The End." Another group used a graphic organizer, drawing a circle in the middle of the paper and putting eight lines with smaller circles radiating out from the center. In the center they wrote, "What makes a good ending?" and in each smaller circle wrote the characteristics that they found in the books they examined. The last group divided the chart into four sections, writing, "What makes a good ending" at the top. In each quarter of the page, they put the title of one of the four books they examined and then listed the qualities of the last page of those stories. Each group presented their chart to the entire class.

Most of the children were not at the point of writing endings, but they were discussing finishing their pieces almost every time we wrote. They were excited, saying things like, "I can't wait for my family to read this!" "I'm almost done with mine." Ramona was the student that inspired the study of endings because she was approaching the final section of her draft. After the discussion of endings, she went to her desk and wrote three different endings (Figure 7.1).

Ramona's willingness to play with text indicates her growth as a writer. Rather than rush through to finish someone else's (a teacher's, test's, or program's) 'work,' she invested in her work, something she appropriated as her own out of love and respect for her father. Other students also engaged this

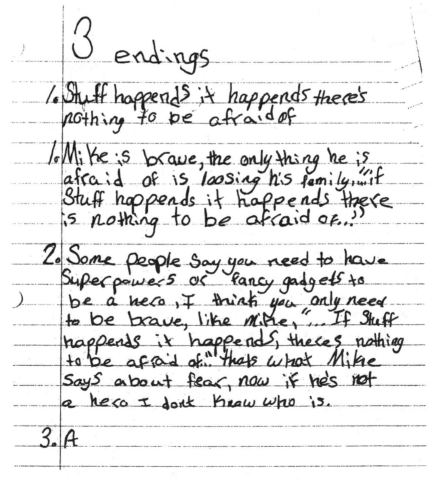

Figure 7.1 Ramona's draft of different endings.

way, taking time to try different things with their writing. Sometimes three students printed out their pieces and read each other's, writing notes on the printout about what they read and then discussing their notes. These discussions sometimes led to changes in the piece and other times led the author to assert that the piece was fine in its original version.

Featured Fifth Grade Authors

Chuck and Estevan had similar composing processes, both taking a bit of time to get started and both eventually engaging with increased commitment and seriousness.

Chuck, the Humorist

Chuck is a quiet fifth grader who has a notebook at his grandmother's house in which he practices gang tags. He asked me to invent a handshake that we could use, so when we first saw each other each week, we'd slide our palms together and then knock our clenched fists on each other's. Then he'd say, "Hey Dr. M." Other students soon joined this practice. Chuck took a long time deciding whose biography to write, thinking he might study his grandmother but abandoning that idea when he couldn't gather sufficient data. He selected his father, learning a lot about him that he hadn't previously known. Right after the discussion of leads (Chapter 4), Chuck copied the list that the class generated. We distributed folders in which the students could store their biography work and Chuck kept his leads list in his folder. He also brainstormed to find his perfect title. At first, he thought of calling his piece *A Boy Turns into a Hard Working Man*, but eventually chose *A Boy in the Desert Turns into a Hard Working Man*. He enjoyed and benefited from the slowed-down process because the pacing fit his ways of thinking and writing.

Chuck used information from his interviews as his lead, originally writing, "A little boy in the desert with his home made bow and arrow chasing snakes and rabbits. Eugene was born December 21, 1966." After meeting with Barbara, he changed the order and worked on the fragmented first sentence, writing, "Eugene was born December 21, 1966. He became a little boy in the desert with his homemade bow and arrow chasing snakes and rabbits." He learned about "homemade" being a compound word. But, by far, the most remarkable discovery that Chuck made was the litany of mischief in which his father was involved. The class looked forward to each part of Chuck's work because of their fascination with his father as the 'bad boy' at school. Chuck's dad popped a bag in class, scaring his teacher; glued an apple to his teacher's desk; cut the wings off bees and put them in flowers that he gave to his teacher; shot off a firecracker under another student's desk; and put smoke bombs in the school vents, causing an evacuation for which he got suspended. The last page of the biography shows a photo of Chuck's family with his dad, mom, Chuck, and his younger brother. Chuck writes:

Eugene finally got married the second time after getting a divorce. Now he's forty years old and has two boys, a wife, two dogs, and a cat. He still enjoys the outdoors.

Chuck included photos of his dad, family, and some pictures he imported from the Web, such as an exploding firecracker, a glue gun, and bees. Although his eight-page biography is among the shortest in the class, it is by far the one that his colleagues considered the funniest. Their shocked faces inevitably crumbled into laughter at the antics of Eugene. Chuck's process as a writer also involved a lot of socializing with others in the classroom. He seemed to want their approval for what he was finding out as he tentatively presented each of his dad's adventures, engaging with others with whom he'd previously had little contact. He was writing and learning about writing as he composed draft after draft in the context of lofty discussions about his writing and the topic of his writing, his dad. He built an ever-widening network of colleagues as a vehicle for ensuring that the work was truly funny, composing himself as a humorist.

One morning, Chuck printed out the first four pages of his PowerPoint, sat with six fifth graders at a rectangular table at the front of the room, and distributed the printout that had all four pages minimized to fit on one sheet of paper. He asked them to write what they liked and what questions they had, the two part strategy we introduced to the children as a way of celebrating what worked and gently nudging each other to address what did not. After they wrote, each person read what they wrote. Sometimes Chuck asked a follow-up question, such as "What do you mean?" when he did not understand the written comments. The students gave their comments to Chuck after the meeting so that he could think about them further. Some of the fifth graders' comments follow:

> I like how it said, "and bang!"
>
> I like how she [the teacher] ran out screaming.
>
> Why is there snow in the background?
>
> What did he love to do as a kid?
>
> I like the title.
>
> What kind of other stuff did your dad do at class?
>
> I like how you said that he was the class clown.
>
> Are you going to get [make] more slides?

Chuck knew that his father was the 'bad boy' at school, but that knowledge had not previously been important or useful in the school setting. His home and family life, indeed his home and family identity, were kept separate as he engaged in schoolwork. Originally, I thought Chuck was also a minimalist, seeking to do as little as he could to appease the demands of the school setting without overexerting himself. His false start in thinking he might study his grandmother was typical of the way he operated in school, perhaps used as a way of postponing (with the hope of never completing) his assignments. The time he had to explore coupled with the reception of his father's life events shifted Chuck's view of school work, his position in the class, and his identity as a writer in school. As he worked and reworked each page of his final copy (see Appendix 2), it became evident that he appropriated the writing practices that were emerging within the classroom, particularly the space for individuality in style.

Estevan's Hero

Estevan knew from the beginning of the project that he wanted to study his father, Javier, but Estevan seemed hesitant to engage. Many of the immigrant families of MVE worried about being the focus of too much attention. Eventually, he interviewed his father in Spanish and brought to the class another remarkable story of immigration in hopes of finding a better life in the US. Estevan's dad quit school in the ninth grade "because his [Javier's] family didn't have money to pay for school" (Estevan's interview, translated) in Mexico. He learned how to install carpet in Mexico and, at the age of 16, he traveled through Mexico in a van to cross the border to find work. Estevan wrote about his dad, "He hid under the van's carpet when they passed the border because he didn't want them to not let him pass." Javier became a US citizen, although Estevan does not tell us how that occurred.

Estevan was caught up in the idea that the person being studied had to be a hero, inspired by Ramona's father, the veteran of the war in Iraq. Estevan worked to craft his father as a hero, although he hadn't accomplished feats typical of heroes as portrayed in the classroom and in the broader media. Estevan wrote three endings in his quest to resolve this issue (see Figure 7.2).

Estevan enjoyed meeting with fifth grade colleagues to examine drafts of his work. He took four pages of a handwritten draft, gleaned from information he learned in his interview with his dad, and met with some students. In one sentence of the draft, Estevan inserted an editorial carrot and wrote "Why" in response to his classmate's queries about what was written. They wanted to know why his father left school, information that Estevan returned to his father to find out and later inserted into the text. He crossed out pieces of text and rewrote them to clarify his intended meaning or eliminated them completely. Estevan learned that his first draft was not his final draft in need of teacher approval; rather, his first draft was his first attempt to make sense of what he'd learned and demanded responses from other readers and writers as a way of ensuring clarity. On another occasion, Estevan brought to his colleagues successive drafts explaining how his mom and dad met in Mexico. The belief in love at first sight and the commitment to family (by becoming pen pals, by

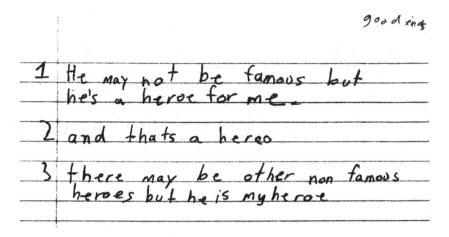

Figure 7.2 Estevan's ideas for endings.

working hard at a job, by crossing the border to find a better life) were woven into Estevan's writing. Drawing upon his interview data, Estevan presented Javier's dedication to the family by incorporating into the final piece a quote from Javier:

> Javier kept installing carpet and working hard for his family. As he said, "I had always installed carpet and I'm going to die installing carpet."

Although Estevan lived with his family and saw his father's commitment to working hard for the family, it was the writing of a biography that led him to pause and reflect on his family's values, partly because he asked his father to reflect upon and discuss them. Listening to the tapes of Estevan interviewing his father, I heard other family members in the background negotiating the meaning of the questions and answers that would address them. This collective negotiation of meaning as a discursive process also emerged in the classroom as the students discussed (in Spanish and English), wrote, and presented what they had collected. The students, their families, and the classroom functioned as thought collectives with processes that were similar and ongoing for the first time in the fifth grader's school lives. That similarity, particularly in a legitimate fashion in the school setting, contributed to new structures of participation (Philips, 1971) in the classroom community of practice. This involved the composing of themselves as inquirers, authors, and critics. They changed their school identities—revised their school masks—through conversation and composing. Estevan's final piece is in Appendix 2. Meanwhile, the sixth graders worked to re-present voices that were part of discursive communities far from the school site.

Sixth Grade Poets' Dark Poetry

It was early March and I arrived to find that the sixth graders hadn't worked on their biographies since my last appearance. I asked them to look at the poems I'd distributed during my last visit, part of my backup plan of always having something ready that I thought was passionate, important, and would contribute to the sixth graders' uncovering of who they were, where they were from, who was important to them, and why that mattered in school. Sonia Manriquez, age 17, wrote *Dark Waters* (in Ochoa, Franco, & Gourdine, 2003), a poem in short pairs of lines and one final line, a total of eleven lines for the entire piece. Some of the sixth graders liked the efficiency of being done in eleven lines. I agreed that the piece was short, but explained that length didn't always relate directly to ease of composition. I thought out loud about the old woman, alone, making tortillas for her family, sweating and crying at the same time. I asked the class why they thought the woman was sweating and crying.

"It's hot in the kitchen," one offered.

"They're poor, really poor, so she's sad," another said.

"She's sad to work so hard."

"She's sad because she's alone."

"Why," I asked, "is she alone if she's making tortillas for twelve people?"

"Because they're not there yet. She's alone. They all left home."

"Got married."

"Or went away to school."

"And the steam in the kitchen?" I asked.

"She's making frijoles, beans."

"That might be," I said.

The discussion is one of the longer ones we've had and I tell them that even though the poem was only eleven lines long, it made us think and reminded us of things in our own lives. "Maybe your grandmother is alone or cooks alone," I say. I was amazed and relieved at the lack of silence in response to this poem. They were publicly forthcoming about their thoughts. We had slowly moved from silence, to very short responses, to a brief but sustained conversation. This was progress. Even my suggestion about a grandmother living alone was not left untouched.

"No. My grandmother is never alone. She lives with us," one student says.

"Mine lives alone," another retorts.

"You see. Just a little bit of writing goes a long way. It makes people who read it want to talk and it makes them think about things, people, and places in their own lives."

"Today, you can use this poem as you write your own poem. But yours doesn't have to be about dark waters. It can be about whatever you like, but it has to make us think."

The poems that follow are the "dark" poems, labeled as such because of the choice of titles and content. The idea of darkness spread quickly through the class as the students discussed their pieces in progress, read over each other's shoulders, and made nonverbal commitments to honor the idea of being honest and truthful in their writing. I offer their "I used to, but now," "where I'm from," and "dark" poems as evidence that the sixth graders were recomposing their portraits of themselves as writers, students, and members of a classroom community and broader communities.

Verdad struggled not only with her uncle's murder, but also with her parents' divorce; her father moved to a nearby home, but she did not see him as often as she liked.

Dark Eyes

When I see into
my mom's eyes I
see darkness

I see understanding
in the steaming room

making food
for my sister and me

as rivers of
tears come down her cheeks

fall down
her face that's when we realized

we are alone.

Juliana's poem is playful as she describes her relationship with her sister. Previously Juliana wrote about her uncle, an alcoholic, and opened her "where I'm from" piece focusing on her father's drinking. In her relationship with her sister, she creates a faux argument and resolves it with forgiveness, the latter something that drives her optimistic spirit. Juliana is also well aware of the socially constructed importance of beauty, a word she plays with to invent a form that she needs as a poet. Part of many of the girls' homework is, indeed, beauty, as they work to follow the norms in their community about beauty, the use of makeup, and the appropriate clothing to wear.

Dark Silence

When I see my sister
when she is mad

I remember when she
is mad she is really silent.

When she would make her
self a snack and I
would bite it.

as she worried of
homework and beautyness.

As she realizes she
couldn't be mad
anymore.

Vianca's use of the word "passed" in the next poem is an interesting, though I
am not convinced intentional, play on words, suggesting the past as well as
someone 'passing' (dying).

Dark Passed

When I think
about my passed

I remember of
my grandfather

He used to
play with me

and take me
to the park

He used to
make me laugh

I know I'm alone.

Jesus' piece has a subtle implication, one that is only verified in knowing he has
very little contact with his father, who was constantly leaving when Jesus was a
baby. He left permanently when his mom's relationship with dad ended
because of dad's drinking and violent behavior.

Dark Cries

When I think about
my dad

I remember
the old stories about him

making me laugh
When I was crying

as he would talk to me
and hold me

in his arms
as he realizes

he has to go.

Ricardo, the gentle and very big sixth grader, seems to have already assumed a patriarchal role in his family, including wondering about the future of one of its younger members.

Dark Future

When I hear my
nephew talk I wonder.

When I see the way
he gets angry I wonder.

When I see the way
he misbehaves I wonder.

When I see the
way he acts I wonder.

When I hear the way
he acts at school I wonder.
What is in his future?

There is ambiguity in absence and relationships in many of the writings by the children in this study. When the poets shared their pieces, I pointed this out. "Poetry does not have to explain every little detail," I offer, after some had read their "dark" pieces. "We don't know the answers to questions like these, unless you tell us: Is an uncle a blood relative or not? When someone is 'gone,' are they dead, in jail for a long time, or has a relationship broken up?" Isaac crafted a poem that led his colleagues to raise questions, but I explained that the poet reads and does not have to elaborate. Isaac chose only to read.

Dark Home

When I look in side my
home.

I see darkness of my uncle
not being there

I open the door I feel my
uncle

but I open my eyes and I
realize no one is there.

that's when I realize
I will never see
him again

Miguel demonstrates (his piece is included in the preface) that when someone is "no longer with us," the meanings are ambiguous; the theme of darkness-as-sadness permeates his piece. Corazon's poem shows that a "dark future" emerges from actions one takes as those actions hurt others.

Dark Future

When I look
into my brother's
eyes

I see him
standing confused in
his room.

Crying loudly
as my mom yells
at him

When he is
Asked why he
Didn't attend school

Being confused he
Realizes he's really

Hurting his own
mother.

Goffman (1959) discusses "dark secrets" (p. 141), an idea that resonates with the dark poems that the sixth graders wrote. These dark secrets constitute what he calls "discrepant roles" (p. 141) in which one's mask is tipped and a glimpse of the self under the mask is revealed. The sixth graders learned to bracket facets of their out-of-school lives (masks), marginalizing or reducing their importance as part of their compliance to school demands. School may serve to minimize or discredit life beyond its walls, coercing children to create dark secrets. Discrepant roles "discredit, disrupt, or make useless the impression that the performance fosters" (p. 141).

As the sixth graders assume the role of insightful poets, they disrupt their roles as compliant children that keep outside lives out of school. The discrepant role lifts the mask and risks disrupting the very essence of what is supposed to happen at school. School creates the "non-person" (p. 151) and works to "show the outcast that he [or she] is being ignored, and the activity that is carried on in order to demonstrate this may itself be of secondary importance" (p. 153). The activity is not as important as the positioning that is underscored through it.

Freeing oneself of this situation usually involves what Goffman (1969) calls "collusion." "Collusive communication" is used by the actors to "free themselves a little from the restrictive requirements of interaction" (p. 190) in the setting at hand. This is followed by a realigning in which the players set out to redefine their roles within the setting. Realigning has to do with the nature of authority in the writing classroom, agency, and children struggling with increased responsibility for bringing authentic life experiences into their writing and for sharing those with each other. There was less struggle in the fifth grade, where the process of bringing home into school seemed more gentle and was more sustained by Barbara's commitment to working on biographies when I was not present. Still, within both groups, there were struggles for identity, voice, presence, and legitimacy. The struggle became very apparent in the sixth grade when I spent an entire day with them.

Sixth Graders' Brief Biographies

In the sixth grade, the students' desire to engage with each other socially rather than academically (two areas Patia viewed as separate and not blendable), led to tension and struggles between Patia and the students. I was not immune to the tension either as, for example, on the day of the fifth grade science field day when Patia suggested that I spend the full day with the sixth graders to get them further into their biographies. The date for the visit to the university was about one month away and they hadn't interviewed, written much in a formal biography genre, or collected artifacts. When I arrived at the sixth grade classroom, I made a list on the markerboard of all the things we'd accomplish on this day: learn to use the digital voice recorders (DVRs), write questions for an interview of someone in the class, and write a brief biography, all in preparation for their work with the person they were studying for the lengthier biography. Patia wanted sixth grade products similar to the fifth graders' work, even though I suggested that the sixth graders' poetry was powerful and presentable. This particular Friday was at the end of their first full week of testing. No tests were administered on Fridays, and the need to release the stress of the week became apparent.

I distributed the DVRs and the directions (in Spanish and English) that came with them. Fifteen minutes later, most of the students knew how to use them, showing each other the way to open new folders, record, and play back at varying speeds. I talked about the qualities of a good question and we generated and posted questions. I grouped the students around the six DVRs. Patia watched from the side of the classroom and demanded that the students be quiet, take turns, and listen politely to me. I brought four poems (Langston Hughes' *Mother to Son*, in Hughes, 1969; *Perhaps the World Ends Here*, in Harjo, 1994; *The Housing Poem*, in Harjo, Bird, Blanco, Cuthand, and Martínez, 1997; Luci Tapahonso's *It Has Always Been This Way*, in Tapahonso, 1998) ready to distribute if anyone said that they were finished interviewing and writing. Near the end of the morning, no one had written a biography, although much conversation was recorded, so I stopped the class and interviewed one of the sixth graders in front of the class. The process was instructive for most of the class as I selected questions from those listed on the board and the child responded. Then, I replayed what he said and asked for ideas of what I should write. On chart paper, I wrote what they suggested. By lunchtime, we'd generated six sentences. I asked the interviewee if he was satisfied with what was written and he wanted some information added, which I did. They left for lunch.

The use of the DVRs, particularly in small groups, was a breakdown in the regularities of the classroom. They didn't typically engage in pair or group work. In the afternoon, I again asked that they select questions, interview someone, and write a short biography that they might use as the "about the author" section of the piece they would write about someone outside of school. They composed short pieces using the questions we'd generated:

What are you afraid of?

What's something sad that happened in your life?

What are your pets?

Who's in your family?

What's the dumbest thing you've ever done?

The following examples, although short, have the intensity and economical use of language that these writers used in their poetry. They mixed the mundane with surprising, the silly with the serious, and the obvious with the subtle. When we shared their pieces, I pointed out how much they packed into the short space of a brief biography.

Mercedes interviewed two people because their group of three wasn't sure how to get each member of the group to interview one person. She wrote:

Vianca and Joanna were the two persons who I interviewed. Joanna wants to be a police when she grows up because she wants to help people by not doing anything wrong. Joanna was born January 10, 1995. She was born in the University of NM. She is afraid of tarantulas because one killed her dog, which is named Oso.

Vianca is afraid of dogs because one bit her on her leg. Vianca was born on June 11, 1994. She wants to be a doctor when she grows up because she wants to save people's lives. Vianca got mad at her friend because she traded her for someone else.

Verdad wrote about Corazon:

> Corazon was born in Albuquerque. Her favorite hobby is volleyball. Corazon is afraid of clowns. Corazon likes to watch "My Wife and Kids." Her favorite movie is "Dead Silence." The season she likes is summer. Corazon doesn't like to read. Corazon likes the United States because people are free. Corazon likes Chinese food. Her favorite singer is Simple Plan. Corazon likes converse shoes. She wants to be in band in 7th grade. She doesn't have a best friend. She likes to eat at China Star.

Isaac wrote about Susana:

> **Everything about Susana**
>
> Susana deepest secret is that she is scared of the dark. She scared of the dark because when she was small they left her alone in the dark. Her favorite show is the new "CW" and "My Wife and Kids." I asked if she has problems at home but she said she doesn't. Susana told me her mind is mostly blank. She likes MVE, but she thinks we need grass.

Ricardo wrote about Carlos:

> Carlos' dad came to the USA under the train and one of his dad's friends froze and died under the train. His mom met his dad in school. His mom works at daycare and his dad has his own company. He wants to be a lawyer and he likes to play the trombone but he wanted to play the saxophone but he couldn't because it was too late so he wanted to play the baritone but when he went to go get it the guy sold it.

They typed these biographies, which did not take a long time. I gave the packet of poems to those that finished typing. I told the children that they could borrow the DVRs to initiate the collection of their interview data.

Things Fall Apart

Later in the afternoon, after some volunteers shared their short biographies, I thought that our study of the more formal structure of a biography had gone as far as it could until the students collected data and artifacts. I explained that to the class and shifted to the poems. I suggested that we talk about them only briefly because I wanted them to use one of the poems as a format to write their own poem, as they've done with *Where I'm From* (Lyon, in Christensen, 2000) and their "dark" poems. Some of the groups that worked on brief biographies in the morning asked to stay together to talk about the poems and possibly write together, which was fine with me. What follows is an excerpt from my field notes, written after the day at school. The notes demonstrate Patia's desire that the students work alone, quietly, and complete their assignments. She also wanted all of her students to have similar opportunities so that no one was privileged.

> I told Verdad that she could work with a friend because they'd been in the biography group together and were getting along so well. Patia came over and screamed that they had to get to work and that they only had one paper [blank paper, to write a poem]. I explained that I said they could co-author a piece. Patia screamed, "Well if you can, others can too. You can't be special. You can't have things others don't have." Verdad's shoulders slumped and she sank into the chair... "I came over here a half hour ago and you still only had this same amount. You have to get writing. You have to get moving. You can't just sit here like you don't have to do the work." Verdad looked at me, then looked at Patia, and said, "We're working on it."
>
> "No," Patia screamed. "You're not. I don't know what you are doing but you are not working on it. You are talking or something but you are not writing poetry." I explained to Patia that I'd told the pair they could co-author. Verdad looked down and Patia walked away and loudly said to the class, "You can write **one** together if you want. They could so you can. You can do that if you want." Verdad looked at her partner and looked away. I touched her arm and said, "I'm sorry your feelings were hurt. I hope you can write a piece."

Verdad usually sits alone and Patia prefers it that way. I disrupted some of the regularity of the classroom by suggesting that partners or groups could write together. Patia's response to Verdad may have been directed at me, although whenever I suggested that she (Patia) could tell me if I was doing something wrong, she never did. Perhaps she could not because of the respect she held for me as a researcher, or her deference to me as a white man. Perhaps my presence undermined her authority, something she worked hard for because, as she explained, many of the students (especially boys) did not respond well to women (particularly Hispanic women) in authority positions. But the disruption for the day had only just begun. My field notes capture some of the disorder that followed my attempts to get the sixth graders to write.

> They struggled with the writing so I had them come together as a large group so we could discuss it. But, it was Juliana's birthday and she had ice cream and everyone kept asking about it. We decided to dish it out. When it was all distributed, I thought we'd talk about the poems but as I started to read one, I noticed some kids with pickles. I looked up and saw Patia with a list and a huge bag of pickles. Kids had paid for them as part of a fundraiser and were now getting pickles. I waited for all the pickles to be distributed and soon realized that no one was paying attention and saw

why. Now Patia and an educational assistant were distributing otter pops [frozen flavored water in a long tube] that kids also ordered. Some kids had as many as 12. The kids were eating and talking and Patia yelled, "OK, you can eat and listen. If you can't eat and listen, you can just listen and not eat, but you can't just eat and talk and not listen."

. . . I tried again to read, but they were really into talking to each other. So I said, "I have to wait to read until you can all hear me." I waited and then read the poems. But the students were pretty hyped up on sugar and pickles and artificial colors. And I sort of liked it. It's Friday and they're exhausted from testing all week and they're partying. They're talking and making faces as I read.

I finished reading the poems, though I couldn't read them seriously even though they're serious pieces. I said, "We're going to write for 11 minutes," having no idea why I chose that amount of time. After they all had paper and pencils, we wrote and it was quiet. Most are light and silly and reflective of the sugar high, but they're great examples of the variety of writing that lies within.

Ricardo's piece captured the mood of the class as the students attempted to write, looked around, thought about next week, and planned for the weekend.

That otter pop was good. R— just traded me a pink otter pop for his green one. It's really good. I can't wait until I get home. I'm glad it's Friday. My nephew will probably call me today and ask me if I want to spend the night. I should probably start thinking if I should say yes or no. Man we still have testing next week. I think it's the science test.

Isaac used language from school (hypothesis; W.O.M.M., for *what's on my mind*):

This pickle is good but I feel like eating [it] at home. Forget it. Mmm. I wonder how many otter pops Verdad bought. Probably 10 that's my hypothesis. I am on the bottom of my pickle. This paper that I am writing reminds me of what's on my mind. W.O.M.M. Verdad could last a year with those otter pops. Wow, Mr. Meyer already has a page [written].

Jesus' sense of humor and the passing of time show up in his piece:

Today was really cool. I don't know why I said *was*, the day is still not over. So far we have went to music, PE, and have been writing with Dr. Meyer. We have had pickles, otter pops and now we are writing for 11 minutes. Hopefully the rest of my day goes like the way it's been. Who am I kidding?

We still have about 50 minutes of school left. The day has gone by very slow. I wish it would go a little faster at least until I get to my house. I hope I get to interview my grandmother. I wonder if he is going to lend us the camera and the tape recorder. Two more minutes left. I don't know what else to write.

Some of the students used their time to write a letter to me, including a status report on their biographic thinking. Esperanza wrote two letters, one about a story in Mexico:

Dear Mr. Meyer

I'm writing this letter to tell you that my dad got happy when I told him that I'm interviewing them about my grandma.

Esperanza

Dear Mr. Meyer

I'm writing about otter pops. One day when I was in Mexico, it was last summer so it was so hot. My cousin told us let's go buy pops. I said OK. When we got to the store, she came out with a big big otter pop. I started to laugh and she asked me why was I laughing. I said because I haven't seen big otter pops. She told me that I was dumb but I didn't care. I was laughing and laughing. When I got home, my mom told me "*Mensa*" [and above "*mensa*" she wrote "Spanish" to let me know it's a Spanish word; it means "dummy"].

Esperanza

Corazon offered some corrective information as well as providing a status report.

Dr. Meyer, I'm really happy that you picked our class for the project. I'm having lots of fun and expect to do my best on the project. Before you came everything was so boring. Sometimes it was probably because we didn't do nothing but accelerated math. But now I enjoy writing poems and w.o.m.m. I think before I used to not enjoy writing what I know. Based on the project I wanted to ask you if we can take pictures of the person it's based on. Well, any way, I just wanted to say thanks for everything.

Your friend

Corazon

[Then she put an arrow from her name and wrote]: please don't spell my name wrong it's C-O-R-A-Z-O-N not C-O-R-O-S-O-N

Juliana wrote in prose-like fashion, using line breaks to create a poetic form:

When I was a baby

When I was a baby I cried
a lot. When I was a baby I
couldn't do anything.
I don't remember but
my mom comes up with a lot
of memories. My mother
would be too busy to work
and didn't pay that much
of attention to me. It's not
like she didn't want to. It's because
she was working. My mom loved
me a lot when I was a baby.
The other day she brought up a story
and said, "I wish you guys were
still babies." The end

Juliana

Isaac, taken with Harjo's poem, seems to be experimenting with mixing his voice with his understanding of Harjo's, paralleling the theme of *beginnings*.

The first day of school is here

The day begins in my room, when the sun rises.
When I feel the sun touching my face, I rise.
It's time, my mom says, time to go to school.
I get ready. I go outside. I wait and wait.
From my eye, I see a yellow bus coming for me.
I jump in the bus and I realize
It's time to learn.

Beginning with the idea of the world beginning and ending, from the Harjo poem, Vianca captured the expectations that children have for school, including the idea that the tables are set for everyone. She suggests the struggle between what goes on outside of school and the requirements within.

My happiness ends here
My happiness ends in the class.
No matter what we have to do in
class we have to live.
The things we have to do in class
are already prepared, set in my table.
So it will be there for all the students
in the class.

At the end of the day as I reviewed all that they submitted, I found some serious pieces that weren't shared. Mercedes related to the Harjo poem, finding parts of her own life that resonated with the images presented.

> The poem I liked the most was *Perhaps the World Ends Here*. I liked it because it has a lot of words that make you draw a picture inside your head. The part I liked was "our dreams drink coffee with us as they put their arms around our children. They laugh with us at our poor falling-down selves and as we put ourselves back together once again at the table." That part reminded me of my dad because he sits down and drinks his coffee by himself in the big brown table. Another poem I liked was *no crystal stair* because it tells how part of the house doesn't have any carpet. I wonder why it said "so boy don't look back." It reminded me of my grandma because she is always mad about her house.

The sixth graders were ready to decompress, having prepared for the two weeks of testing since August. They accomplished decompression by celebrating a birthday, eating pickles and otter pops, and bracketing anything resembling schoolwork. They joked even with their writing, enjoying a party-like atmosphere. The day underscored the struggles the students faced living with multiple masks. The tensions between discourses at school and those outside of school seemed to collide in a festival of food and social conversation. Temporarily, many of the rules were suspended. They could talk, eat, and move around the room with a little more freedom, although Patia periodically pointed out behaviors that she found too extreme for school. Within that temporary social milieu, a few writers remained serious. All writers probably need a space in which to simply relax, but the day signified, or perhaps magnified, the idea that classrooms are not only places in which multiple identities, languages, cultures, and experiences come together. They are places in which these differences produce tensions that may express themselves as struggles in response to the sense that, as Vianca wrote, "things . . . are already set . . . for all the students."

The Classroom as a "Site of Struggle"

Reviewing field notes, listening to students' voices on digital voice recorders, hearing the voices of their families, and engaging with them in the struggle to make sense of the ever-growing body of written work they produced are easy places to romanticize the work of our year together. By romanticize, I mean that the work could tend towards looking like a wonderful (albeit local) success story in which students are transformed from reluctant or non expressive writers to a deeply intellectual community of writers. That did occur to some degree as their writing changed over the course of our year together. However, the tensions (struggles) within the data need to be represented here in order to dispel those romantic notions that too easily reify this work to the level of some popular movie. The classrooms in this study were, in varying ways, constant "site[s] of struggle" (Volosinov, 1973) as we worked to include the students' home lives. The complexity of home as a transnational (Guerra, 1998) and multilingual setting that involved non documented family members (for some), frequent trips between Mexico and the US (for others), as well as the influences of gangs, religion, drugs, prison, health issues, extended families, and changing familial constellations and intimate relationships contributed to the students' struggles to tell their truths as they worked to compose narratives, poetry, expository text, and identities. Much of the students' writing throughout this book serves as evidence of the struggle to bring self, home culture, voice, and meaning to school in ways previously unrecognized, marginalized, unofficial, or not considered relevant. In the following sections, I present some of the facets of our *struggle*, but struggle does not necessitate pain, although at different times throughout the year, all of us experienced pain. Struggle may be joyous, intense, difficult, challenging, oppressive, or liberating because it underscores the presence and possibilities of our own agency, thus giving us a sense of truly being alive, present, and heard.

Struggle and the Use of Time

There was a struggle that showed itself in the way time was used at the school. In the weeks preceding the statewide testing to determine if the school made adequate yearly progress, test preparation was common in many classrooms. Even Barbara relinquished to the administrative pressure to prepare because she wanted her students to be familiar with the format of the test. Regularities such as test preparation, test taking, and prescribed curriculum, were rooted in the official portrait of the school. Schools were supposed to look like places in which children's time was used to prepare for and take tests. The struggle for time—finding or carving it out—was a struggle for space in which to compose or recompose self as a writer and a teacher. Barbara intuited this idea when she committed to doing something that the students would remember for the rest of their lives. Patia struggled with it as she felt the pressure to cover official curriculum because of the demands of administrators and legislators.

The struggle with the use of time represented a struggle for power and control. Barbara struggled to use time to welcome multiple perspectives, knowing that not every child agreed with her or each other, but all sides were heard. In school, where rigid adherence to a schedule may take precedence—indeed is expected to take precedence—over other issues, taking time for conversations about playground fights or the struggles real writers face are "relevant to the present situation of the child" (Miedema, 1992, p. 35). Engaging in such *relevance* is a struggle between teacher and the institution of school, between kids and their idea of school, and between a body of learners, a teacher and their official portrait.

It may seem easy for a teacher to allow time for dialogue, and clearly she is the power figure that does allow for it (or not). If children take time to talk, it is unofficial and vulnerable to being shut down or quieted by the teacher. But when a teacher decides to allow for such space, she is vulnerable. She departs from the standard course and, in schools such as MVE, such departure could put her at a different place in the textbook from her colleagues. Teacher as the power person, grants 'permission' for things to happen. Conversations, the science field day, a birthday party, and the pickle and otter pop distribution are official slots of time in which regular rules are suspended. The biography work within both classrooms was the only time that I know of that was a regular occurrence, built into the schedules of both classrooms, during which regular rules were suspended. Of course, there were norms that were adhered to, but even these were bent (such as project duration, student-developed rubrics, and appropriate topics for written language activity within school).

Writing as Carnival

Many teachers have ideas in their minds of the perfect classroom, a sort of teacher-defined Utopian place towards which they work with their students in a variety of ways: active community building, coercion, manipulation, caring, conversation, love, power, and many others. Each of these ways, when considered as facets of communities of practice, has legitimate forms of participation, again, defined by the teacher, district policy, state mandates etc. But there are times during the life of any community of practice during which community members (teachers or students) resist legitimacy, sometimes sanctioned and other times not. A time of collective refusal, such as a pickle day or a science field day, are officially sanctioned events, although some of the children are not sure exactly which norms or rules are bracketed and find out through gentle correction or sharp reprimand. Officially sanctioned (by the teacher) bracketing was the case with the pickles, ice cream, and otter pops. It was also the case with the science field day as schedules were disrupted and activities were changed. This is Bakhtin's (1984) idea of *carnival*, a time of "refusal to acquiesce in the legitimacy of the present social system" (Gardiner, 1993, p. 35, cited in Kujundzic, 1994). Every carnival, in the Bakhtinian sense, is a struggle because of the fact that permission was given for the event. If no permission were given, if no one allowed the rules to be suspended but individuals *refused to acquiesce*, then, rather than carnival, revolution is taking place. Revolutions don't happen too often in schools. The struggle within the carnival is determining how far the rules may be bent and which rules may even be broken. There is also the inherent struggle between the dominant source of power and the non-dominant participants (students, and teachers, too) to revert to or reinforce the rules or in some way let it be known that the carnival is bounded by time and there is a predetermined end. Pickle parties end; science field days come to a close. Yet, they are real events that demonstrate possibilities of what can happen in school and, as such, find a place in the minds and recollected experiences of all present.

There was a sense of carnival that emerged through our writing as things began to change for or be reconsidered or resisted by the writers and their teachers. The students sensed that the rules were disrupted, but weren't initially sure how to come to terms with it. Vianca knew about school and what to expect, "The things we have to do in class are already prepared, set in my table. So it will be there for all the students in the class." She knew that students were expected to 'eat' what is 'served' at the school table, intuiting that such ingestion occurred regardless of appetite, interest, need, or desire. Paull (1972) understood that children must go to school, everyday, regardless of what happened the previous day or what might happen the next. "From what one must do there is no escape. Tomorrow I would have to go back to school" (p. 10). The writing carnival that I helped induce had some degree of legitimacy in that I was a researcher and the teachers were known in the school for being involved in the study. The writing carnival was a regular occurrence in both classrooms and Barbara was willing to continue it at least once each week when I was not present. The carnival was bounded by time and space and it was brave teacher activity as the teachers either allowed or cultivated the suspension of the usual and moved to unexplored pedagogical territory by suspending traditional borders of space, time, context, and the nature of performance. As with any Bakhtinian carnival, someone had to initiate it and my sense of myself as the invited initiator is an important part of counterportrait activity. I helped influence the use of time as it was spent, the opening of space to write, and the welcoming of the formerly unofficial onto the official landscape. Of course, once this happens new struggles emerge.

Carnivals Breed Struggle

When the borders of acceptability are redefined, even the obvious and everyday raise questions and become vulnerable; redefining, questioning and vulnerability are sites of struggle as individuals and the group search for some resolution in order to function as a community of practice and not a community in disruption. There are struggles over content, time, perfection, multiple drafts, large amounts of data, typing, finding a person to study, honoring the person studied, composing leads and endings, and finding, facing, and writing truths. One of the strategy lessons I taught both classes was something I heard one morning on National Public Radio. Natalie Goldberg discussed writing and said, "two plus two equals Mercedes Benz," when discussing the idea of surprises in writing. I brought this idea to the children and also talked about things that they know that may seem ordinary, but may be quite extraordinary when committed to paper because the everyday to one person seems unique or even extreme to another. The children struggled to write and they also wrote to portray the struggles that they uncovered or realized. Estevan, well aware of his father's love for the family, got a glimpse of such a struggle when he heard his father say that he would install carpet for the rest of his life. His father's struggle led to Estevan's struggle to understand what a *hero* is because his father had not fought in Iraq and did not win any medals. Estevan's struggle led him to uncovering the heroic deeds that love can bare, such as working at a demanding job out of love for family.

The sixth graders' poems revealed struggles with darkness, death, relationships, murder, doubt, and fears. They struggled not only in their lived experiences, but in bringing those into the classroom and acknowledging those experiences within themselves (confirming their realities) and presenting them to others. When Esperanza wept about her grandmother and Juliana cried about her father and others saw, we experienced moments when teasing was suspended, putdowns were sidelined, and glimmers of care shone. When they wrote and read brief biographies, they struggled to understand each other and to compose both written pieces and relationships that were truthful. In their classroom, they struggled to understand the boundaries of safety, between them and their teacher and between each other, having learned to be unsure of what might occur if they revealed something personal.

The invisible presence of a system in motion is not something that is easy to resist. The students in this study have been in the NCLB environment since kindergarten or first grade and resisting what has always been (in school) is a struggle, especially when it demands disruption of strongly, though artificially, imposed borders. Resistance is the struggle to understand to a sufficient extent so that action may ensue. The children and their teachers struggled to create different school masks and to resist the old ones. The struggle to understand what lies within, how it got there, and to believe that it is a powerful source upon which to draw as a writer and a human being is intense work.

Counterportraits, Struggles, Legitimacy, and Possibilities

In this chapter, legitimacy was further born out and articulated in the processes in which the children engaged in writing and the ways in which they interacted with each other, their teacher, and me. Any community of practice has borders, artificial constructions that are put in place typically by those in power. As the fifth and sixth graders explored their writing, their identities, and their interactions, they questioned, stretched, and redefined the borders (Giroux, 1992) with which they were familiar in a school setting. They struggled at the borders of well-defined spaces and their challenges to the borders were, at times, carnivalesque in nature. The typical curriculum and the way in which it was enacted were bracketed during the times that both classes wrote biographic pieces. They redefined what was acceptable—legitimate—within the school setting and, in doing so, initiated a process of exploring possibilities for themselves as writers (part of *identity*) as well as what can happen (*legitimacy*) in school (*a community of practice*). Lave and Wenger (1991) suggest that legitimacy occurs at the periphery for those new to a community. The idea of legitimate peripheral participation is not meant to dismiss or devalue the work. It is intended as a beginning of the exploration of possibilities with a degree of specificity that allows for the uniqueness of each child, family, and community. Counterportraits are explorations at the periphery in the composing of a community of possibilities, possibilities that were not known at the outset and were studied and crafted by all of us as the work progressed.

Wenger (1998) explains "non-participation as practice" (p. 171) in his discussion of corporate life as "making their time at work a livable realization of their marginality within the corporation . . . . It manifests in the instantaneous legitimacy obtained by remarks about looking forward to the weekend or wishing it were four o'clock" (p. 171). We experienced a gradual reduction in non-participation as practice when students asked if they could be excused from recess to continue work on their writing, worked for two hours or more and didn't notice how quickly time passed, or expressed disappointment when our poetry session was over. They talked about finishing their pieces, but not simply to have them completed like 'schoolwork.' They wanted to share it and had authentic audiences such as each other, families, and future teachers in mind. Further, their willingness to read their work to each other in small groups, especially in the sixth grade, to read it to the whole group for input and critique, and to read across classrooms also suggested a change in the community of practice, legitimacy within that community, and the possibilities of what could happen in school. Of course, the nagging question of reliability (measured via replication of the study) in the present educational research environment must be addressed at some point. Quite simply, this study cannot be replicated in the present sense of the word as articulated by documents such as the *Report of the National Reading Panel* (National Reading Panel, 2000). Not only because of its qualitative approach, but because of the findings that are emerging, particularly the idea that locality matters. Replication is about compliance; counterportraiture is about disruption. Allen (1989), twenty years ago as of this writing, addressed the issue by asking us to address two questions:

> How might these practices benefit the children with whom I work? . . .
> How might I study if and how they are of benefit? The answer to the first
> question will reduce the risks for some children immediately. The answer
> to the second will lead to policies that may one day reduce the risks for all
> children. (p. 16)

Any counterportrait is evidence of a struggle to resist the official portrait. It is a struggle rooted in actions that honor children's lives within and beyond their classrooms. At present, such work must be done in the cracks that exist between the tectonic plates of required curriculum and high-stakes testing

(Ohanian, 2001). The local work is a site of hope. The goal is that as such cracks yield results that matter locally and other locales engage in counterportraiture as well, the work will be accepted and influential (perhaps even disruptive) in official forums as evidence of authentic learning that cannot be addressed in standardized curriculum or captured on a single test or in a single moment.

Chapter 8

Writing Places as Hybrid Spaces

> Mexican-American students . . . have not had the opportunity to develop academic discourse skills in their primary language in a school context that supports their full linguistic development. The irony is that schools often require from these linguistic minority students precisely the academic discourse skills and knowledge bases they do not teach. It is what we call a 'pedagogy of entrapment,' in which even in contexts where teachers are well intentioned, they often fail to explicitly teach the academic discourse necessary for school success.
>
> (Macedo & Bartolomé, 1999, p. 59)

Pedagogical entrapment has moved to pedagogical crisis in 'failing' schools, particularly when teachers are held hostage by curricula that claim to be based on research, even though they are not (Coles, 2003) and, further, do not meet local needs. In our many discussions of the qualities of writing, using language about writing that the children eventually appropriated, we made advances towards pedagogical liberation by composing, with children, places in which their truths were the points of origin. These were hybridized spaces (Bakhtin, 1981) in which multiple meanings, languages, and pedagogical opportunities contributed to the use of *academic discourse* as a necessary tool, but not for the sake of the tool, rather for the sake of the work.

Just after the middle of March, the tone of the school changed because the state mandated tests were over and the pressure to achieve adequate yearly progress (AYP) assuaged. There was, in the air of the school, a celebratory pause between taking the tests and knowing the results. I arrived on the Friday of the week after the tests and learned that it was weird hair day in addition to being St. Patrick's Day. It seemed as though the end of testing was officially the beginning of some very different events at the school. Field trips were taken, games were played, and the teachers seemed more at ease. Although the teachers would eventually feel renewed pressure because of the still-to-come district level (now that the state level was over) reading tests and a different computerized test for some other assessing, today green hair and strange hairdos were all over the school. Patia was feeling pressure to have her students complete the biography narratives because the visit to the university was approaching quickly. Barbara's students were approaching completion of their pieces and were wondering what to do once they were done.

Sixth Graders Get Serious

As the date of our work at the university came closer, I stopped bringing poetry to the sixth grade class and worked more to have them focus on expository pieces. I wrote a schedule on the board, which Patia copied, listing the dates that each child would have a digital voice recorder over the following two weeks. Before I arrived on one Friday in early March, Patia and Roberta had written a list of interview questions without input from the children. It was a list of a dozen questions that the students would take with them when they borrowed a recorder. Hoping to inspire the sixth graders' interest in the search for artifacts, I brought some artifacts from my childhood and demonstrated how the artifacts were part of a biography I'd written about my mom, including some quotes from my sisters, who, I explained, I interviewed over the phone. I read about my father, whose temper was sometimes explosive, my mother's sense of justice, and my life now as it related to being my parents' son. My document was two pages long and I showed the sixth graders how I used the storyboard (Appendix 3) to move the text into slides. The finished piece, with Yiddish and Hebrew songs as backdrop, seemed to motivate a lot of the students. They wanted to get to work on their biographies, but I wanted them to have a written record of what they needed to do.

"What do you have left to do to finish your biographies?" I asked.

A lot of them started to talk at once and I suggested that they write what they have left to do. I explained, "Just write it down. It doesn't have to be long. Just write what you have done and what you need to do. It's a status check about your biography work. Write how it's going. And, when you finish that, turn it over and tell me anything else that you're thinking that you want me to know." I wrote on the board: *status of my biography* and *what else I want you (Dr. Meyer) to know.*

Esperanza wrote to both of the prompts and then lowered her head and began to cry. I went to her desk and she showed me her pieces (Figure 8.1). She explained that it was hard to write about her grandmother because she loved her so much. I suggested that her love for her grandmother made it important to write the piece and she agreed as her crying subsided.

Jesus sat near enough to Esperanza to hear the conversation that she and I had. He already decided to interview his grandmother and his sensitivity (see, for example, his *dark* poem in Chapter 7) seems to resonate with his classmate (Figure 8.2).

On the other side of Figure 8.2, Jesus wrote:

> My grandmother is so sick. I hope she gets better. She has to have something on her arm because it hurts so bad. She wants me to interview

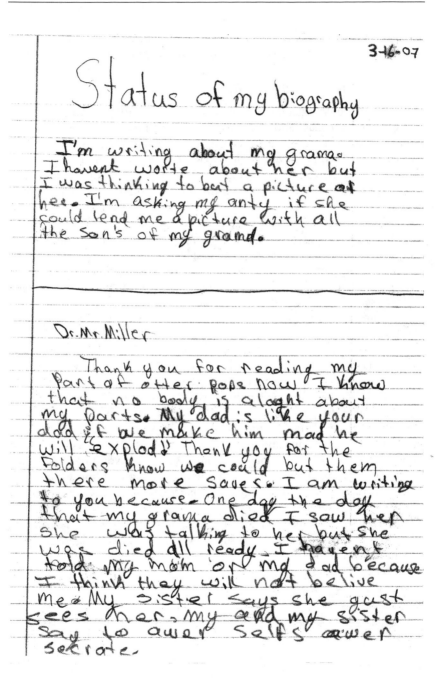

3-16-07

Status of my biography

I'm writing about my grama.
I havent worte about her but
I was thinking to but a picture of
hee. I'm asking my anty if she
could lend me a picture with all
the son's of my gramd.

Dr. Mr. Miller

Thank you for reading my
Parts of otter pops now I know
that no body is alaght about
my Parts. My dad is like your
dad if we make him mad he
will "explod" Thank yoy for the
folders know we could but them
there more saves. I am writing
to you because. One day the day
that my grama died I saw her
she was talking to her but she
was died all ready. I havent
told my mom or my dad becaue
I think they will not belive
me. My sister says she gust
sees her, my and my sister
say to awer selfs' awer
secrate.

Figure 8.1 Esperanza's status and needs.

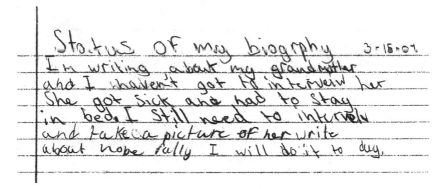

Figure 8.2 Jesus' status and needs.

her to see what I can do. My grandma is so nice. She always wants the best for me. I want the best for her, too. My grandma is fun. She likes to have flowers. She is always cleaning. She laughs almost all the time. She loves her house and she used to clean houses. She had little cards that would say what she does. It had like a cartoon person that looked like her.

Miguel sees value in getting the story of his mom's crossing into the US (see Figure 8.3).

Mercedes (Figure 8.4) has her cousin on her mind even though her biography is going to be about her mom. The emotional tenor of the room as they write their truths sometimes brings up ideas that seem unrelated, but they are actually moments of attention to life-influencing moments that were formerly bracketed in school, including the guilt survivors feel.

Verdad wrote about not writing about her uncle and then surveyed and reported on her colleagues' activity.

I'm writing about my uncle and I haven't done anything. I need to do: what I need to do is write the questions down. Record the people I'm going to interview.

I wonder what we are going to do after this. I hope it's something. I wonder what we are going to do in band. I wonder when I'm going to take the recorder to my house. I wonder why F— isn't writing so is A—. I wonder what [the teacher] is writing about. A— started to write. I wonder what L— is writing about. She's almost half way in her paper. [The teacher] is past half way. E— is just playing with his pencil instead of writing G— is talking to E—. Ms Roberta is reading the book Dr. Meyer wrote [The children asked to see one of my books, which I brought and showed.] She's smiling.

Verdad

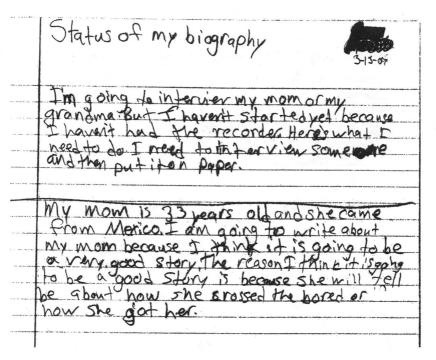

Status of my biography
3-15-07

I'm going to interview my mom or my grandma But I haven't started yet because I haven't had the recorder. Here's what I need to do. I need to interview someone and then put it on paper.

My mom is 33 years old and she came from Mexico. I am going to write about my mom because I think it is going to be a very good story. The reason I think it's going to be a good story is because she will tell be about how she crossed the border or how she got her.

Figure 8.3 Miguel's status and needs.

Corazon has "nuthing" (Figure 8.5) done, but she has a plan.

But there's more to Corazon's writing for the day. On the reverse side of Figure 8.5, she wrote:

> I am thinking how stupid I am cuz I'm always getting in trouble. Today I almost got in a fight with this girl. I guess I just can't keep stuff to my self. Every time I see her pass by me I feel so mad. I just hope I wouldn't do something dumb the next time I see her. Ohhh and the principal also told me that if I was to get another write up or warning slip they were going to suspend me. I just feel really bad cuz I'm not listening to my mom and getting into more and more times. "I'm sorry mom." I am feeling so bad right now. My head is hurting and I also have a really sore throat.

Corazon is articulate about her rage and the struggle to contain it as she works on a biography about the very person for whom she is working so hard to contain that rage.

After the status reports, which I collected if they wanted a response, the students got busy with their biographies. The following week I was greeted with, "Did you write back?" The following are a sampling of responses to their

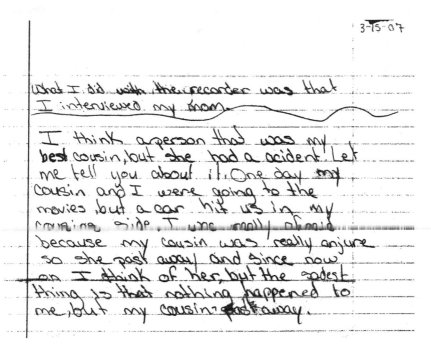

3-15-07

What I did with the recorder was that
I interviewed my mom.

I think a person that was my
best cousin, but she had a accident. Let
me tell you about it. One day my
cousin and I were going to the
movies, but a car hit us in my
cousins side. I was really afraid
because my cousin was really anjure
so she past away and since now
on I think of her, but the sadest
thing is that nothing happened to
me, but my cousin past away.

Figure 8.4 Mercedes' status and thoughts.

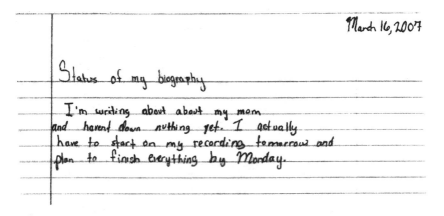

March 16, 2007

Status of my biography

I'm writing about about my mom
and havent down nuthing yet. I actually
have to start on my recording tomorrow and
plan to finish everything by Monday.

Figure 8.5 Corazon's status and needs.

status writing. Such interactions helped to solidify our relationships and provide them with evidence I hoped they would appropriate as part of their disappropriating of their official portrait.

Esperanza,

The story of your grandmother's life will make a really good biography. There's so much to learn about her and to tell about her. I wonder what your mom remembers about her. To be honest, I don't really understand what happens to people when they die. I'm not sure how she could talk when everyone thought she was dead, but I also know that you are smart and you see things with your own eyes and you trust what you see. Do you think you'll put that part in the biography? I hope you can get some pictures of her to scan in. The most important part is the story. Get a lot of information and write the story. It will be great.

Thank you for always being such a serious and good writer.

Thanks for working on this,

Dr. Meyer

Jesus,

I think that the things that you listed that you have left to do are a good plan for you to follow. You need to interview her and maybe get a picture. I'm sorry she's sick. If she's too sick to talk, maybe you could interview other people about her life so far. What do you think? Can you get it done? The things you wrote on the back of the page are really good. You already know a lot about her. That's a great beginning. Keep going!

Thanks for working on this,

Dr. Meyer

Miguel,

I think the story of how your mom got here will be a really good story. There are so many different stories about crossing the border and all of these stories teach us about how people get here and also WHY they want to come here. What questions will you ask your mom so that she tells the interesting parts of the story? Good luck with this. You are doing very important work.

Thanks for working on this,

Dr. Meyer

Mercedes,

I hope you get to interview your mom soon. I am so sorry about your cousin. And I'm sorry that you had to be in the car when this happened to her. I'm also glad that nothing happened to you because I might not have gotten to meet you if something happened to you, too. I don't know why bad things happen to good people, sometimes, but it's true that it does. I think that something like this helps you understand how precious life is.

Thanks for working on this,

Dr. Meyer

Verd, [her nickname for herself]

The story of your uncle's life is very important. It will help others know what kind of a man he was. It will also let the world know that other people loved this man and now he is gone and he is missed. I know that this is a sad story and it may be hard to write, but it's a story that will make other people stop and think about how important life is.

Thanks for working on this,

Dr. Meyer

When I returned these pieces, the dialogue was over. They didn't write back to me and I didn't want them to because they had other writing to do.

During a late March visit, the sixth graders used the entire time to transcribe sections of their interviews, compose drafts of their autobiographies, or confer with Patia, Roberta or me. Patia was very anxious about having final pieces completed soon, particularly because the fifth graders' pieces were so close to completion. Most of the sixth graders did not bring artifacts or photographs, nor were some willing to borrow the disposable cameras that Barbara purchased for them to use. The ones that did borrow the cameras often returned them with a host of reasons for not having used them: the person wasn't there, they went away for the evening, they got home too late, they forgot it was in their backpack, and many more. They also, to a much greater degree than the fifth graders, began to express fear about the trip to the university. They wanted to know how many people they would speak in front of, who the people were, what the room was like, if the people would be standing or sitting, if there would be restrooms, and if there would be food for them. I responded to all their questions, but the fear was not assuaged.

Two weeks before our trip to the university was another day of panic for Patia as she anticipated the presentations. She decided that every child needed at least five PowerPoint slides. "You need five slides. Only five slides," she said, for her to consider the piece complete. Five became the goal for many children as a way of being finished with the work. The work of the sixth graders changed for two reasons. First, the move away from poetry was not easy because they'd learned that poetry could be accomplished in short bursts that often yielded satisfying results; second, the goal of completing five slides became the standard. They were still truthful, but the drive to learn about their families diminished for some of the writers as meeting the goal set by their teacher took precedence. It was a realistic goal in that we had limited time to reach a product for presentation. Esperanza wrote about her grandmother; she wrote honestly, but the pressure nudged her into brevity as she wrote the title and two other slides.

[Title page, Slide 1] My *Abuelita* Sylvia [photo of grandma in the background]

[Slide 2] My *abuelita* was born on November 15, 1952 in a big city in Casas Grandes. Casas Grandes is by Chihuahua where my dad [dad's name] was born. [Dad's first name] is the one on the left [in photo].

[Slide 3] My *abuela* [endearing way of referring to her *abuelita*, like 'Gran' in English] came to the U.S.A. to try to have a better life. Over there in Mexico they used to have work but no money. So they came to the USA to work and get money.

I went to MVE both Thursday and Friday of the week before our trip to the university. In my field notes about that final Friday prior to the trip, I wrote:

I . . . met with kids [in the fifth grade] one at a time [to review their final pieces] and then went to Patia's class for part of the morning. I told the sixth graders that we'd do a rehearsal [to get ready for the second rehearsal with both classes] and that's what we did. Each one got up and read their biography. They were terrified, mostly afraid of what they'd hear from their friends in the class. One child got up to read, but a slight click of the tongue from one of his friends caused him to fold into laughter followed by refusal to read. Their old habits—old masks—seemed to flow back as pressure to produce dissolved the sense of community (and perhaps safety) that had begun to evolve. I hoped that the fifth graders would encourage them a little later in the day.

Jesus refused to read and I wasn't sure if he had anything to read. Patia insisted that I meet with him, as she took him and me into another room while Roberta watched the class. "Tell Dr. Meyer why you aren't reading anything? Do you even have anything?" Jesus looks at me and his eyes fill with tears.

"You don't have to read anything if you don't want to," I say.

"But she said I can't go on the trip if I don't read," he whispers, pointing towards Patia with his chin.

"You can go," I say, "but I'm worried. I am worried that you'll get home on the night after the trip and everyone else will have read but you. Then, what will happen? You might feel really bad and won't be able to do anything about it then. It'll be too late. What are you worried about?"

"I'll be embarrassed."

"I know how that feels. I talk in front of lots of groups. Why don't we do this . . . why don't you just look at me, and not anyone else. You look at your writing and at me."

His eyes are really full now.

"Well," I say, "just think about it. It's totally up to you, ok?"

He shook his head up and down just the slightest bit.

The rehearsal with both classes took place after lunch. It ended abruptly when a group of children arrived at Patia's class for reading and others reminded her that they needed to leave.

Jesus was secretive about the contents of his biography and didn't allow peers to see it; he did allow Roberta to help him edit and, at one point, she even took dictation as he spoke so that he'd have a product to bring with him. I know that Jesus completed five slides and printed them off to read at the university, but he did not attend because he got into a fight with Ricardo; both were placed on in-school suspension and not allowed to attend. Ricardo's eye remained black and blue for weeks. Perhaps Jesus found an honorable way to stay behind. The hard copy seemed to have disappeared when I asked Jesus if I could see it.

Jumping ahead for a moment, I continued to visit MVE after the field trip and found that fighting increased as spring arrived and tempers seemed to flare easily in the sixth grade. The children grew increasingly rude to Patia and at one point, as she yelled at Jesus for not getting some work done, he left the typically quiet and withdrawn role that he assumed when being reprimanded and screamed, "Shut up!" at her. She immediately told him to go to the office where he was put on in-school suspension. Somewhere in all this turmoil, perhaps in anger, he lost his slides about his grandmother and the contents of his folder on the computer.

When finishing became the focus of the work, the revising process was not allowed to flourish, but still the students struggled to bring important information to their texts. "Even if it's short, it can say a lot," I said on that last day as they struggled to complete five slides. Patia told them that they "represent the school and need to have good pieces to read." I regret now not having pushed some of them to bring an anthology of their poetry, which could have been framed as writers bending a genre. Some of them, such as Ricardo, wrote pieces that were clearly reflective of the questions that he asked the person he was studying (his dad), questions (from the teacher-generated list) including:

Where were you born?

What was your first job?

Why did you come to the US?

Have you ever been caught by immigration?

Who helped you?

Where do you like to live?

These questions yielded some long conversations on the recorders, but the children had to reduce them to finish the task at hand. However, rather than focus on the negative aspects of such rushing in school, it is important to consider that the communication within the families involved the children being reminded or learning more of the details of the stories of their families.

Ricardo's slides contained the following, including the title page and each titled slide but no photos (although he and others used colorful backdrops on their slides):

[Slide 1, title page] My Dad by Ricardo

[Slide 2] Childhood

My Dad was born in Cuauhtémoc, Mexico. My Dad had a fun childhood. He was going to school for a few months about a year. He used to help his dad working on the ranch in between school. He had a lot of fun helping his dad and going to school.

[Slide 3] A New Life

The first job my dad had was in construction. My dad's purpose for coming to the United States was to work. My dad got to the United States by walking from El Paso to Las Cruces. My dad didn't come to the US with family. He came to the US with his friend.

[Slide 4] Rough Times

Some people helped him out by letting him stay with them. They also helped my dad and his friend find a job. My dad has been caught by immigration. When he was working they came and asked for papers. My dad didn't have any papers so they took him back to Mexico.

[Slide 5] The Past And The Present

My dad can help his family in Mexico more in the US than if he was in Mexico. He can help them more because he makes more money in the US. That's the difference between the USA and Mexico. My dad's happiest memory was when he was 27 and he met my mom. My dad's fear is to be sick and not be able to support his family. My dad's dream is to win the lottery and retire early. That's my dad's story of his past, now is the present.

Many of the students in the school are, like Ricardo, transnationals living much like Oscar Martínez described in chapter 2, in two worlds, both important but neither sufficient. Ricardo's father knows that he is responsible for the family and Ricardo understands his father's feelings of not having a safety net, such as disability insurance, that can be counted on if he becomes hurt or ill. Ricardo is accurate in writing, "now is the present," because in those words he captures the fragile nature of the connection between two worlds as well as the vulnerability of his father who serves as the bridge—or, more accurately, the lifeblood—between those worlds.

Miguel made ten slides and included some quotes from his interview with his mom. My reason for interchanging the words 'page' and 'slides' is that the children eventually printed and bound their PowerPoints, a process that produces quite professional looking books. Rather than feeling undermined by the pressure to finish, Miguel engaged with a fervor that some other students expressed, too. He used time efficiently and his lengthy piece is presented in the next chapter.

Poetry in the Biography Genre

The fifth graders' pieces averaged about 15 slides and included many parts of a book. The fifth graders worked with Barbara during a mini-lesson to brainstorm the parts they might include in their books: cover and title page, dedication, copyright (part of dedication page), table of contents, body of the biography, last words and final thoughts, important dates/timelines, and "all about the author" as the closing page of the piece. They discussed whether or not a glossary should be included, ultimately deciding that it was not necessary. There were many conferences that focused on revising and editing, with their teacher, their peers, Roberta, and me. Between my visits, they had discussions about writing, revising, dialogue, sequencing, beginnings and endings, and design and layout, revisiting some of these topics with newfound relevance as they reached certain points in the work. These topics were presented to the whole group, small groups, or individuals as Barbara, Roberta, or I (when I was present) thought appropriate or as students self-identified needs.

"I'm done," came the amazed call of Ramona one Friday morning. And she really was. She had met with Barbara and colleagues, revised and edited, determined the sequence she liked, and even argued, in a thoughtful and scholarly way, about some parts of the piece. For example, she didn't want to change this rather convoluted and quite condensed history of her father's love life:

> Later after high school Mike got married to his other best friend in a Las Vegas chapel. Shortly after, Mike noticed it was a mistake and left her for his true love, Vicky. Vicky already had a child, Nicole, from an abusive boyfriend.

The question that loomed was this: once the children were done, what would they do?

The children read many of the poems that I read with sixth graders, quite often on the same day that the sixth graders used the poems as inspirations for their own writing, but the fifth graders had little time to discuss or use the poems as points of origin for their own poetry. After Ramona was finished with her biography, I explained in a quick mini-lesson that the sixth graders used the poems as a way to begin writing biographically. Barbara suggested that the fifth graders write a poem to include as part of their biography. The writers that chose to do so were, then, involved in writing multiple genre (narrative and poetry, Romano, 1995) biographies. A new section was added to many of the books as the children composed poems and added them as one of the final pages of their books. Poetry was a way to rework the piece into a more condensed and, for many, intense form. In some ways, the poems reduced the work, consistent with Dyson's (2003) interpretation of Bakhtin's (1981) view of poetry:

> Poets' common aspirations to select each word in the light of some hoped for singular expression, some symbolic unity . . . led Bakhtin (1981) to view poems as limited in their potential for orchestrating the diverse voices of everyday life.
>
> (p. 163)

But in other ways the poems served as a final signifier of a long journey, almost a memento, yet at the same time a final tribute to the person being studied. Contextualized within a multiple genre piece in which the narrative voice and the poetic voice of the writer complement the goals of portraying a loved one, the poem has significant power and presence. Within the classroom, among fellow writers who watched the work evolve into a narrative biography and, subsequently, into a biographic poem, there was much between the lines that the in-classroom community knew. This specificity created a sort of 'in-house' joy as the writers celebrated each other's accomplishments. Damico (2005) refers to this as "the transformative potential of poetry, where students engage with and use poems towards what June Jordan calls 'a foundation for true community: a fearless democratic society' (in Christensen, 1994, p. 6)" (p. 145). Perhaps both Dyson and Damico help articulate what the poems did. The poems were, to some degree, limited to local understanding, yet they also reflected an increasingly "fearless democratic society" of truthtellers that was emerging during our writing time.

A counterportrait built with such poetry as data needs the support of thick descriptions (Geertz, 1973) to (hopefully) gain presence, acknowledgment, and validity in more official domains, such as state departments of education. Perhaps, then, Bakhtin (1981) was correct when, referring to the "stylistic devices" of poetry as "too narrow and cramped, and cannot accommodate the artistic prose of novelistic discourse" (p. 266), particularly when such discourse is the gold standard. However, oral works were composed in both classrooms during the telling of many stories before, during, and after the children wrote. I came to see the many conversations about life outside of school as the truer, thicker descriptions and retellings of life events. The children's writing captures some of these events, but not all. The sixth graders began with poetry and moved to the more traditional expository form of a biography. The fifth graders moved in the opposite direction, but both groups created multiple genre pieces by bending the traditional genre of biography to include oral histories, poetry, and expository text. Had more time been available, we may have used digital means and incorporated segments of the recordings that children made, brief film clips, and more in order to include more full and elaborate versions of what the children collected.

Ramona portrays her dad with an intuitive understanding of the many masks (Goffman, 1959) that he wears.

Dad

When most people think of my dad
They think army man
When I think of my dad I think
Dad, who helps and loves me
So yes he is an army man but
He's much more too
He's my brown hair brown eyed

Dad
He's my adoring, loving

Dad
He's my funny, smart

Dad
So don't only think army man also think

Dad.

Poem by, Ramona

Debi's study of her mom, presented in the next chapter, is saturated with quotes, photos, and the drama that she seems to attract or manufacture. She was originally going to study her grandmother but the work became too emotional for her. Crying, one day, she said that, "I just don't want to do this. I miss her so much." Her grandmother lives in England, where Debi's mom was born. Debi was one of the few Anglo children in the study and her mom was a teacher at the school.

Neat Freak

Blond hair, blue eyes
"Clean up your mess."
Get out of my sight
No! Clean up,
then get out of my sight.
Clean up that smoke,
clean up,
clean up,
clean up
This Neat Freak,
ladies and gentleman,
Is my mom.

Debi, Marisol, and some of the other children used the strategy of repeating something three (or more) times, an effect that Barbara learned at a writing workshop she attended. Marisol brings in the Spanish spoken in her home by using 'dichos,' which are expressions meant to teach or advise, such as "do what's best for you and not for others."

Best Father Ever

Broad shoulders, strong legs
I hear my father's words –
"do what's best for you and not for others"
I hear him call my name –
"Marisol, Mija, Mowgli, Jungle Book"
He gives himself –
Love, advice, hugs to his dog
I hear his words – "don't get in trouble anymore"
Lots of Love
Lots of Love
Lots of Love
And that is the "Best Father Ever"

By Marisol

Although I haven't presented much of Rosa's work (her entire biography of her dad is in Appendix 2), her father's love of his family fills the pages of her writing. She ends her book with her poem about her dad:

Jon's Poem

He comes back home
He comes back home
With some advice and love from work
He loves me so much that I cry
And he still loves me as millions and millions of hearts flying
above us in the sky
And loves me forever and ever

By Rosa

Consuelo incorporates Spanish into her poem because it's the language in which she knows her mom. Her mom tells her to be good, help to clean up, and do her homework. Woven into those motherly demands are Consuelo's understanding of her mom's strength, goals, and dedication to her family.

The Giving One

I see my mom
with curly hair
wishing to get her papers
and never giving up
and as I hear her say,
"Se buena,
Ayudame a limpiar,
Y haz la tarea."
as I hear inside her head
that she will give
love and attention
to her children and husband
Never gives up learning English
-Never gives up teaching her children to do good
-Never gives up getting her papers
-Never gives up opportunities to get a job

Estevan's poem seems to start in the middle of a sentence or thought, as though there were other phrases describing his father that might have come before. He does use quotations to indicate dialogue, but quickly goes back to the free form suggestive of a collage of his father's looks, voice, and actions, ending with advice for his children.

Bio Poem

he has a mustache
and he is tall

I hear him say, "Let him,"
because he doesn't want my little brother to cry
I hear him say my name,
"Estevan"
he gives me
love
love
love and
chocolate
my dad gives me games if I do a good job
he tries to beat me in racing games
(that's all he buys me)
he wishes for an education for his kids

By Estevan

Hybridized Texts and Contexts

Each piece of writing, conversation, strategy lesson, and discussion about writing process and content contributes to the counterportrait within each writer, teacher, and me as a researcher. Each presentation of first draft, subsequent drafts, and final piece contains some element of surprise (Murray, 1985) that nags at the inertia of the official portrait. The composing within each classroom is about the writing of individual pieces and the writing of new spaces in which composing occurs. These are the spaces in which counterportraits are composed, almost invisible to official forums and absent from the official portrait, but present nonetheless. In Chapter 3, I wrote about third space as a 'contested' space in which a different and unique opening is created for students to write, a space that considers institutional as well as out-of-school realities; in Chapter 7, I discussed the classroom as a site of 'struggle' because creating the opening for a third space may meet with much resistance, both from students and their teachers, as well as school, district, state, and federal contexts. The children initiated the work tentatively because their understanding of what is supposed to happen in school was challenged as school changed and they were unsure of what the new parameters would and would not allow. Uncertainty was part of the hybridized space that the children were articulating, exploring, and in which they composed.

Bakhtin's (1981) idea of "hybridization" is explained as "The mixing, within a single concrete utterance, of two or more different linguistic consciousnesses, often widely separated in time and social space" (p. 429). The idea of "mixing" is apparent in the writing that both classes completed. In nature, a hybrid is typically a genetically different organism that thrives more efficiently or effectively where others may not survive as well or at all. The fifth and sixth graders' writing, much like the writing of the students studied by Dyson (2003) was unique in that:

their new length and diversity contributed to the complexity and power of the children's texts as communicative means and, moreover, as dialogic hybrids (Bakhtin, 1981); these hybrids recontextualized material from diverse social worlds within official literacy practices.

(p. 94)

Even though the sixth graders' minimum acceptable length for final pieces was determined by their teacher, their pieces were longer than most pieces they'd written for other assignments during the year. I also interpret length dialogically, meaning, "as a part of a greater whole [since] there is interaction between meanings" (Bakhtin, 1981, p. 426) and across contexts. The students' writing signifies a hybridized space because of how it was composed, the content, and how it was received.

The hybridized contexts of both classrooms were evident because there were subtle and not-so-subtle shifts as the ethos of, and activity in, the classrooms changed. The changed contexts subsequently supported a change in the possibilities of what could be brought to the classroom and the nature of the composing processes, drafts, and acceptable products. The teachers welcoming me into their classrooms was significant in the process of hybridization of context because of their willingness to talk, explore, and try strategies. In their own ways and to different degrees, the teachers allowed the students to have increasing amounts of input into the ways in which writing was used in their classrooms. This involved a shift to writing that centered around the children's lives, a shift from students as objective recipients of curriculum (Freire & Macedo, 1987) to a more subjective space for writing. Clarke (2005) reported a similar shift that students in a classroom made once they and their teacher realized that they were the objects of a "narrowed curriculum focused on tests and skills [that] had left students without important understandings" (p. 154). Freire's conscientization (1970a) is an important facet of a hybridized space, hybridized relationships, and hybridized activities because consciousness supports knowing and understanding. During strategy lessons with the writers, we presented and discussed what other writers in the class were doing, initiated conversations (such as a consideration of the parts of a book in Barbara's class), and discussed with one class what the writers in the other class were doing. When the students presented their pieces across grade levels, borders between classrooms were crossed for an engagement in mutually pedagogical activity.

Both texts and spaces, then, may be hybrids and the masks (Goffman, 1959) that the students brought to these social contexts changed, providing evidence or expression of the hybridization. Hybridized space and activity had a degree of organicity as different identities emerged within the contexts and texts that mutually supported risk taking, changes in the community of practice (Lave & Wenger, 1991) in school, and shifts in the institutional regularities (Sarason, 1972). For example, Esperanza, Juliana, and Debi cried in school about the content of the curriculum, perhaps because that content was an emotional and cognitive hybrid composed of representations of two social worlds. Referring to Bakhtin (1981), Dyson (1997) describes students like the fifth and sixth graders, "beginning in an enclosed space and . . . experiencing freedom as they move beyond that space . . . becoming more aware of diversity and . . . of different languages linked to different social worlds" (p. 166).

Many of the children at MVE lived in social worlds that were not only *different*, but devalued by interpreters of test scores and socioeconomic indicators. Perpetrators of NCLB see the children as *less than, fragile, deficit, dysfunctional, disadvantaged and broken*—and certainly not as any kind of official asset, especially in any systematic sustained way in school or society. "Dialogic theory situates children not simply within a particular studied practice, but on a landscape of interrelated voices" (Dyson, 2003, p. 12) and the landscape and voices of many of the students' homes do not fit into the classroom unless that space is hybridized in such a way that texts and contexts—social worlds—are not just acknowledged but are welcome as central to the curriculum. Dyson continues:

> Thus, our texts are formed at the intersection of a social relationship between ourselves as composers and our addressees and an ideological one between our own psyches (or inner meanings) and the words, the cultural signs, available to us . . . Composers, then, are not so much meaning makers as meaning negotiators, who adopt, resist, or stretch available words.
>
> (p. 4)

The fifth and sixth graders arrived at school with fairly clear notions of what could be 'negotiated' and what could not. As the "social relationships" between all those present in the classrooms changed, the "composers" and "addressees" changed. Their relationships changed, and the possibilities for acceptable "meaning" changed. These changes were individual and social, cognitive and emotional, perhaps even spiritual.

When the stuff of home becomes the stuff of school, social worlds can be recognized and considered legitimate across different spaces. The voices of home, brought to school literally on digital voice recorders, became curricular events, suggesting a new level of importance and respect for those voices and the stories that they told. The 'peer-governed' in the hybrid space became a governor of curriculum, dialog, and interactions between and among writers. But mostly, the hybrid space was a writing space, seemingly a private space (from mind to paper) but not really private because it is composed of and within the multiple voices of homes and colleagues in the classroom. Hybridized spaces enable writers and thinkers to reconsider what is acceptable in schools, "adjustments" (Goffman, 1961) that allow for "something everybody wants—for someone to see the hurt done to them and set it down like it matters" (Kidd, 2002, p. 185) or to celebrate joys, record events, and discuss (in writing or orally) relationships previously not brought into school. This is a social space in which there were ongoing negotiations through conversations.

Jesus pushed the hybridized space too far, thus jeopardizing his survival as a member of the class, when he told his teacher to, "Shut up!" engaging in what Goffman (1961) refers to as a "disruptive secondary adjustment" (p. 199). He brought the space down around himself with many fights and by refusing to engage in (resisting) the official curriculum that his teacher felt must be covered. Hybridized spaces have borders that each participant must figure out while also deciding how to stretch or redefine them. This can make the hybridized space one in which the identity of a student (or teacher) may be vulnerable because of the subjective nature of the space. It is for this reason that Hagood (2002) refers to identity as "subjectivity". "Subjectivity highlights the tensions of betweenness not as one identity or another or as multiple identities, but in the transitional state of transforming" (Hagood, 2002, p. 257). The idea of "the reader [or writer] as a subject marks the site of a struggle for existence, knowledge and power" (Hagood, 2002, p. 255), especially in terms of who one is or may be within a space.

Moje offers a brief but articulate view of adolescence as a time of upheaval physically, socially, and politically. She then suggests that the "raging hormone model of adolescence" (p. 215) is accepted because we fail to understand the complex ways in which adolescents use text. She explains that adolescents "use literacy to navigate, synthesize, and hybridize multiple spaces" (p. 217). It is within these hybridized spaces, in which they have agency, that they compose, reflect, plan, and act and supporting such spaces in school may make the classroom a place in which multiple subjectivities are welcome, negotiated, and constantly recomposed.

Hybridized Spaces and Counterportraits

Hybridized spaces are not easily assessed by criterion-referenced tests and as counterportraits grow increasingly complex and rich in detail, the official portrait remains a homogenous smear. This school is still a 'failing' school and the children remain 'at risk'. However, in this chapter the students' writing goes closer to their hearts in hybridized spaces, even though in the present restrictive test-driven climate it is nearly impossible to demonstrate to a larger public that these spaces exist, that they are complex places, and that they matter. It is impossible to demonstrate, except in scholarly journals and books that are dismissed (Taylor, 1998) that hybridized spaces are places of struggle and resistance, and that, as such, they are not always predictable, neat, and tidy. We have more work to do to demonstrate that these spaces matter because of the ways in which identity, power, and agency (Lewis, Enciso, & Moje, 2007) play out in them.

The official portrait stays in motion, maintaining its officialness, because that motion is supported by the official texts that appear in the media and are appropriated by schools and communities. Counterportraits are, by their very nature, unofficial and, as such, political acts that work to undermine the hegemony of the official portrait. The local nature of counterportraits is both their strength and weakness within the current educational climate. Local counterportraits are evidence of responsiveness to the various and tentative subjectivities that enter a school and are composed in, while concomitantly composing, hybridized spaces. That's their strength. That local apparition is also a weakness in that we are still faced with issues of legitimacy beyond the local; therein lays the political nature of the acts that we would now commit as a group of fifth and sixth grade teachers and students. The move to presenting their work in venues in which such work has not been previously presented is part of the political activity of having hybridized voices heard in official spaces. Further, the students are the experts in those spaces, feeling the power, prestige, and agency that expertise carries. In the next chapter, the counterportraits from the hybridized space of the classrooms give birth to momentary glimpses of officiality, as the children's writing gains legitimacy in the eyes of others beyond the school (local) site.

Chapter 9

Products, Presentations, and Power

> Let me here just recall an incident that happened to me when I was thirteen years old. Once my science teacher walked up and down between the rows and taught the class that, in the final analysis, life was nothing but a combustion process, an oxidation process. I jumped up and, without asking permission as was customary at that time, threw him the question, "What meaning, then, does life have?" Of course, he could not answer, because he was a reductionist.
>
> (Frankl, 1978, p. 37)

Frankl's work focused on the meaning that we bring to, compose, create, or find in our lives. He suggests that meaning is not stagnant, but exists with a certain degree of organicity, something that has a sense of present, past and future. Earlier in the same work, he wrote, ". . . those most apt to survive the camps were those orientated toward the future—toward a task, or a person, waiting for them in the future" (p. 34). Our work in the fifth and sixth grades was about making meaning and making sense of the past and present. Yet as I considered the children's futures, I wondered about the importance of a strong sense of self and the importance of the ways in which self influences others. The children gained in confidence and self-esteem (even pride) as they presented their writing in three venues, described and discussed in this chapter. In two of those venues, they read the work they'd written at school. In one, they composed relying upon a familiar format as they wrote and presented slam poetry. In the analysis at the end of the chapter, I discuss the children's work using the idea of 'spheres of influence' to consider the far or not-so-far reaching effects (influence on extant inertia) of their writing. Their individual and very local sense- and meaning-making have been discussed in almost every chapter; their influence on the official portrait is the focus of the spheres of influence discussion. Some spheres of influence are present in our lives, but others are a potential, an *orientation toward the future*. I found no professional literature on spheres of influence, but Tolle (2006) refers to them in writing about human spirituality and the ways in which we influence other's lives.

Our First Public Venue

On a Friday late in April, the children and their teachers piled into a school bus to be the keynote speakers at a conference for one hundred preservice teachers. The fifth and sixth graders were the first group to present, demonstrating that there were spaces of hope and possibility and that the ways in which children, their teachers, and their schools were portrayed in the popular press did not fully capture what children could do as readers and writers. The students had practiced reading their pieces in front of both classes, but when they arrived at the university's conference center, entered the auditorium, and saw the college students sitting at tables facing a podium, most of them panicked. I met with them quickly to address this and explained that they didn't need to read to the whole group; we'd break into smaller groups and they could share their work at the tables. A huge sigh of relief was heaved by all, but I asked if any one wanted to share with the entire group, reading from the podium. Two sixth graders, Miguel and a girl who was not in the study, volunteered. I introduced the teachers and explained the work that the students had been doing for the past months. The children stood around the edges of the large room, a pronounced contrast apparent between the mostly white crowd and the almost entirely brown writers. Then I presented the *I used to, but now* PowerPoint (Chapter 4) consisting of the children's words in a slideshow with music and pictures. Some of the preservice teachers grew wide-eyed and some cried as they read the children's poems. I also presented a slideshow of the children at work, using the digital voice recorders, transcribing, writing, reading, conferring, and working at the computers. These two slideshows totaled about ten minutes. Then I introduced the girl to read her *Where I'm From* poem and the text of her biography of her mother. After listening, the crowd clapped quite a bit. Next, Miguel read the text of his mom's biography from the bound printout of his PowerPoint.

My Mom's New Life

[Page 1] My mom was born in a small village called El Azulillo, Jalisco Mexico. She came to the U.S.A. to work so she could help her parents because they were very poor. The people there were all very poor. She said, "They needed me to help them."

[Page 2] Her first job was cleaning offices. Then she meets her husband and she stopped working. She met her husband in Phoenix; she lived with her brother in the same apartment complex where they met, and then got married. She didn't want to live in Mexico because she wanted to work over here. She came to live with her brothers and her sister-in-law in the United States.

[Page 3] Her childhood was very amazing with her family and in school because she played with a lot of kids. My mom said "I went to school with my neighbors and we had to walk for one hour to go to school and we liked the walk." She went to school until the 7th grade because there wasn't enough money to keep on studying.

[Page 4] When she crossed the border, she said, "It was easy when we crossed the boarder because someone took us in a car and it took a long time." She has never been caught by Immigration.

[Page 5] She said "I am very scared of snakes. I can't even see them from a distance." When she came to the US she stayed here. She didn't go back until recently. Her happiest moment was when her mother came to visit after a long period of time. She didn't have her papers and they gave her mother a passport, so that is why she came to visit.

[Page 6] She thinks that living in the US and Mexico is very different. "There is so much poverty over there," she says. If people don't work in Mexico, they don't eat; and here, if people don't have food, they still get help. She also says that the US is prettier.

[Page 7] Her goals for the future are to strive for her children to have a better life and that they get what they want and need.

[Page 8] Her happiest moment was when my sister E— and I were born.

Miguel looked at me when he'd finished reading because the room was quiet. I went over to the podium and leaned into the microphone. "You can clap," I told the future teachers. And they did, as the intensity of both children's writing penetrated the audience. "You can discuss [the girl's] and Miguel's work with them when they visit your tables. I've asked the rest of the children to read to you at your tables," I explained. "Their teachers and I will help them find a table. Since these are final copies, you may tell them what you liked or found interesting and you might ask questions if you want to know more. They may not provide answers for you because some of them have written all that they want to tell. Also, some of the writers have poems that they've written based on this biography work. They'll read those, too."

Reading Their Work in Small Groups

Patia, Barbara, Roberta, and I directed children to tables and they began reading their pieces. Some of the future teachers were initially somewhat paralyzed by the content and fumbled to find questions or engage the writers in conversation about the writing. At one table, Verdad (a sixth grader) read her piece, but it was not finished. In the narrative, she hadn't written the part about her uncle being murdered, but his murder was in the poem she'd written before she composed the narrative. That poem was included as the final page of her book. She read to the group in Spanish and, with the help of Roberta, she translated the piece. At other tables in subsequent readings, she translated her piece herself. Verdad's book had a Mexican flag on the cover and title page. She put drawings that she found on a clipart web site on the other pages. On the page entitled, "He Came to the United States," she found an online photo of the border with a corrugated metal fence and two men helping each other over. On the page entitled "Immigration," she found a photo of a border patrol vehicle and pasted that as the background. The rest of the pages have smiley faces, sad faces, hearts, and other colorful clip art.

My Uncle

[Page 1] Where He was Born

My uncle was born in a ranch in Durango, Mexico. It's a beautiful place where there's an abundance of natural beauty and animals. Everything is very beautiful.

[Page 2] My uncle came to the United States to work, to live a better life. The first job that my uncle had was working in a restaurant. He worked washing dishes for a couple of months. Later he worked in a factory that made paper. He stayed there for a couple of years because he liked that job and they paid him much more than his first job. Also, he made a lot of friends.

[Page 3] He Came to the United States

He came to the United States from the border of Juarez, Mexico, but he had to cross the Rio Grande. My uncle said the Rio Grande has plenty of water. But another friend helped him cross the river to the other side of the border that is El Paso, Texas.

[Page 4] An Experience

The experience that my uncle had was that coming to the USA is not an easy thing because there's various obstacles on the road. Like for example when he crossed the Rio [River] it was a very sad experience because the current almost took him. But at the end, he was able to cross fine.

[Page 5] A Special Memory

A special memory was when my uncle met the woman of his life. It was very special because they met in a park. It was a rainy day. And both of them went underneath a tree so they would not get wet. And from there they met each other and then they got married.

[Page 6] Immigration

My uncle has been arrested by the immigration. It was a day when he left his home to go to work. And when he was waiting for the bus, the immigration arrived and then they took him to Mexico.

[Page 7] He Met his Wife

My uncle met his wife in a park. It was a very rainy day. And that's where they got to know each other more. Until they decided to get married.

[Page 8] Childhood

My uncle's childhood was very special because in his house he behaved very well with his parents and his siblings. He was a very intelligent student in school. His teachers liked him a lot because he always did his homework. And he would help out his classmates with their work.

[Page 9] Something peculiar that scared my uncle was when he was a young boy. He was 8 years old. His father asked him to go to the corral so he could feed the animals. Before he knew it, he was inside the corral and he was almost gored by a very big bull. Then he was very frightened.

The group of seven future teachers listened attentively and then asked a few questions about Verdad's uncle's wife and his schooling, seeming to avoid discussing immigration. They were polite, kind, and thanked her for reading. She hesitated a little as she looked at me and I asked her to read her poem. She read:

My Uncle

My uncle was a cool guy
He never gave up no matter what
He was a really good guy
He got mad when he didn't do things right
He was happy when it was his birthday
I use to talk to him and he would understand me
I use to tell him all my problems I had
He was a really happy guy
He use to take me and my sister shopping
His dream was to become a firefighter
But now he's dead
His dreams are gone
My uncle was the coolest guy in the world
No one can take my uncle's place

I listened and thought of the other drafts of this poem that I'd heard over the course of the year. In one draft, she wrote about him being in a "happier place," where he would be "loved forever." In another version, he was in a "better place," but in this version, the one included in her book, Verdad's uncle's "dreams are gone." As she finished reading, she lowered the book to her lap and looked at it. The future teachers remained quiet. "Sometimes a poet tells you more, and sometimes she does not," I said to the future teachers. "Do you want to tell them anymore about your poem?" I asked her. Verdad slowly moved her head to indicate that she did not. I looked at the future teachers around the table, their eyes riveted on this sixth grade poet, and said, "You are very fortunate because today you got to hear an amazing author and poet tell you something very close to her heart." I walked with Verdad to the next table at which she read her pieces. "You did really well," I told her. "It made some of them cry and some of the other ones didn't know what to say. That's what good writing does, sometimes. It leaves someone who hears it speechless." She sat at the new table and held up her book for the college students to see, her expertise at presenting growing with her confidence.

Carlos, a sixth grader, wrote his book in Spanish and Roberta sat with him as he presented in order to translate for him. Carlos wrote the biography in the first person almost entirely with his father's (Luis) transcripted words. He'd listened over and over again to the recording, selected which particular words would be put into the biography, and transcribed those exact words. Carlos also used a Mexican flag for the background of one page and then shaded each of the other pages. His dad's story is another one of immigration, learning about America, and living in two worlds.

Luis [Louis] T—'s Life

By Carlos T—

[Page 1] Childhood

I was born in Chihuahua Mexico. As a young boy, it has always been work since I was in elementary school. I believe I started working when I was seven years old. I would go to school and then I would go to work. Then I went to middle school and I had to pay each month and for books. I finished the second year of middle school, then I didn't want to return to school. People started to go to the US. They said that in the US you got a lot of money and that it was easy. Pure lies.

[Page 2] The Way to the US

When I came to the US, I came by train as a wetback. There were eight of us and they arrested us twice, they took us back to Juarez and the second time we got together with seven other people, then we were 15 and that night we were able to cross over here again. In the train we would put ourselves into some boxes [cargo crates]. The temperature was so cold; it rained and it snowed. We got off in Rincon, NM because the border patrol started to inspect the train and we had to get off so they wouldn't be able to see us. Then we waited for the border patrol so we could get back on the train and then we grabbed onto the freight boxes of the train then we got inside a trailer of the train. And that's how we traveled.

[Page 3] The Border

It was raining we were all wet and we were holding onto the door of the trailer because if it closed we would be trapped. When I arrived here we met a white man and his name was Pete from [a town] A friend of ours knew him and that is where we stayed for a while. One ugly thing that happened was that when we were trying to cross the border in El Paso from Juarez, the gangsters were trying to steal our sneakers and clothes.

[Page 4] I Meet My Wife

The purpose why we came to the US, it wasn't much [we didn't give it much thought] but our friends that came [back to visit] they would always arrive with a lot of money. They would only speak of the wonderful and good things but never would talk about the battles [struggles] to make the money. My first job was cleaning apartments of construction [debris]. I met my wife at a trailer park. That's where I lived, we became boyfriend/girlfriend and then we got married.

[Page 5] The Way to Albuquerque

One of the experiences I remember is arriving at the V— Hotel in [town], NM. We rented a room there and a friend of ours that had a car took us to Albuquerque. We paid him 70 dollars; there were 15 of us and 16 with the driver. At that time it was a lot easier to travel back and forth to Mexico; today it's a lot more difficult to return. Today people really have to think about returning to Mexico frequently.

[Page 6] Plans

Here the border patrol has never bothered me. One time they arrested me with my brother but I already had papers and my wife took them to me where they were holding me and they did not deport me and I didn't have any problems. My brother was taken and they took him for being illegal. His [Luis', a brief switch to third person] plans for the future were to finish his house. He still wants to buy a home in [another town] because of all the gangs that are close to our home. [Now he switches back to first person.] I would like to see my children do very well in school and I do not want them to be involved in any gangs. The end.

In the sixth grade classroom, Carlos's work, like others', triggered discussions about how students' families arrived in the US, their feelings towards the country, gangs, and stories from Mexico, including many stories of crossing into the US for work and back into Mexico for family. Most of the college students knew about their families' journeys to the US, but for many the stories were two or more generations in the past. Yet the stories of the children resonated with some future teachers' pasts because they were the first in their family to attend a university.

Vianca (a sixth grader), telling the story of her grandmother whose name is also Vianca, was the only student to write about herself as part of the immigration story she told as one facet of her grandmother's crossing. Vianca wrote in Spanish and also colored her slides; she didn't include photos or clip art. She read her piece in Spanish and translated it herself.

Vianca de —

By Vianca —

[Page 1] The Land Where Vianca was Born

Vianca de — was born in Chihuahua Mexico on a ranch called Beautiful View. She told me that there was a lake with fish and there was a temporary farm [planted seasonal vegetables]. The ranch had elementary schools and it was very beautiful.

[Page 2] Why She Came to the United States

She came to the United States to be with her children. Her children came illegally in 1990. She said that when they came to the US there were four adults and one girl, who was me. It took us a month to pass the border through the desert. We were detained by immigration two times. We were coming in a truck. She told me that the first two times that we were detained by immigration were when we were crossing the border. The third time we passed (entered) fine into the US.

[Page 3] Why She Lives Better Here Than There

She told me the difference between living in Mexico and the US is that in the US there are more commodities and more jobs than in Mexico. "You live better here," she said.

[Page 4] Where She Works

My grandmother's first job was as a maid in Chihuahua. She was only fifteen. She liked that job a lot because she also worked at that [kind of job] in El Paso.

[Page 5] Her Youth

My grandmother Vianca met my grandfather when she was 25. He met her when he was driving through the ranch where she lived. My grandmother's childhood was happy because she was with her family, her friends from school, and on her ranch.

[Page 6] Her Special Memory

A special memory that my grandmother remembers was when a man paid for the hotel when we were crossing the border. Then on another day, a man put a bill in my grandmother's hand because he saw her crying and praying that we would cross fine. Another man took my grandmother and us to his house and we stayed three days in Chihuahua in his house.

[Page 7] Happy Memory

A happy memory of my grandmother's was when she was young because she enjoyed her youth. My grandmother's plans are to keep on living, to enjoy her children and grandchildren.

[Page 8] About the Author

Hello, my name is Vianca. I am 12 years old. My teacher is Ms —. My best friend's name is Mercedes. What I like to do in school is to read.

There is a dark side to Vianca's life, one that she wrote about in the poem (Chapter 3) that she did not put into her book. As she read and translated her biography to the future teachers (some amazed at Vianca's fluency in two languages), Vianca' stature changed. Her shoulders slipped back, she sat up straighter, and her voice grew louder. She attentively responded to questions about how old she was when she came to the US, where her grandmother works now, and why she chose to write the book in Spanish. "Because it all happened in Spanish," she told them.

Debi's (a fifth grader) story is the one with which many of the future teachers were comfortable because it is the story of a fairly mainstream family. Debi's mother is an assistant at the school and Debi is one of the few white students at MVE. Debi scanned photos of her mother that were incorporated into her book. Debi's penchant for drama is clear throughout her work and it evoked laughter from her audience of college students.

Sara G—:

The Story of Her Life

By Debi G—

Dedication Page

Debi G— is dedicating this book to her mom, Sara G—, and her dad Bob G— who is in the US Air Force, and her sister Katherine G—. She would also like to dedicate this book to her grandmas and her aunts and her uncles also her cousins, and her cousins in England, and Debi's godfather and his kids.

Table of Contents [sixteen lines long, each line being the title of one of her pages.]

[Page 3] A Birth of a Baby Girl

Sara was born in Blackpool England. She was born September 27, 1968.

[Page 4] Sara's Parents

Sara's dad and her mother were married for 40 years. Her first child was 2 years old when Sara's father passed away. Sara was so sad when he passed away. Her mom was devastated that her husband has passed away.

[Page 5] Memories

Five years later her father-in-law died. She was very upset. She will carry on her memory of her dad and her father-in-law and all her family remainders especially if her mom dies or her brother. She will still have her memories to pass on to her grandchildren and maybe her great grandchildren.

[Page 6] Growing Up

Sara grew up and was a flower girl at their aunt's wedding, and in the picture below you will see that she is on a hillside with her brother, Andrew.

Sara grew up and married a man whose name is Robert W. G—. He was stationed in England when he was in the US Air Force. Sara's last name after she married Bob was G— which is a German name.

Then 8 years after that she had a beautiful baby girl named Katherine. She was 2 years old when her little sister Debi was born.

Sara wanted to be a teacher or assistant teacher.

[Page 7] Moving to New Mexico

Sara's daughter was 2 months old when they moved to New Mexico. Sara and her family lived in Albuquerque for one year then they moved to [town]. Sara's family moved to [town] because it has mountains and skies that are beautiful and the mountains are so high and the plants are so green.

[Page 8] Sara's Accident

Sara had very many injuries, like the time Sara fell through a bridge and bruised her knee. It was swollen and painful. The reason she fell through a bridge is because there was a hole in the middle of the bridge. When they got back to [town] she had to go to the hospital to have it checked out. So she came out of the hospital in a wheelchair. She had it for 3 months. Thank goodness she had a pair of crutches. Sara had them for almost a month. She had to walk all over the place with her crunches on.

[Page 9] Debi and Katherine do Everything

Debi and Katherine had to make dinner and also run Sara a bath and it was all fun until she got in a lot of serious pain so we had to give her a lot of pain relievers so the pain could die down so she could feel not very much pain. That is why she had a very bad injury that she had to go to the doctors. It was very hard taking her to the doctor's office she would moan and cry because of all the pain.

[Page 10] Sara's First Job

Sara's first job was babysitting at the age of fourteen, because their next-door neighbors finally decided to trust her.

[Page 11] Sara's Second Job

When she was thirty-four she got a job as an assistant at a place in Albuquerque. It was not a good job. Debi and Katherine did not get to see her except when she dropped them off at school. She would be tired when she got home she would get mad. When it would start to get loud even when it was getting quiet she would yell. After a few years she decided to quit.

[Page 12] Sara's Third Job

She got another job at [MVE] as a work room person. After two years she got a job as a teacher's assistant at [MVE]. She still remains to this day a teacher's assistant.

[Page 13] Pictures of Sara at Work [photos]

[Page 14] PTC Mom [Parent Teacher Committee]

Blonde hair, nice smile

I smell cookies.

"Time to bake cookies."

"PTC mom says it is time to bake cookies Debi."

"Makes cookies for others."

Oh no the cookies are smoking.

Give some to the dogs.

Baking cookies,

Baking cookies,

Baking cookies

That is a PTC mom

[Page 15] Neat Freak [This poem appears in Chapter 8.]

[Page 16] About the Author

Debi loves her life so much. She loves her family, her pets, her friends, and her stuffed animals. Debi G— has changed this world since she was born.

Debi's heroes are her parents and teachers because they are so nice and loving. When she grows up she will be a teacher because she admires her mom. Hopefully, Debi will become a successful teacher, and maybe, she will even become a popular soccer player. We'll have to wait and see.

Consuelo's (a fifth grader) work, based on her translated interviews with her mom, was received with tears and laughter.

The Life of a Mexican Immigrant

This book is dedicated to my hard working mother.

Copyright© 2007 Consuelo Ramirez

[Page 1] The Troublemaker

My mom was born on March 7, 1969, in a crowded house and poor family in a place known as Juan Aldama, Zacatecas, Mexico. She had 5 sisters (including her) and 4 brothers. She had fun in her childhood because she would get on the roof of the *Mesquites* (a huge tree), but after a while she would lose her fun because her mother would come after her and take her down. Then her mom would tell her, "Get off because you're going to get hungry or end up having to go to the bathroom."

[Page 2] The Dog

She got bit by a dog when she was just 6 years old. She was walking past the house where the dog was and the fence was open. So the dog started to follow her. Then my mom started to run because she was scared. The dog ran after her. It bit her until the owner came to control the dog.

[Page 3] Living with her Grandma

My mom lived with her grandma for most of her life. She lived with her since she was 9 until she turned 16 years old. My mom learned how to cook when she was 9 years old.

[Page 4] Her Childhood

When she was little she would play with girls pretty much her own age. They would play *el patio de mi casa* (the path of my house), *la cebollita* (the onion), and *brincar la cuerda* (jump rope).

[Page 5] Suy

My mom's first pet was a cat. It was fat and it was named Suy. It would get rabbits and eat them at the windowsill. Suy would leave half and eat it when it was hungry. It would sleep on one side of my mom. It was an Angora cat. It was so fat it could barely fit through a window her mom had.

[Page 6] The Memory

My mom's memory is her grandma because of how long she lived with her.

[Page 7] First Job

When my mom became 16, she had to leave her family to go work in a store selling clothes. Many of her brothers and sisters left to work at a very young age.

[Page 8] Education

She didn't have a very good education. She went to 7th grade and 8th grade at night. If my mom had a better life, she would have become a lawyer. [See Figure 9.1.]

[Page 9] She Leaves Her Home and Family

When my mom passed by *mojado* (illegal immigrant [literally: wetback]) it was a hard and fascinating adventure. It was a risk in her life because you don't know if you will get here safe or you will get stuck in the middle of nowhere like any other immigrant. My mom had to walk for three days without sleeping. The first thing she thought when she got here was to thank God that she got here safely.

[Page 10] Love is Found

My mom met my dad through one of his aunties. She presented him to her. They met when I was just about to become two years old. They have been married for nine years.

Figure 9.1 Consuelo's photo of her mom from page 8 of her biography.

[Page 11] A Better Life

When my mom first came here she was an immigrant. Now that she met my dad, she is going to become a citizen (in two years or more). While she waits to get her papers she is learning English and getting a GED to become a teacher's assistant.

[Page 12] California

A little while before my mom met my dad she lived in California. California reminded her of where she lived in Mexico because it was green and pretty. The only difference was that there was earthquakes. SCARY!!!

[Page 13] A New Life

A long while after she met my dad she started to understand that life in the US is better than in Mexico because there are more opportunities, like better jobs, better pay, and better education.

[Page 14] The Family

My mom is proud of her husband and kids.

[Page 15] The Giving One

[see poem in Chapter 8]

[Page 16] All About the Author

I was born on March 28, 1996. The idea for this biography came from my teacher. She said that we could pick anybody in our family so I picked my mom. I am glad because I got to know my mom more than I used to. If I had an opportunity I would have done the whole family, but it would have been a lot more work. If you do read "All About the Author" I hope you enjoyed the book.

Mercedes (a fifth grader) preferred to work with her mother, at home, on her biography of her mother. The first draft that Mercedes brought to school was copied from a website about a fetus's right to live. This strong anti-abortion piece included language about women and their children that was highly politicized. My concern was that it was neither her own work nor a biography and I explained that to Mercedes. She was very welcome to include her mother's views on women and unborn children, but she had to figure out a way to do that as part of her mother's story. Mercedes could not attend the day at the university, but we could include the work in this book.

The Story of My Mom

My mom and I decided to write about a not born child because my mom had a story that seemed like that one. Let me tell you about it. When my mom was 17 years old she found out that she was pregnant. My mom was very excited. One day my mom tried to do something she couldn't do.

When my dad got home my mom was crying, my dad was scared and he was asking her what had happened. A few minutes later my mom told my dad that she had probably lost the baby. My dad asked my mom what she had tried to do. My mom had tried to pick up a box with heavy stuff. The next day my mom went to the doctor and he told her that she had lost the baby.

My mom was very sad and didn't want to eat. My dad was very scared because my mom didn't want to come out of the room. About a week later my mom decided to come out again. Now my mom got over it. It was her first baby, but now my mom has 4 kids and she is very happy.

Some of the biographies the students read appear elsewhere in this book (Appendix 2 and other chapters). I wrestled with the placement of these pieces and chose to place as many as possible within the context of the narratives of what we did, rather than isolate them in an appendix. Some, however, are in the appendix in response to suggestions to keep the chapter from becoming too unwieldy. I apologize to any writers that feel that their work has been banished, as that was far from my intention.

Slam Poetry

The fifth and sixth graders were out of time and I announced that we needed to line up and leave. The entire room rose, giving the students a standing ovation. The children walked to the door of the auditorium and as they exited they were given university box lunches from the catering service. We took the schoolbus to a university classroom to eat lunch and work with two poets from the Albuquerque slam poetry team. As we walked to the bus to ride to the university classroom, the students were quiet. I walked along with them and asked a few what they thought. "It was scary, but it was good," Consuelo told me. Marisol smiled a huge smile and said, "Good." Ramona said, "I don't think they could hear me that well because so many other kids were reading theirs."

"Did they ask good questions or say kind things?" I asked.

"Yes," she smiled.

"Then I think they heard you," I offered.

When we reached the bus, they were typical fifth and sixth graders again, clamoring to sit with their friends and talking about what was in the boxed lunch. Some were shaking their cans of soda. Some of the children ate inside the classroom and others ate outside, running around between bites and sips. When the poets arrived, we called them all into the classroom.

"I say 'poetry,' you say 'rocks,'" said one of the poets. "POETRY!"

"Rocks," the voices of the fifth and sixth graders almost whispered back at him.

"What?" he asked the group. "WHAT? Did someone say something? I said, when I say 'poetry' you say 'rocks.' POETRY," he screamed.

"ROCKS!" came the scream back in unison. The fifth and sixth grade writers smiled. Jesus, the poet, (pseudonym) was a strong, tall, broad shouldered Chicano with a voice and tenor that radiated his history as someone who's been on the street, knew his way around, was bilingual, and was so comfortable with who he was that his presence drew out the students' and poets' shared cultural and linguistic roots. He explained slam poetry as being performance, without props, that has to be about "your real life." I couldn't contain myself, calling out, "You gotta tell the truth." The poet, kind to an old professor, paused, looked at me, and rubbed his chin thoughtfully. "Yeah," he said, "you gotta tell the truth." Then he told us that he would perform a poem. Poetry slams are competitive and Jesus explains that you can "boo the poem, but not the poet," and that if you like something you hear, you might call out something or snap your fingers. Poems must be three minutes long, or less. He performed a poem, from memory, which impressed the children. "He doesn't have any paper in front of him," Ramona noticed. "I know," I said, "amazing." The poem was about friends of his that chose gangs and drugs, some of whom died. It was a powerful piece and contained words with which the children resonated and eventually used in their poems, such as "Querque" for Albuquerque and some Spanish.

Isaac (pseudonym), the second poet, performed a poem from memory as well. His piece was about living in this part of the country, including references to low-riders, what happens on the streets, and family. Jesus said, "Now it's your turn." He explained that we would write and perform poems. "But maybe you think you can't do it, but I'll help you. Here's how you do it. You begin each line with 'I come from' and then you write about something or someone that you come from. You can write about places, and families, and things that have happened to you." Many of the students look around the room to find me because we'd written "Where I'm From" poems. I felt as though I became a bit more legitimate as they heard from a Chicano that this is one way that poems are composed. And, as I circulated during the writing, I saw many familiar lines being written again with slightly revised twists. They wrote quickly and when Jesus asked for volunteers, Verdad raised her hand as she called out, "I'll go first." She read what we all knew to be somewhat familiar lines, but she did so with a force, beat, and clarity that we hadn't heard before. She appropriated the rap qualities of slam poetry, including beat, tempo, and intonation. Other students volunteered to read as well, also with force, beat, and clarity. Both slam poets commented on each piece, telling the children the lines of the poems that they liked and why they liked them. "That's a powerful line," Jesus the poet said, "because I really know where you come from. Your mom and your small home and your neighborhood with gang signs. I can see it. That's good poetry," he told Chuck.

The children, disappointed at how quickly the time passed, needed to leave in order to be back at the school at dismissal. The poets thanked them and the children stood up and applauded. Then, as though some quiet announcement were made, they approached the poets and asked for autographs. "Keep writing," one of them offered. "We will," replied Chuck. Later that evening, Barbara sent me an email about a very resistant writer, one that was not in the study, but who "wrote poetry almost all the way home, then he sat at his desk and continued to write instead of cleaning his desk." Other students wrote on the bus and upon return, but they took those pieces home and I never got hard copies to include here. It was the power of voice that changed that afternoon as their work was legitimated by two poets with whom the children resonated linguistically, culturally, experientially, and spiritually.

For Families

Barbara and Patia met over lunch one day prior to my first visit after the trip to the university. They wanted the children to present their biographies to their families and decided that the school's "Showcase of Excellence" night would be a good venue. The Showcase is held yearly in the gymnasium and families can view art and literacy work on display prior to performances by the band and some other school groups. Barbara and Patia sent notes home to families inviting them to arrive at their children's classrooms an hour and a half before the Showcase to hear and see biographies.

We expected families at about five o'clock, but by four thirty they began to arrive and brought food. These were not simple snacks, but platters and pans of Mexican food and spicy chili and salsa, fried tortillas with cinnamon and sugar, fresh tortillas, and more. We quickly pulled together some tables outside Patia's classroom, in the small commons area shared by the four classrooms in the sixth grade pod. Families—including aunts, uncles, cousins, and children from a few months old through early high school—listened to their students' work, but first they loaded paper plates with food. Although all of the food was in the commons outside Patia's classroom, plates were loaded and brought to the fifth grade classroom, too. During and after eating, the families listened to the writing, viewed PowerPoints, and talked about the work. The adults answered their children's stories with more stories, discussing different parts of the story that the child didn't know or had omitted. There were tears, hugs, laughter, and many smiles as the adults shook their heads in recognition of either their contributions to the work (if they were the subject of it) or knowledge (or learning) about the person whose story was being read. Some children read their work in the corner or off to the side, while others read aloud to larger groups or the whole group. The event seemed to orchestrate itself as families shifted from focusing on one reader at the center to multiple readers at the sides.

At one point, I watched as Consuelo tugged gently at her mom's sleeve and walked her towards the fire door in Barbara's classroom. She spoke quietly to her mom and then opened her book and read it, translating each page into Spanish. Her mom stopped her from turning the page too soon so she could look closely at the photos, reread, or ask questions about what Consuelo had written. Consuelo looked at me after reading to her mom her poem, *The Giving One*, and mouthed, without a sound, "She's crying." Consuelo's mom wiped her eyes and hugged Consuelo close to her and held her, looking at the cover of the book, rubbing her hands over the Mexican flag. I walked tentatively over and smiled at Consuelo's mom; I asked Consuelo to introduce us, which she did. I said, "Mucho gusto" [glad to meet you] and then asked Consuelo to tell her mom that she (Consuelo) is very smart and a wonderful writer. Mom answered [in Spanish], "I know."

I showed the families the PowerPoints that the future teachers saw, and many of the students translated for the family members and, noticing the need, Patia translated for all to hear. When it was time for the families to adjourn to the Showcase, Patia and Barbara presented me with a gift. It was a 12 by 18-inch picture frame with each child's and teacher's thumbprint made into a tiny animal or silly 'thing.' They had eyes, ears, whiskers, legs, and other arms and the artists wrote their names next to their creation. As the families adjourned to the Showcase, I thanked them for letting me work with their children. I hugged some, shook some hands, high fived, and when Chuck and some of his friends walked by, we slid hands and clunked fists. Driving home, a collage of faces and lines of print passed through my mind. I stopped the car and took some photos of the mountains turning pink as the setting sun hit them.

Counterportraits and Spheres of Influence

In these final chapters, I work to understand how counterportraits may influence the official portrait that perpetuates poverty and positions of power-lessness among children such as those at Mesa Vista Elementary. Poor, mostly immigrant children have become pariahs through institutional regularities (Sarason, 1972) that claim to be working one way (for children), but in reality work in very different ways (Polakow, 1993; Carger, 1996). Public schools are supposed to be the great equalizers, making any dream a possibility, but in reality they work to maintain the status quo for many children. Of course, we all know the aberrations, stories of someone who "pulled themselves up by their bootstraps," but many of the children at MVE do not have boots, 'boots' being a metaphor for support structures that enhance the possibilities for access. Like the gang members in Smith and Whitmore (2006), the children in this book "enacted literacy . . . but their shifting status in each context means their actions as literates moved them along the trajectory towards membership or denied the legitimacy of their participation" (Smith & Whitmore, 2006, p. 178). The trajectory is along an unpredictable vector that does not guarantee success in the future, the way it appears to for more economically privileged children (Delpit, 1988). Learning the genres of power may not mean one has power in the spaces in which the official portrait is composed. We need to teach in ways that consider spheres of influence (discussed below) as well as personal meaning making. As we moved along our trajectory as a community of writers, power dynamics shifted because the children found reasons to write, think, and share. Previously, writing was work that needed to be done at the mercy of a teacher's demands, but now writing made sense in new ways with different demands from themselves, each other, the content, their teachers, and me.

In the rest of this chapter, *spheres of influence* is used to explain the ways in which one person or group has some kind of effect, impact, or power over other people or groups. An official portrait, appearing from a seemingly faceless author, is composed by groups of people that have a huge amount of influence, affecting public opinions, financial appropriations, legislation, access, and subsequent influences. A sphere of influence in which one resides may affect the senses of meaning and purpose that an individual or group has. Likewise, a sphere of influence in which one does not reside may affect one's life as well. Spheres of influence are webs of discourse (Gee, 2000–2001) and the power and inertia created, co-opted, or appropriated within them. The student authors' and poets' writing affected each other, preservice teachers, slam poets, and their families. The children were listened to and respected in the small spheres of influence of their lives, spheres described as small only because their voices would not carry to official settings where the official portrait is composed. The children's use of writing contributed to their identities as writers (González, 2005) and repositioned them in each other's, their families', some future teachers', and their teachers' (including my) eyes. Yet, in terms of a counterportrait that would gain recognition as an articulated and accepted response to their official portrait as 'poor and failing,' there was little influence beyond the very local.

Using language, power (Foucault, 1970, 1972a), identity, and the way those changed as the young writers presented their work to multiple audiences, their official portrait—in the minds of their audiences—were nudged. That nudge influenced their views of themselves, cultivating their self-confidence as months of work culminated in authentic responses of joy, tears, legitimacy, and credibility. The children saw the influences of their work; the audiences felt the influence; and I wondered about the idea of such a local influence—specifically how to extend it beyond those that were writers and witnesses.

Small spheres of influence are multidimensional and are composed at the nexus of language, identity, culture, power, knowledge, and agency. They are hybrid spaces because of how they are composed, what can happen within them, and whom they affect. The children in this study used language and composed language to find their own and other's knowledge, re-present it, and re-compose their own knowledge. They exerted or cultivated their agency as they acted on the social worlds of others by presenting their writing and thinking to each other, their own teachers, future teachers, slam poets, their families, a group of principals (via the principal of MVE), and a researcher. The fifth and sixth graders gained insights into their power as writers as they witnessed audiences respond to their writing. They felt a sense of collegiality with slam poets who confirmed what writers can do and how they can do it with a personal, social, political, and cultural edge. The poets, having strong cultural and linguistic commonalities with the children coupled with the way they embraced the children's writing and thinking, gave the young writers the sense of being part of something larger—a larger sphere of influence.

'Small' spheres are small because they are inchoate and have little influence beyond individuals present and involved. In contrast, a law such as NCLB may have been drafted by a small group but its influence is exerted far beyond the site of composing (therefore a large sphere of influence). The law is a political act with far reaching effects, ultimately making its designers part of a larger sphere of influence. Each sphere has a qualitative essence that is signified by how far reaching that influence is. The 'larger' the sphere and its influence, the more capable it is of affecting many others' lives—and influencing inertia. This leaves me wondering about our next steps in composing counterportraits with increased influence in official domains, such as legislatures, school boards, and the larger public. This may involve returning to a school to think and act further with children, their teachers, and perhaps their families to address the political realities that perpetuate the status of immigrant, economically poor, linguistically different from the mainstream, non-white children.

The year following the formal study, I continued to visit MVE regularly and work in the fifth and sixth grade classrooms with, for the most part, new writers. The work was not part of a systematic study, as I was spending the year analyzing data from the previous year's work. Barbara had retired and Roberta taught fifth grade; Patia remained a sixth grade teacher. Only two children from Barbara's class were in Patia's sixth grade room. One of them was Consuelo. One day, I gave her a blank postcard and suggested that she write to me about anything she wanted me to know. She wrote:

Hi Dr. Meyer,

Every night I stay awake and think about why did my dad left me without meeting me. Since the day he left me, when I was born, I lived with my auntie for two years. Since then, I have lived with my stepfather and treat him like my real father. Now that I understand, I don't want to meet him because my mom said he would drink and change his name so the DWI couldn't get him.

This is life in a small sphere of influence—Consuelo's life is huge and rich, although its influence in official spaces remains small. Consuelo's decisions about her father may change over time, but the important thing is that she thought about him, asked about him, and wrote about him because those actions influence her position in the world, her sense of agency, and her sense of power as a writer and a thinker. I call this a small sphere not to demean this

writer or her colleagues, but because the world did not make a huge and significant shift because of what they wrote and how they thought of themselves as
writers—at least not yet.

When Small Spheres Align . . .

There are many small spheres of influence within the stories of the children in
this book and beyond. Belenky, Bond, and Weinstock (1997) studied small
groups of women "working to make the whole society more inclusive, nurturing
and responsive to the developmental needs of all people—but most especially of
those who have been excluded and silenced" (p. 13). They chronicled the work
of women engaged in social action for justice and democracy, but who did their
work by distributing responsibilities and leadership. That distributive nature
made the work difficult to 'name' as belonging to someone or some specific
movement because, among other factors, of the nonpresence of a charismatic
leader. The groups worked locally, often without much recognition beyond the
communities in which they were involved. These are small spheres; they
occurred within and in spite of the ongoing life of communities. And, they
changed those communities because of the influences they had on the quality of
lives of disenfranchised people. Belenky et al. imagine what their work would be
like if it were enacted in a school setting and I believe that our work over the
course of the year resonated with their dream that:

> the teachers would be skilled at drawing out the students' questions and
> reflections; they would listen with care so they could better understand
> their students, their histories and cultures, their accomplishments, as well
> as their hopes and aspirations. They would document what they see and
> re-present their findings so the students could reflect on their strengths
> and dreams. (p. 308)

Altwerger (2005) points out the historical roots of the present oppressive
situation in schools dominated by tests, standardization, and legislation. She
recognizes the systematic growth of relationships and partnerships that have
led to schools being sweatshops (Meyer, 2005) for large corporations. The
corporatization of schools was a process of entrepreneurs collaborating with
each other with the promise of mutual gain (Poynor & Wolfe, 2005), typically
financially but also perpetuative of the economic situation of minorities and
the poor. The collaboration made the sphere of influence qualitatively large,
meaning it had effects not only on profits for certain corporations, but also on
legislation, curriculum materials, professional development, and methods and
criteria used to determine the status of school performance and the quality of
oppressed people's lives.

Our spheres of influence (the teachers', the students', and mine) may be
small, but they serve as points of hope (Liston & Zeichner, 1996) and possibility

for a shift, a turning point as more and more counterportraits surface and apply pressure to official forums. Such a shift could threaten those with power and wealth, making the work much more difficult than it might seem on a common sense level. It is for this reason that I offer a caveat. It seems I am, to this point, laying out an argument that suggests that students and their teachers are the ones to lead the political activity of legitimizing counterportraits in official settings, including legislatures, the press, and state and federal departments of education. To some degree, this is accurate, but it is also unrealistic in light of US education history, although Shannon (1990) does offer some examples of progressive teachers as activists. It may be too much to expect children and their teachers to become activists to the point of near-rebellion, although that certainly has been evident in other countries (Freidberg, 2005). In the US, the change, if it is to occur, will have to occur in multiple forums. Writing to make meaning, to understand the world in which we live, is crucial. Counterportraits, if they are to gain legitimacy in composing larger spheres of influence, extend beyond writing to make meaning to writing to recompose what is allowed in school, whose voices matter, and how those voices are expressed.

Chapter 10

Suffering, Struggles, and the Community

"Yet when you are aware of human suffering, you can't simply stand by and say nothing. As we learned from the Holocaust, indifference is a murderer too."

(Tan, 2003, p. 365)

Poverty, cultural, and linguistic differences from the mainstream, gangs, drugs, violence, high-stakes testing, curriculum constructed far from the children's lives, and teachers and children held hostage by these last two are all contributors to the suffering I saw. Many teachers are forced or coerced (Meyer, 2001) into doing things they do not believe, adding to their own and their students' suffering. I presented some of the fifth and sixth graders' writing to a group of teachers and, when we were well into discussing the children's thinking and writing, I stopped and asked the teachers to write about what they thought so far. One teacher wrote:

> Education—where are we going with it? What are we doing to kids as we teach under the influence of NCLB? I, as a teacher, feel like a prisoner in my teaching. Forced to teach kids to read 40 words in 1 minute. Read nonsense words in one minute. What is this? There isn't time just to enjoy reading; no time to immerse children in stories. What am I doing to kids? I want to teach kids to love learning not in one minute either. At the beginning of summer I ask the Lord to forgive me for what I've done to his children and at the beginning of [the] school year I ask for forgiveness for what I'm going to do to them.

> Why don't we teachers revolt against all this?

Humans—teachers and children—are suffering in schools and simply can no longer 'say nothing,' especially when typically compliant teachers use words like "revolt."

The children in this study began to name—in writing and aloud—the things that needed to be said to find their voices as vehicles for naming their own and institutional *indifferences*. Through their biography work and soul-searching writing, they came to understand more of who they were, where they were from, and what they could be. In this chapter I present their final self-evaluations and some of the thank you notes that they sent to me as further evidence of their growing awareness of their situations and agency. Before presenting that writing, though, I present some of my growing awareness of the conditions in which the children in this study live.

Home Visits

Over the course of the year, I learned about children living in homes with no natural gas, which means there was no heat or hot water unless they had a working fireplace or woodstove, which a few of the trailers did have. Some children worried with their families about not having sufficient money to pay rent, having to move, and then facing the same lack of funds. Children knew that their family members were drug dealers, thieves, chronic gamblers, alcoholics, coyotes (leading non documented citizens across the US–Mexico border), and gang members. They knew that their family members were gardeners, grape growers, construction workers, plumbers, religious church-goers, and more and that they were willing to help others in the community with these skills. They also knew that family members had short tempers, owned guns, got into fights, were stressed, held grudges, were separated, and worried about money. They knew so much, and perhaps because of that knowledge, very few of the sixth graders had photographs to incorporate into the pieces they'd written.

"What if," I asked the sixth graders one afternoon, "I were to come to your house and take some pictures? Would that be ok? Would that get you in trouble?" There was almost a chorus of "you wouldn't come to my house" in a cacophony of variations. "Why wouldn't I? If you don't want me to come, I won't. I was just offering to bring a camera and take some pictures." No one said anything. "Well, I'll come this Sunday," I said. After we worked on final drafts of the biographies for the remainder of that day, I packed up to leave. "You're not really coming to our houses, are you?" I heard someone say. "Well, yes, I'll come, but if it's not a good time you can just tell me that and I won't stay and I won't take any photos." There were more challenges as the sixth graders suggested that I would not really visit their homes. I asked Roberta, the teacher hired in March, if she'd join me on Sunday because she was familiar with the community from her years of home visits as a Head Start teacher.

Roberta and I met in the early afternoon at the gas station/convenience store near the school. When I pulled up to park, Roberta was already there and Carlos, a sixth grader, was with her. She said that he was there with his family when she pulled in and they said he could come with us to help us find houses. The family were going to Wal-Mart and his mom said that the fewer kids that go, the less money they will spend because the kids always ask for things. I'd brought two waters, two apples, and some nuts. I gave one of the waters to Carlos and told Roberta we could share the other one. Carlos started to drink his as we pulled out and nursed it for a few hours. We didn't finish visiting homes until 6:30, as we returned for me to get my car.

Roberta knew some of the children well because they were in her class years ago. Some of them still called her Miss Roberta, reminiscent of those preschool years. She knew the kids and their families, especially their moms because that's the person she met with seven or more years ago during home visits or family activities that were part of Head Start. We left the store and traveled for less than a half-mile; then we turned right and entered a web of dirt roads. Carlos knew where everyone lived because they were on his bus and he pointed out where his cousins lived and waved to one that was sitting outside on her front steps. The roads were lined with trailers, mostly single wide and many with exteriors that showed signs of wear, such as rust, broken shutters, missing windows replaced with plywood or other things that didn't match the original construction material. I noticed very few power lines and we decided that the lines must be buried, especially since every house had a TV set, some of which were on when we arrived.

We pulled off the road onto Vianca's dirt driveway where she lived with her mom in her grandmother's trailer. Roberta sat so I did too. Carlos, said, "Beep beep," wanting her to blow the horn to let them know we were there. Most interactions were in Spanish so my translations are via Roberta, Carlos, and what I understood. "Vianca," Roberta called from the open window of the car. An elderly woman appeared in the doorway. The door was propped open to the inside, with the rusting metal exterior and rotting plywood front steps making the trailer look abandoned. The elderly woman asked what we wanted and Roberta asked if Vianca was home. The woman shook her head no and Roberta explained that we were her teachers. They talked about why we were there and then the woman came down the steps of the trailer and approached us. Roberta introduced herself more formerly, introduced me, and said that Carlos was one of Vianca's classmates at school. She explained that we were taking pictures for the project that Vianca was doing in school and asked if Vianca had talked about it at home. She said that she was Vianca's grandmother (also named Vianca) and knew about the project because Vianca had interviewed her a few times. She sent her boyfriend to get Vianca, who was with some friends at another house. Grandma said she wasn't ready for a photo and that she'd have to do her hair and change her clothes. She wore a kerchief over her hair, a sweatshirt with the arms cut off, and a pair of jeans. Roberta said she looked beautiful but she insisted and disappeared into the trailer. We waited outside.

Vianca returned, saw us and her jaw dropped, as she opened her mouth but no words came forth. Roberta told her that we were here to take photos for her biography project. Just then grandma reappeared and told us to come in so I took the camera as Carlos, Roberta, and I climbed out of the car and walked into the house. As we entered, I noticed that the heavy front door etched a quarter circle deep into the plywood floor. Some of the layers of plywood were worn through. The kitchen chairs just about touched the counter space, with little room to move around. The cloth that had covered grandma's hair was gone and her hair was styled. She had on a dress and held three different hats. She cleared an altar area of some other things so that the poster of the *Virgen de Guadalupe* would show in some of the photos and told Vianca to come over and have her picture taken with her (most of the families were practicing Catholics and had special shelves or other small areas dedicated to their beliefs. These included statues, posters or framed paintings of the Virgin of Guadalupe as well as family-specific items, such as photos of loved ones that have passed away and other artifacts of spiritual significance). We took a few pictures and since Vianca's cousin was also there, she was included in the photos. Grandma wanted her photo with some of the other hats, so I took those as well. Figure 10.1 is one of the photos.

Once outside, Vianca did not want more photos taken and kept covering her face. I think (hope) she was fooling around because I did take a few. We thanked everyone in the trailer as we stepped out (Vianca and Carlos went out before Roberta and I) and we talked with Vianca before leaving. I said that now she had photos for her biography. She said, "No," although I was not sure why and she didn't explain when I asked. I said that I'd get them to her. When we left to find the next child's home, Vianca and a friend appeared on a four-wheeler and followed us to the next few visits. Although the students had access to these photos, few actually put them into their biographies. I think they may have felt 'done' with the work.

At almost every house we visited, families welcomed us in and offered us something to eat or drink. Carlos and the student whose house we visited went outside after photos were taken and the adults stayed inside and talked about their families. They were very interested in the biography project because some had heard about it from their children. They wanted to see the final pieces; we assured them that those pieces would be sent home after the family night's events. They talked about the love they have for their children, dreams of their children graduating high school and going to college, and they imagined their children getting good jobs. In many of the homes, I told families about their children's writing and one mother cried as she explained that no teacher had ever visited their home before. An uncle at that home told us that no teacher seemed to care enough to visit.

At one home, we saw the grape plants that a father planted the day his son was born and a map of where the family originated in Mexico. As we drove down dirt roads, I photographed gang graffiti, trailer homes that had blown over, huge amounts of trash in people's yards, old cars, vans, trucks, and buses parked in yards and porches attached to the trailers (Figures 10.2 and 10.3). The porches were made of wood and suffered the results of being exposed to the intense dry heat of the desert. At each stop, if someone was home, I asked

Figure 10.1 Vianca's Grandmother.

the children what they wanted photographed and took the pictures that they requested: family members, friends, and pets. Many of the families had dogs that I was much relieved to see tied up because they were ferocious, barking and pulling at their chains as we drove up. When I next visited the school, I joked with some students about their dogs and the students were quite willing to share with the class how afraid of their animals I seemed to be. Most of the trailers had some kind of fence around them, constructed with wire, corrugated metal, cinderblocks, or wood rails.

Roberta was really hungry and she wanted me to see the small store that many of the children talked about in school. We returned to the paved road and drove up to a store that was about 1,200 square feet. It was packed with

Figure 10.2 One of the student's front yard, this one with a wooden fence.

fresh baked pastries and there was a deli and butcher shop at the back. The
butcher was cutting thin slices of uncooked beef as a woman working there
took our orders. All the signs and conversations in the store were in Spanish.
We took the food to go and ate at Roberta's house, which was on the other side
of town. Roberta described her area as more stable, with families not moving
in and out as much. Roberta's children went to a different school, not MVE.
Roberta's house is a home that she and her husband built, having bought the
land for cash, built the house a little at a time and lived in it as they finished it.
She showed me the certificate she got from one of Mexico's *normales* (schools
where one learns to teach). It was 18 by 24 inches, lettered by hand in
calligraphy. She was an eighteen-year-old student, born and raised in Mexico,
when she earned it. Carlos, Roberta, and I ate together and I talked about how
confident and visible Carlos seemed outside of the classroom. In school, he's
quiet, almost invisible, but today he helped us find homes, cracked jokes, and
seemed quite comfortable and sure of himself. Carlos smiled and I thanked
him for helping us. Different contexts and relationships meant different masks.

Juliana's mom visited with us outside of her trailer and said that Juliana
would not come out because her hair was not done. Mom didn't let us take her
picture for the same reason, but I told her that when I saw her at family night
I'd take her photo then. She smiled and said that would be all right. Juliana's
dad is constructing a 2,400 square foot house behind the trailer. They are still
living in the trailer, but the house is far along and will be ready as a dwelling
within a few months of our visit. It is a one story building with a master suite,

Figure 10.3 Gang tags on a metal fence.

separate bedrooms for all three girls, and a big kitchen and living area. A few of the families owned their land and trailer, like Juliana's, but many more were renting. This visit inspired me to ask Juliana more about her dad and led her to revise a poem (Chapter 3). We visited a few more homes before driving Carlos to his house and talking with his mom.

We did not discuss 'human suffering' at any of these visits. None of the families brought up the subject, but the conditions under which they lived were very far from satisfactory in the US. I was stricken by the contradictions of rural poverty. At one point, I faced a dirt road with a long line of trailers and when I raised my eyes a little bit, I was taken by the beauty of the valley leading to a dramatic mountain range to the east. The desert vegetation is sparse, but has its own brown beauty, hot and dry. Seemingly plunked down in one little area of this vast setting is this community.

Bringing the Community to Sixth Grade

The fifth graders did take photos so we didn't visit their homes. I wondered what the sixth graders thought of their community so I put the photographs from that day into a computer slide show that I presented to them during my next visit. We made a semicircle of chairs facing the TV monitor that was mounted in one corner of the room, near the ceiling. I explained to the class, "This past Sunday, I visited some of you and I want to show the photos I took." There was mock-terror in some of the kids' eyes. Vianca especially did not want me to show her photos, yet once the first slide of her was shown she seemed to enjoy the attention. "OK, let's see what we have. These are not in the order we went to the houses . . . If you want me to visit your house, let me know and I'll come next week, especially if you need photos for your biography." I talked about each home, what we saw, the stories we heard and explained that these were things they saw everyday, but for me, it was interesting and the first time I'd heard many of the stories that families told. I joked with Vianca about her hiding her face from the camera and acting all shy but then following us around on her friend's four wheeler. We laughed together. I told stories I'd written in my field notes from that day. When we came to the photos of the roads and houses we'd passed, the children called out the information that they knew about the site. Verdad named all the gangs whose tags we saw. "Oh, that's Eastside and that's Sur 13, and there is Juaritos Mara Villa, and that's Westside."

The children shared what they knew about each other, the roadsides, the abandoned trailers, and the places where people lived. They talked about relatives and friends and people they didn't like. Someone said the wind had knocked over one of the trailers shown on its side and others agreed. "Yeah, I saw that and now it's right side up again," someone said with much authority.

"What else do you know about it?" I asked.

"It's very dented and rusty," Ricardo said.

They talked about their community as being poor, comparing their homes to the ones they see in Albuquerque, the nearest large city. Some of the children knew about homes on the side of town where Roberta lived and some newer homes along the highway that they described as very expensive and big.

They took turns, cross-talked, and I asked questions. "Who lives there? Why is that tagged? Which gang is that?" And there were answers and some discussions.

"I know who painted that one," came a voice from the crowd.

Silence.

No one would say the name and that probably was for the best; they knew not to reveal any information about gangs. I didn't tape the conversation, which was a big mistake from a research perspective because the talk was both factual and reflective and I found myself thinking that we'd begun an important conversation linking their lives, the community, and the things they see and hear each day (Freire, 1970b). Driving home, I thought that this was a beginning of something, a new direction—one that left me wondering what we would do if we had more time. We named and discussed the 'facts' of their cultural artifacts as the children saw them, things such as homes, roads, and gang tags. What, I asked myself, happens when children become aware of their suffering, when their lives are used by themselves as points of reference as they consider possibilities for what they might do now and in the future? In an earlier chapter, I discussed communities of practice as places of possibility and limitations. From a funds of knowledge perspective (Moll, Amanti, Neff, & Gonzalez, 1992), the community has capital. I wrestled with this idea in a comment within my field notes as I wrote about the sixth graders:

They were changing in many ways and I knew it was too late. The year was over. After viewing and discussing the slide show and an hour of writing and telling them how much we'd accomplished (individually, as I worked to edit pieces with them), the day was over. What was won and lost this year? That was the theme of the ride home as I studied this community so isolated in so many ways, wearing masks in school and in town. I had seen the underbelly last Sunday. They knew and I knew and it became official curriculum as we talked about it in class using the slides as a point of origin for the discussion. Amid the silent and voiced struggles with suffering, there were suggestions of hope, rooted in our accomplishments during our year together, and those hopes were evident as the children reflected on themselves as writers.

Writers' Reflections on the Year

After all the writing and presenting were over, I asked the fifth and sixth graders to complete a four-question survey in which I asked:

1 As you think about the writing we've done this year, what did you learn most about yourself as a writer?
2 What did you learn about writing?
3 What is something that you'd like me to know about biographies, poetry, or anything else?
4 What would you want to work on next if we were going to keep writing together?

Overall, the responses were brief because we had only a little time and because I left only a little space for writing (about one fourth of the page per question). Yet, reading their responses helped me realize the power of asking them what they thought about their accomplishments as writers over the course of the year. They felt included in an evaluative and reflective process in which they typically did not participate. This was an opportunity to respond to open ended questions in which they could self-select and compose descriptions of their writing, learning, and performance. Conscientization (Freire, 1970a) was inherent in this process because the children were actively included in thinking about who they were, using their own work as artifacts, perhaps even evidence, that supported the (very brief) case they were making about their learning. They were, then, involved in a metacognitive process in which they reflected upon their learning and could thus be instrumental in becoming conscious of the masks they constructed and presented to the world.

With the fifth graders, Barbara and I periodically stopped to encourage them to reflect on their progress and accomplishments. They rated their performance with rubrics and even had small group discussions about accomplishments and goals. The fifth graders had quite lofty conversations as they developed their own rubrics for different parts of the biography (ends and beginnings, for example). For the sixth graders, this was the first time we used time for them to think this way. For both groups, their thinking about their work over the year provided some insights into their inner thoughts and feelings about what they'd done.

Reflections on Self-as-Writer and Counterportraits

In response to the first survey question, a few of the students wrote quickly to complete the task at hand, somewhat contrary to what I've just written above. Estevan wrote, "Everything," and Chuck wrote, "I learned that I am a good writer." Both of these boys tended to write *just the facts* throughout the year, including in their biography pieces. Still, Estevan's biography was quite moving and Chuck's had the entire class hysterical. Perhaps, then, Chuck did learn that he's a good writer. He learned that he could write well for an audience, gather data, compose a piece that made sense, and capture his father's personality in a very entertaining way. And perhaps Estevan did learn *everything*—if everything includes writing proficiency that moved his mom to tears as he read it.

Debi, consistent with whom she was the entire year, wrote, "That being a writer is a lot of hard work," complete with angst and drama. She abandoned writing about a grandparent because she became too sad and felt too abandoned because that grandparent lives in another country. Ramona, whose biography contains the tragedies and victories of her soldier-father and his impact on their family (including the complex web that was woven before her parents finally married), wrote, "I learned that I had fun writing." Ramona had fun with all things difficult. So very contrary to Debi's tears and deeply furrowed forehead, Ramona's large round blue eyes squinted as they resonated with her smile, typically answering, "Fine," when asked how the work was going. And, typically, she'd follow up *fine* by asking probing questions about her writing process or the content or sequence of her piece. For Ramona, *fine* meant she was getting to work on something in which she enjoyed investing time and energy. Identity, then, is a part of the counterportraits that these officially 'failing' writers drew upon to recompose the portraits within. Those places within had, for many of the students, become saturated with their official portrait to the point that many of them believed they were failing writers, readers, and people.

Some of the children moved into an evaluative mode. Andres wrote, "That I'm pretty good, well at least better than I thought I would be." Here we get a sense of the way Andres learned to elaborate and qualify as a writer, characteristics of his writing in the biography he wrote. Ricardo self-evaluated by writing, "That I'm a better writer than I thought." Although the words seem simple enough, the depth of them cannot be underestimated. The responses of his colleagues as he read his funny poems (about eating paper) or wondering about his family members taught him that he is a good writer. Jesus self-evaluated and also moved into a consideration of genre as he wrote, "I learned that I could write poems better than I thought I could." Jesus, who wrote about his brother being shot and subsequently getting a smaller gun for safety, found more than poetry; he found a soft and gentle voice that he put into writing. Consuelo self-evaluated and set goals, writing, "That I was a better writer than I thought and I can still improve in my writing." Coming to the realization that they are good writers, writers with voices and goals, is the beginning of understanding the power to redefine who they are and how they are positioned, and thus is a way to address suffering and to act upon it. Elbow (1981) knew this:

> if we are brave and persistent enough to sing our own note at length—to develop our capacity for resonance—gradually we will be able to 'sing ourselves in': to get resonance first into one or two frequencies and then more. Finally, we will be able to sing whatever note we want to sing, even to sing what note others want to hear, and to make every note resound with rich power. But we only manage this flowering if we are willing to start off singing our own single tiresome pitch for a long time and in that way gradually teach the stiff cells of our bodies to vibrate and be flexible.
>
> (p. 282)

Voice, then, is political, requiring the bravery and tenacity to which Elbow refers. The children needed to locate their voices as part of understanding genres, including the genres of power (Delpit, 1988).

Esperanza also learned about genres and was thankful for the space in which to compose herself as poet and writer. She wrote, "I learned that I never knew I could write poems or even a book, so thank you." Esperanza's learning resonates with Halliday's (1978) idea that we learn language, learn through language, and learn about language—pretty much all at the same time. Learning about language this way continues for life; three other children also intuited these multiple ways of learning to be writers (learning writing, learning through writing, and learning about writing). Marisol, the fifth grader that sat with many pieces of her data, wrote, "That I never knew that I could learn so much about a person just by a biography and that I never knew I could write that much to make a story like mine." Isaac wrote, "I didn't know I could write that much about someone else. Now I have more ideas about writing." Writing, then, leads to more writing, almost an urgent call from within this young author to keep writing. Vianca wrote, "What I learned about myself was that I did not know that I could write what I wrote." This brief reflection could be referring to content, genre, length, or topic. Perhaps the keyword in Vianca's thought is "I," reflective of her learning about herself.

She continues:

> Muchas gracias por estar con nosotros en la clase. Era muy divertido. Gracias también por ayudarnos a escribir poemas y nuestro proyecto. Siempre lo vamos recordar. Lo vamos a extrañar. Muchas gracias por todo.

[Thank you very much for coming and being with us in the class. It was a lot of fun. Thank you also for helping us with our poems and projects. We will always remember it. We will miss you. Thank you for everything.]

Vianca also suggests that she learned that writing is relational; we wrote together and learned from each other. Juliana suggests that we learn writing, learn through writing, and learn about writing, noting, "What I learned was how to get all my thoughts and writing them. I learned how to write more than I did before. Well I actually didn't write a lot, but now I write because Dr. Meyer showed me how." Recall Juliana's struggle to write about her father and finally having her truth confirmed by another student in the class. Verdad showed that she learned the *why* of writing, noting, "What I most learned about myself is that I wrote from my heart and that I wrote to express my feelings."

Power comes from identity, voice, expression, and audience (response). These young writers felt valued, or perhaps more accurately, revalued (Goodman & Marek, 1996) as evidenced by their understanding that their truths matter. The writers that they buried within, for safety and protection, the voices that they silenced to avoid vulnerability were brought forward and expressed and they were well received by multiple audiences and changed because of it. Their work as presenters is consistent with grassroots organizing (Kahn, 1991) in which forums are created for the silenced to speak; such is the stuff of an individual's and a group's agency in composing counterportraits that may eventually change how an official portrait is composed and used.

Reflections on Writing and Counterportraits

The goal of the second question was to move the children from thinking about themselves to focusing on what they learned about writing, a subtle shift and some of the writers wrote very similar answers for both questions. Still, categories emerged as I analyzed their writing. Estevan, consistent with his response to the first question, simply wrote, "Everything." I discussed his use of that word above. Isaac, like others in the class, wrote that he learned what a biography (the genre) is, stating, "Now I know what a biography is and how to do one." Marisol also learned some of the specifics of the genre and intimates the importance of revising and editing. She wrote, "That it takes a long time to get a story good without any mistakes." Debi's response resonated somewhat with her response to the first question. "Yes, I learned a lot about writing because as a writer, it took a long time to write a biography." Membership in this literacy club (Smith, 1988) demands space in which to write and time to compose.

The fifth and sixth graders learned the meaning of 'biography' by engaging (Cambourne, 1984) in the genre: doing research, writing drafts, and producing a completed piece may be life changing for learners. A shift occurred as the students took metaphorical control of the 'press,' consistent with Delpit (1995):

Literacy can be a tool of liberation, but, equally, it can be a means of control: if the **presses** are controlled by the adversaries of a community, then reading can serve as a tool of indoctrination.

(p. 94, emphasis added)

Learning this genre meant controlling what went to press and what became of the pieces produced (the audiences that received them). Over twenty years prior to my writing of this chapter Delpit (1988) wrote:

merely adopting direct instruction is not the answer. Actual writing for real audiences and real purposes is a vital element in helping students to understand that they have an important voice in their own learning processes.

(p. 288)

Merging the ideas of controlling the press and having voice leads to a heard presence, by which I mean that the students' voices were listened to as part of their construction of counterportraits. By being voiced in their community and beyond (and now in this book), they work on undoing the official portrait.

Three of the students wrote that writing is fun. Ricardo wrote, "That you can have fun writing." Vygotsky's (1978) idea that children at play are a head taller may be transposed to include the idea that writers that have *fun* are a head taller, meaning they perform in ways more advanced than may be expected. Andres brought up fun and his mind, writing, "It is fun and it makes you think." Chuck brought up the affective side of writing, "That it's fun and another way to let out your feelings." It's interesting that Chuck, who is very efficient with his use of words, brought up the emotional side of writing. He seems to have learned that his colleague-writers in the class wrote about things from a broad emotional spectrum and also understood his use of humor as a way of gaining audience recognition and approval.

Vianca also brought up feelings, "What I learned about writing was that you express your feelings." Juliana, who admitted she "didn't write a lot," wrote, dotting her 'i's' with little hearts and circles, "I learned that writing is beautiful" (Figure 10.4). Verdad took what she learned about herself (writing from her heart) and generalized it, writing, "What I learned about writing is that some people write to express their feelings to other people." Jesus, "learned that writing the truth is best. Also that you could write about anything." The importance of the truth and one's heart came up for Consuelo, too, "That you can write of what your heart feels. You can just let the story flow." Esperanza wrote along the same lines, explaining that, "Writing for me is like a hobby. But like making a poem it comes from your heart and that is true."

Fun [play], angst, fear, drama, hurt, healing, trauma, joy, and hope were all part of writing the space and the writing in the space. I found myself constantly confirming with the children that their feelings were legitimate and welcomed

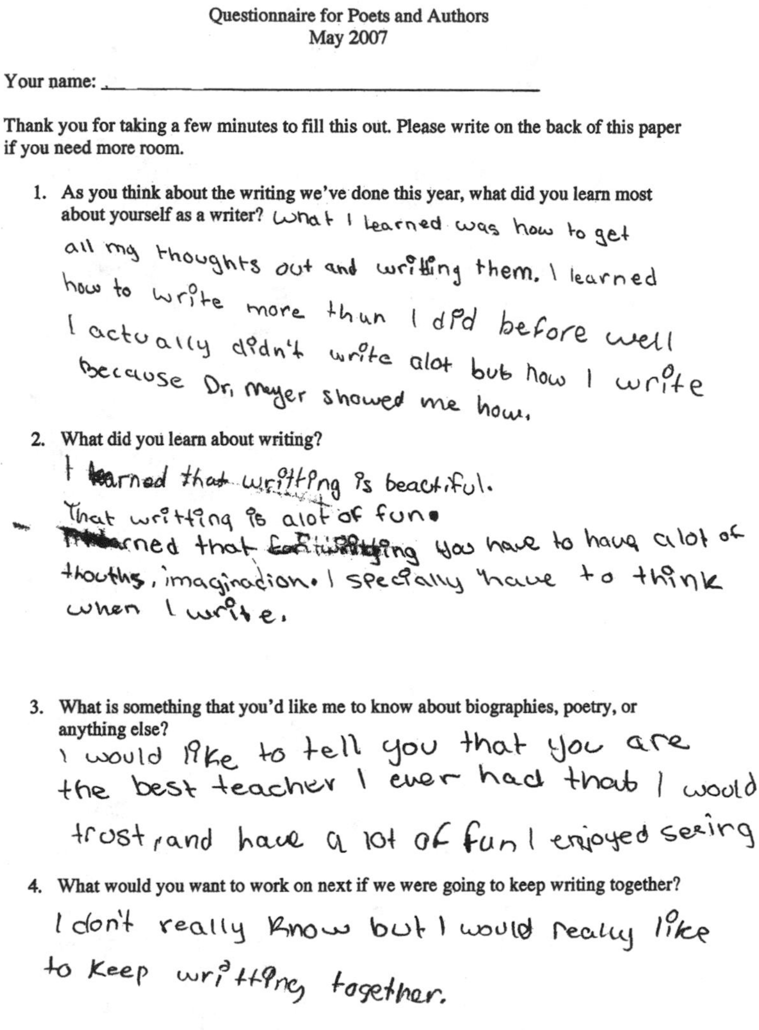

Questionnaire for Poets and Authors
May 2007

Your name: _____

Thank you for taking a few minutes to fill this out. Please write on the back of this paper
if you need more room.

1. As you think about the writing we've done this year, what did you learn most
    about yourself as a writer? What I learned was how to get
    all my thoughts out and writing them. I learned
    how to write more than I did before well
    I actually didn't write alot but now I write
    because Dr. mayer showed me how.

2. What did you learn about writing?
    I learned that writting is beautiful.
    That writting is alot of fun.
    I learned that writting you have to have alot of
    thouths, imagination. I specially have to think
    when I write.

3. What is something that you'd like me to know about biographies, poetry, or
    anything else?
    I would like to tell you that you are
    the best teacher I ever had that I would
    trust, and have a lot of fun I enjoyed seeing you

4. What would you want to work on next if we were going to keep writing together?
    I don't really know but I would really like
    to keep writting together.

Figure 10.4 Juliana's self-reflection on writing.

and needed to be part of the experience to keep it honest. The space that Freire
(1970c) worked to create among marginalized groups was an emotional space,
as well as a cognitive and political one. That emotionality, interrogated as a
vehicle for deeper understanding of cognitive and political issues, led to a sense
of power because they composed different masks for school and maybe for out
of school as well. Every time that children write, it is a political event because
that event will affirm or oppress, expand or compress, enhance or diminish
the students' identities, their self-worth, and the real, present, and potential

spheres of influence in which they dwell. Each event confirms and perpetuates the official portrait or challenges it, interrogates or ignores it, and undermines or supports it to some degree—affecting both inertia and spheres of influence. No writing act or act of teaching writing—including refusing to write—is neutral.

What Else, What Next, and Counterportraits

There was quite an array of responses to my request to tell me something that you'd like me to know about biographies, poetry, or anything else. Three students, Isaac and Chuck (predictably) and Ramona wrote the word, "Nothing," the latter adding, "Just that I enjoyed it." Jesus left the question blank. Initially, this might seem dismissive of the question, but I'm more inclined to think that they have a sense of agency and if they have nothing to say, they'll tell me that with a word or no words at all. Two of the students reported fun or pleasure. Andres wrote, "I had fun making it into a book." Debi, continuing her angst-ridden view, wrote, "That writing a biography is not as easy as it sounds. It is very difficult." Once again, the sense of a writer's identity seems to pervade the smallest or grandest endeavor. The joker is consistently the joker, but a deeper look at such an identity reveals that it is broad, encompassing compassion for others. The student that sees everything as a chore, seems fairly rooted in that subjectivity, yet her sense of accomplishment comes through (granted, with a strong reminder about the difficulty of the endeavor).

Esperanza wrote about family and surprise (Murray, 1985). "What I like of biographies is that you could write about your family. I learned a lot of things of my family that I never knew. Poetry, I like it, especially slam poetry and I like it because you get it from your heart." Estevan's response hinted at the many untold stories that remained within the oral texts of small and large group discussions or in private subtexts well out of range of the written text that he produced. He wrote, "I didn't write my whole dad's life." Writers made choices, exerted ultimate control over text. Ricardo's response suggested bending the biography genre, as he wrote, "That poetry can tell a story."

There were, in this group of writers, a couple of philosophical treasures. Marisol wrote, "To always listen to the words because you can probably find something in that paper or words that you hear can relate to your life." Her response reflected her own process of writing in which she listened closely, returned to text, returned to the source to listen again, and learned about the roots of who she is. And in an ambiguous "you-voiced" piece (leaving me wondering if she's addressing me, colleagues, or some collective group learning from her), Verdad wrote, "I would like you to know that people just don't write for fun; they write to express to other people," (Figure 10.5) which is why she wrote about her uncle. At first, she told me, "He's dead," nodding her head *yes* when I asked if that was the whole story. But she learned that the story is more than an internal state of knowing; it involves the impact of others knowing.

Questionnaire for Poets and Authors
May 2007

Your name: ▄▄▄▄▄ ▄▄▄▄▄ ▄▄▄▄

Thank you for taking a few minutes to fill this out. Please write on the back of this paper if you need more room.

1. As you think about the writing we've done this year, what did you learn most about yourself as a writer?

    What I most learned about my self is that I wrote from my heart and that I wrote to experss my feeling.

2. What did you learn about writing?

    What I learned about writing is that some people write to express there feelings to other people.

3. What is something that you'd like me to know about biographies, poetry, or anything else?

    I would like you to Know Know that people just dont write for fun they write to express to other people.

4. What would you want to work on next if we were going to keep writing together?

    I would like to work on writing about people that I care for and people that care about me.

Figure 10.5 Verdad's responses to the final questionnaire.

Three of the students interpreted the question as an opportunity to write something directly to me. Consuelo wrote, "About biographies I would like to thank you because you taught me how to understand my mom a lot, more about poetry. Thank you for telling me about white space and punctuation," recalling specific strategy lessons. Juliana wrote, "I would like to tell you that you are the best teacher I ever had and that I would trust and have a lot of fun. I enjoyed seeing you." Vianca wrote, "I want you to know that you are a really good person." The children understand that even though they were working on pieces about their families and themselves and the worlds in which they lived, they were in relationships. We cannot separate the writing that the children did and the relationships they had with each other, their teachers and me. Each of the completed pieces has many subtextual stories, but not just stories specific to the focus of the particular text. Those subtextual stories included the tales of the multiple relationships around (as well as within) the texts they composed. Juliana understood that writing is relational, noting, "I don't really know but I would really like to keep writing together." She understands that relationships matter because it is within the contexts of those relationships that we find or cultivate the power within self and the group. It is within relationships that we establish a place to name our suffering and it is that power that may be used to change the views that writers have of themselves and that others have of them.

Eight of the students wanted to engage in biographies again, perhaps because it is now familiar territory. Some wrote:

> More biographies because I really learned a lot about my dad. (Marisol)
>
> Another biography. (Estevan, predictably brief)
>
> I would want to work on another biography of a different person. (Vianca)
>
> I would like to write on your best friend or some of the teachers. That would be so cool. (Esperanza)
>
> I would like to work on writing about people that I care for and people that care for me. (Verdad)
>
> I would like to write about our lives. (Jesus)

Ricardo wanted to write "An autobiography of ourselves," and Andres's wish was, "Probably another poem," staying within the familiar. Ramona wrote, "I would want to write a fiction book," and Isaac wrote that, "I'm going to get a folder and write little stories and put them in there," making a commitment to continue his writing.

Thank You Notes, Relationships, and Counterportraits

I was moved to think more deeply about our accomplishments following what originally seemed like perfunctory thank you notes that the children gave to me on my final visit of the year. Their notes, which both teachers decided to require the children to do, were dutifully appreciated by me upon receiving them, but it wasn't until a full year later as I sat reading them that I realized their significance. Esperanza wrote on the inside of a piece of paper she'd folded into fourths.

> I used to have a brain
>
> Without words
>
> But now
>
> I do
>
> (Esperanza, May 2007)

She drew upon a format we'd used during the year to condense her understanding of her growth as a human being and writer into a strong assertion and acknowledgement of what she'd accomplished. Verdad wrote, "Thanks to you we learned to write from our hearts." These final brief pieces suggest that the children have agency in developing and understanding counterportraits. Juxtaposing *brains without words* with *having a brain with words* shows the internal shift from feeling as though one has little capital (Bourdieu & Passeron, 1990) to feeling a sense of possibility of interrupting or even disrupting the official portrait. The work begins within self and community and addresses struggles through action, in this case the action being the recomposition of self.

Benjamin Barber (in Goodlad, Mantle-Bromley, & Goodlad, 2004, pp. 7–8) wrote that, "Public schools must be understood as public not simply because they serve the public, but because they establish us as a public . . . [yet] society undoes each workday what the school tries to do each day." School, then, is a place in which a public is composed (Bomer & Bomer, 2001). Goodlad et al. go on to suggest, "it is folly to talk about educational excellence apart from the influence of the cacophony of teaching that is going on in the culture" (p. 8). The suggestion that schools are working towards a democratic citizenship perpetuates the meritocratic myth that many families and students in this study held: if one simply works hard enough, success will ensue. School does work to create a public, but it cultivates the reproduction (Bourdieu & Passeron, 1990) of a public—complete with power structures, values, language, and distribution of wealth—that already exists, thus perpetuating the essence of the greater society.

I do not mean to portend that teachers and the school system set out intentionally to maintain the often-tragic conditions in which the families and children in the MVE area live. However, larger agendas are at work that tacitly undermine the hopes and dreams that many families have about American schooling, particularly immigrant families such as those that send their children to MVE. Spring (2002), McLaren (2007), and Augusto, Allen, and Pruyn (2006) offer elaborate explanations of the hegemonic realities of schooling. Willis and Harris (2000) argue that "literacy and politics have worked hand in hand as barriers for many people of color, the poor, and females throughout the 20th century" (p. 75). Stuckey (1991) wrote that, "much Western comfort comes at the expense of the poor and minorities" (p. 113) making it essential that schools perpetuate socioeconomic class and status in order to preserve the comfort of those already comfortable. Those suffering stay suffering.

Levine and Nidiffer (1996) studied 24 college students from high poverty settings and the people that influenced them in order to understand how at-risk (of failing in school) students were successful in getting to, and through, higher education when so many of their peers did not. Predictably, and perhaps interpretable as hopeful, they found that influential individuals, learning to navigate a new discourse, and programs early in schooling focusing on academics and strategies for surviving socially were important contributors to success in higher education. Success, then, appears to be a matter of serendipity because if a student happens to have a mentor, if they are informed of strategies for reading and thriving in a new discourse, and if they experienced some early education programs, they have a greater chance of 'beating the odds.' Jordan (1996) critiques Levine and Nidiffer's work because:

> the possibility of institutional racism being an actual barrier to college enrollment among African Americans and Latinos is not handled by the authors. The underlying assumption is that individuals, with proper support and guidance, can overcome poverty in the face of broader structural inequalities.
>
> (pp. 29–30)

Like many of the children, Isabel wrote a full page thanking me and then ended by writing, "but the best thing that you gave us was trust. I mean trust is very important." Juliana began, "thank you for everything that you did for us," and then added, "You knew that we could write. I had never had a teacher that I would trust as much as I trust you." The trust that I have in the children is that they can use their power to make change. That's a huge expectation, yet, fully believing that "the master's tools will never dismantle the master's house" (Lorde, 1984), I'm beginning to understand that my hope is that as the children appropriate writing as their own, they will use it the way it was used by Martin Luther King Jr., Caesar Chavez, Gloria Steinem, and others in the important movements that reshaped our country.

Even though the children and their families may seem confined by hegemony and inertia, I am not ready to "quit on democracy" (Kohl, 1998). Kohl writes:

> When schooling is sparse, minimal, and obsessed with skills without content you get the impoverished thought and marginalized imagination that show up, as children enter adolescence, in terrible test scores and scorn for school and everything it represents. Without conviviality, school comes

to resemble a minimum-security prison, a depressing holding pen . . . . It is disheartening to see people abandon the public schools . . . . For me it is a dangerous way of quitting on democracy and is bound to increase the tensions and violence our children will have to live with in the future.

(pp. 262–263)

Perhaps the work of this year will help contribute to centralizing imagination, conviviality in school, and a deeper belief in democracy, enabling students whose families believe that the US is "pure lies" (Carlos's dad) to find possibilities here. When Juliana writes about continuing to write together, I see glimmers of such possibilities.

Such hope is hard work at the present time, but it is the hope that is rooted in critique that can lead to action. Edelsky (1999) discusses school as a pipeline for prison, but still I cannot give up hope because, as Esperanza says, it is possible to move from thinking you have a brain without words to having one with words. Our work in the classrooms was about disappropriation of the portrait that kids appropriated from official sources, the result of a web of relationships that perpetuate suffering. The idea that relationships are an integral facet of teaching and learning literacy is understandably troubling in the present educational climate. The push to rely upon published programs to standardize teaching— programs for the economically poor with scripts that must be adhered to with little or no variation—is a push to make school activity "teacher proof" (Jackson, 1968). The relational nature of our work suggests that the teacher does matter. Both classrooms wrote biographies, but the tact (Van Manen, 1991) and tone (Van Manen, 2002) of the classrooms were different because of the complex relationships between: teachers, teachers and me, students, students and teachers, families and schools, the school and the state, the state and the federal, and all of the permutations and combinations of these. The relationships in our work mattered because truths mattered, honesty mattered, and taking risks mattered and all of these are characteristics of relationships. When relationships matter, ideas like *standards-based tests* dissolve and leave exposed the reality that literacy is quite a bit more than some adopted program. This threatens publishers because it threatens profits; it threatens administrators because it demands a level of trust in teachers that has been undermined by a "manufactured crisis" (Berliner & Biddle, 1995) in education. Relationships that are truthful and honest (and threatening) may inspire hope for the suffering.

Critical Literacy, Hope, and Counterportraits

Inspiring hope for children living at the nexus of multiple crises—economic, linguistic, familial, cultural, educational, to name a few—necessitates different kinds of curricular processes, ones we initiated by finding and naming the individual truths that children bring to school. The situation demanded mov- ing our discussions about texts and oral stories "from the personal to the critical" (Lewis, 1999, p. 164). I now believe that we did more of the work of Freire's (1970a) *conscientization* than I'd previously thought. The consciousness-raising in which we engaged was at the heart of the work because it served as the point of origin for a sense of agency as the children understood who they were and where they were from and eventually worked to understand where those around them are located in the larger portraits of family and community. Lewison, Flint, and Sluys (2002) offer "four dimensions [of critical literacy]:

1   disrupting the commonplace,
2   interrogating multiple viewpoints,
3   focusing on sociopolitical issues, and
4   taking action and promoting social justice."

(p. 382)

Counterportraits may be enacted as counternarratives to widely held beliefs (Comber, 2001) and may include all four dimensions, as ours did.

In the telling of truths, we found ourselves disrupting, interrogating, focusing on sociopolitical and sociocultural issues, and engaging in actions. Part of that work was identity work, rewriting the selves that they had come to be and were forced into being in school; part of it was uncovering the truths in families and rural neighborhoods; and part of it was informing others as a way of continuing the raising of consciousness that occurred in the classrooms. We engaged in critical literacy through acts of poetry consistent with Bomer and Bomer's (2001) discussion of poetry as being the only medium that "has the grace to reside at funerals and weddings, to mark the transformations in peoples' lives, to say what cannot be said" (p. 3). Espada (1994) understands this firsthand as he writes in the preface of a collection of poems (we read) from Central and South America about three poets "murdered for political reasons" (p.18), including one that was burned alive, nine [others] that were jailed, five forced into political exile, and one that the US attempted to deport. Poetry is about "political resistance" (p. 18) because it is about exposing the false fronts that compose the official portrait, peeling off the thin layers of paint to show the bold colors beneath, and presenting the counterportraits that expose inequities, injustices, and stories of pain and suffering that embarrass a nation's claims of decency and caring.

Esperanza had words in her mind before we began writing the truth, but she didn't have help in decodifying and codifying (Freire, 2005). When we wrote, talked, shared writing, and discussed the photos of their neighborhoods and families, our discussions involved:

[d]ecodifying or *reading* the situations pictured [or written, which] leads them to a critical perception of the meaning of culture by leading them to understand how human practice or work transforms the world.

(Freire, 1991, p. 26, emphasis in the original)

Freire explains further:

> I have always insisted that words used in organizing a literacy program
> come from what I call the 'word universe' of people who are learning . . .
> their anxieties, fears, demands and dreams . . . . We then give the words
> back to the people inserted in what I call 'codifications,' pictures repre-
> senting real actions.
>
> (pp. 25–26)

The children pointed out the familiar and obvious (to them), and also showed
they understood the rules within their community, including what could be
discussed and what could not. They briefly lived life in a writers' collective
in which "anxieties, fears, demands and dreams" were named and, to some
degree, interrogated. They codified their lives in and into words others could
read and hear.

Another part of Juliana's thank you note read, "Some of us decided not to
write, but when you came, most of us started to write a lot. I am really thankful
that you taught me how to write all those poems . . ." But it wasn't just me. It
was Juliana who was willing to engage in a relationship with her colleagues and
me, to be honest and to write and talk and generate text that demanded that
she learn. She was willing to place those demands upon herself and engage in
much the same way that Freire (1970a) had learning-to-be-literate adults
understand the deep cultural importance of a brick or a clay pot within the
contexts of their lives. Juliana's struggle with a poem, sitting for fifteen minutes
with one line, was her process of beginning to understand who she was and
where she lived.

Our codification involved looking at the themes of our lives and inquiring
about those themes within our selves and, later, within others. When the theme
of *life in our family* arose, it became clear that many children live with violence.
"My uncle was murdered," Verdad said, almost challenging me to make the
murder legitimate school stuff, later asking, "Do I write about that?" As she
wrote about him, and eventually interviewed others about the murder of her
uncle, she began to understand (decodify) the ways that the murder upset her,
her family, and the community. Other children in the class knew about the
murder and offered some input, although Verdad's anger and pain—her
suffering—was something she had to decodify and codify to understand and
legitimate in order to make reflective decisions as a writer and a human being.

Verdad wrote that her uncle was "in a better place." Understanding "better
place" meant facing her reality that the present place is not that good for family
members. In August 2007, Verdad's father shot himself in the head and died,
another sad and powerful demonstration to a twelve-year-old girl that the
present locale is not a good place. We may have ended the school year with
Verdad thinking that the "better place" is not in this world and her father's
suicide may have confirmed that theory.

The group of truth-tellers with whom I worked were willing to engage as Alice Walker (2006) wants us all to engage:

> Sit for a moment and consider what it means to be aware; let yourself feel the many ways you have been morally and politically manipulated and tricked. Consider your own part in this.
>
> (p. 14)

Walker hopes to inspire us to understand and act upon our sense of complicity and to move to a sense of agency as we consider the inequities with which we live. The suggestion that we have a "part" in our own feelings of being "manipulated and tricked" may not be comforting but is indicative of an important sense of responsibility in counterportraiture. In the present climate of standards (Ohanian, 1999) and high-stakes testing, the search for the spaces in which teachers, researchers, and students can do the thinking necessary to develop their senses of agency and freedom are in jeopardy, as Greene (2000) articulates:

> To narrow the spaces accessible to young people and to keep them from breaking with intellectual or physical or social confinement seems to me to be an outrage. At the very least, their growth may be blocked; they are stopped from becoming different, from discovering a project, from creating an identity (p. 9) . . . the notion of uniform standards in a moment of unprecedented diversity cannot but erode the teacher's choices among alternative approaches to pedagogy, even as it cuts into the freedom of youth . . .
>
> (p. 11)

In an earlier work, Greene (1995) captures the passion and intensity with which we might approach counterportrait work:

> I think of how much beginnings have to do with freedom, how much disruption has to do with consciousness and the awareness of possibility that has so much to do with teaching other human beings. And I think that if I and other teachers truly want to provoke our students to break though the limits of the conventional and the taken for granted, we ourselves have to experience breaks with what has been established in our lives; we have to keep arousing ourselves to begin again.
>
> (p. 109)

For many years the children at MVE learned that "what they know is not important enough to incorporate into [classroom] praxis" (Willis & Harris, 2000, p. 81), evidence of teachers complying with demands placed upon them, particularly recently under the guise of scientifically based reading instruction

(Coles, 2003). Further, we know that "learning to read will not ensure a more equitable or socially just world" (Willis & Harris, 2000, p. 83), at least not until such learning is deeply rooted in the realities of students' lives and strategies for acting upon their worlds.

Many of the thank you notes gushed with sentimentality about missing me, having fun, loving biographies, and writing things "we never would have written." I submit these reflections as evidence of counterportrait work in third space (Gutierrez, Rymes, & Larson, 1995) as voice, power, presence, and authority emerged:

> in the face of a rigidly monologic teacher script [first space], the relevance of students' counterscript [second space] to the processes or topics discussed in the classroom has little influence on the teacher's script. The only space where a true interaction or communication between teacher and student can occur in this classroom is in the middle ground or 'third space' . . .
>
> (p. 447)

We are complicit in our own and other's suffering unless we actively (and in some schools, secretly, under cover or 'in the cracks') carve out places in which to think, write, and honor the truths of our students' and our own lives. We owe it to ourselves and to our students to resist or struggle so that they and we do not withdraw, drop out, comply, self-medicate, and engage in other high-risk (to self and others) activity. It falls to us to engage in some projects that we can identify as counterportraiture for "literacy and justice for all" (Edelsky, 1996).

Chapter 11

Writing Spaces for Better Times

When I think about student resistance and the limits of education, I have the impression that one of the main difficulties is a dichotomy that exists *... between reading the words and reading the world ... the world of* American education, the school, is increasing the separation of the words we read and the world we live in. In such a dichotomy, the world of reading is only the world of the schooling process.

(Paulo Freire, in Shor and Freire, 1987,
p. 135, emphasis in the original)

Freire's dichotomy was evident in our work as we saw changes in the children and ourselves when we *decreased* the separations between words and worlds and supported the children in drawing on both, legitimately, across the many contexts in which they live. In this chapter I present the themes of counter-portraiture that may apply to classrooms and serve as areas for further research to support the creation of classrooms in which writing is an integral part of a democratic project. These themes are the result of thematic analyses across the data and domains (see Appendix 1) from the previous chapters. I do not offer specific ideas for further research or classroom applications because such suggestions run counter to the relationships inherent in and context-driven specificity of counterportraiture. Counterportraiture is, ultimately, evidence of the democratic process when democracy is considered as both an ideal and a political project. As an ideal, democracy can never be achieved because of the continually changing contexts of our world, but as a political project we can use writing to help children and ourselves engage in an ongoing understanding, clarification, interrogation, and enactment of this ever-emerging ideal.

This research began as an investigation of truths. Ultimately, the truths of some were found to be more powerful, influential, and even intrusive than the truths of others. The official portrait is a manufactured truth that carries significant weight across school districts, the state, and the country. That truth is composed of demographic and high-stakes assessment data presented as an absolute and accurate portrayal, which, in turn, influences the setting of standards, which are then assessed. This self-serving cycle continues to selectively exclude and include groups as a function of those groups' current positions and roles. Simply put: the rich remain rich and very few of the poor have access to wealth. The official portrait excludes the ways with words (Heath, 1983) of most of the writers in this book and by doing so dismisses their ways of thinking, experiencing and knowing their worlds. It turns out that they can read the word and the world and the differences between their worlds and the official one that Carlos's dad called lies. They also wrote their worlds as a way of interrogating and making public their truths, which stand in opposition and resistance to the official. Opening writing spaces meant opening places to think, consider, react, compare, wonder, rejoice, regret, and compose better times by opening spaces for legitimation.

The Purposes of School, the Search for Joy, and the Spirit of the Child

These three themes (purposes of school, the search for joy, and the spirit of the child) overlap so consistently across the chapters that I place them together in this section. Schools should be sites of struggle, resistance, searching, and joy. *Resistance* (as Freire used it, above) is one expression of struggle, a theme that we faced daily, *we* meaning the children, teachers, families and myself. When I began the work with the children, I asked one thing: that they tell their truths. The work became a study of the nature of truth and whose truths matter, to whom, and the ways in which mattering are operationalized in day-to-day life. There are the truths that bring some people peace and comfort, those that perpetuate wealth, and those that are dismissed and essentialized. Some truths seem to not possess sufficient capital to initiate or overcome their inertial state, especially if that state is non English speaking, non white, and non wealthy. There appear to be genres of the wealthy and powerful that work tirelessly to maintain the official portrait of the students at MVE, a portrait that influences the truths they compose, the struggles they face, and the ways in which they face them. Rosen (1986) explains:

> Genres may be the house-styles of contemporary capitalism. But those legitimized forms, endorsed institutionally, are constantly being subverted and eroded. **Writing is itself a site of conflict** and ferocious subversive play is possible within its boundaries. We can foster that kind of play or outlaw it.
>
> (p. 10, emphasis in original)

Calling genres "house-styles of contemporary capitalism" suggests the current distribution of wealth (in this case literacy capital) and profit is right and good, but only for some, and that there is ongoing pressure *within its boundaries* for subversive activities that challenge that distribution. I offer that the use of "boundaries" implies obstacles that have always been present (like mountains), but 'borders' may be a more accurate (and more vulnerable) description because these are artificially drawn and may be redrawn under a variety of conditions (evolution, revolution, and treaties, to name three).

Freire's words at the beginning of this chapter apply to the writing that occurs in school as well as the reading. The young writers in this book read their worlds and composed by using their worlds, a significant departure from what many students in schools are experiencing. Their words and their worlds—often translated—functioned, to some degree, to lessen the separations that Freire discussed. They composed poetry, narratives, and expository texts, and they composed themselves, writing places, and relationships. Freire questions and then reminds us as teachers and researchers that we need to focus our work in such a way that we are present as partners in literacy work.

> How is it possible for us to work in a community without feeling the spirit of the culture that has been there for many years, without trying to understand the spirit of the culture? We cannot interfere in this culture. Without understanding the spirit of the culture we just invade the culture.
> (Paulo Freire, in Bell, Gaventa, & Peters, 1990, p. 131)

Part of such a partnership is respect for the 'spirits' of students, which are the places in which their passions, curiosities, and senses of the deep connections between all human beings are composed and reside. The work of this research evolved into the search and re-search for the spirits of children, teachers, to some degree families, and myself during hard times. The expression of one's spirit is an expression of trust and may only happen when a writer finds a safe place to compose. These spaces nurture or confuse, and even challenge, but they shut down or never open when the space is legislatively constructed and bounded. Every writing space is political because of the issues of power that saturate it, making writing space vulnerable to corruption. These constructed spaces may be places of caring (Noddings, 1984), but because of the pressures under which schools like MVE exist, caring may be forced into the margins as test performance assumes central importance. The official portrait overwhelms children's and teachers' spirits, leaving in its wake frustration, resistance, struggle, and, most often, appropriation of the official 'inadequate status' inherent in the judgment: not making adequate yearly progress. The effect of the loss of children's and teachers' spirits was put quite simply over twenty five years ago when Goodlad (1984) asked, "Why are our schools not places of joy?" (p. 242).

Echoing Goodlad, Bomer wonders:

> Shouldn't an education for democracy be working to make such apathy unlikely and rare, rather than fostering it? . . . . It is true that the bureaucratic priorities of the education system do not position students as

competent citizens or teachers as educators for democracy .... It is
unlikely that any government, ever, will beg the schools to teach students
to struggle for social justice. Teachers are the ones who will advance that
idea. Or no one will.

(Bomer, 2007, p. 304)

Ultimately, living with the children's and teachers' struggles to live life in the
shadows of an official portrait that felt mean-spirited, blaming, and angry
reduced to this question: What is school for? Wolk (2007) offers that, "Our
children go to school to learn to be workers. Going to school is largely
preparation either to punch a time clock or to own the company with the time
clock—depending on how lucky you are in the social-class sorting machine"
(p. 650). Yet he challenges his own statement by suggesting that, "If school is
not helping children to consciously shape their cultural, political, and moral
identities, then we are failing to educate our children to reach their greatest
potential" (p. 652). One of the very basic questions about school (what it is
for?) became one of the central struggles we faced in our work at Mesa Vista
Elementary, but there were other struggles as well.

In this section I did not specify a purpose for school, how to find joy, or the
specificities of nurturing the spirit of the child. There's no curriculum here and
there shouldn't be because it is up to individuals and sites to appropriate and
individuate these themes and others that they find specific to their contexts. For
example, joy may become a heuristic or question used by teachers, students,
and researchers to pose to a classroom or school. Where is our joy? How do we
know it? What evidence do we have of it? Such questions and reflective activity
would be my preferred use for applications of the present work to other local
engagements in counterportraiture. In the following sections, the themes of
struggles and responding to struggles are explained. Inherent in struggling and
responding to struggles are the three themes discussed above. The struggles
with time and activity (carnival) were presented in Chapter 7 and the struggles
as part of suffering and community were discussed in Chapter 10. In the
following sections, I present the final layers of analysis of *struggles* as themes of
counterportraiture.

Inner Struggles

Some of the struggles that the writers faced resided within their innermost
thoughts and feelings. Some of the children, being in a school that struggled to
respond to the tensions between lives inside and outside of school, were
"suffering a personal defacement" (Goffman, 1961, p. 20) or "curtailment of
self" (p. 14) because of what they learned to silently relinquish upon entering
school. Some felt "assaults upon the self" (p. 35), such as Juliana being elected
president of the student council, but "messing up" (p. 51) resulting in
punishment that included the confiscation of her office, or Jesus' struggle to

please, yet maintain a sense of who he was, building to his scream of, "Shut up!" to his teacher. In prisons, when the punishment is viewed as unjust, a "get even" (p. 62) mentality emerges, just as it did at times in the sixth grade classroom. Ultimately, inmates face the "sense of a watered down life" (p. 68). In school, children may sense life as watered down, as their priorities, needs, interests, and differences are dissolved in a standardized curriculum that makes little or no sense in their non-standardized worlds. Increased consciousness or an intuitive sense of conditions gives rise to struggles within.

Subjectivities are created by institutional practices that do the work of making individuals appear to others and perhaps themselves in a particular way, as intelligent or incompetent for example (Walkerdine, 1990). Institutional practices are designed, for the most part, to deny access to resources to specific groups of people (minorities, children, teachers, etc.) as a way of maintaining power over them. The 'help' that has been offered to MVE comes with a subtext because all present know that there are interventions for the *failing school*. The range of subjectivities available tends to be limited and the available subjectivities are, often, "self-pathologizing" (Walkerdine, 1990). In other words, in order to participate in the educational institution that is the supposed roadway to prosperity, one may come to see oneself as powerless, dis-eased, or a failure in need of compliance and conformity. Words like "disadvantaged," "poor," and "from little Juarez," were imposed on them by the state, the federal government, the school district, social service agencies, and some teachers. Rather than feeling valued and learning in a school that cultivated the funds of knowledge (Moll, Amanti, Neff, & Gonzalez, 1992) that were inherent in the community and the children as agents of the community, the students were reified into categories of the official that forced them and their teachers into a limited repertoire of tones, colors, and hues. Their official portrait is the official truth functionally and operationally as it serves as the reasons for the way things are, the reasons to blame certain people (teachers, economically poor children), and the justification for specific interventions supposedly designed to bring equity, equal opportunity, and success.

Lee (2008) argues, "that to generate robust and generative theories about how and what people learn, we must attend to issues of diversity based on conceptually complex frameworks that position diversity as essential or fundamental to the human experience and not as some wayward pathology" (p. 272). We as teachers and researchers are faced with the struggle to move ourselves and students away from pathology- and deficit-based assessments, pedagogies, and ideologies, issues that go much deeper than a life in school and penetrate to the very quality of life available to an individual. Teaching may seem to some (and is sold to some) as neat and professional looking as the slick boxes in which programs arrive at a school, but in reality it's very messy and very personal.

The teachers felt pathologized as well, facing inner struggles with standardization that came with pressure to achieve adequate yearly progress. Tension was created when teachers felt pressure to force children to be standardized in ways that did not acknowledge the children's individualities. Patia would not have expressed it this way, although Barbara would. Patia was so deeply pressurized that she was stuck between compliance and the realities that she saw in the classroom and the community. Standards, as they were written and evaluated, constricted the children's thinking and their teachers' activity, limiting the possibilities for activity within the school setting. Standards constricted teachers, locking them into programs that forced them to turn their backs on what they know, whom they teach, and even each other (isolating them). Of course, content matters. Content is the 'what' of school. Yet the 'how' (the processes) and 'why' (for the purposes of testing or democracy) matter. Many of the standards were covered as we worked, but we had located ourselves outside of the official border of school activity in which adopted programs and high-stakes tests based on standards not only reify what little spirit there might be in those standards, but serve to marginalize and disenfranchise the individual in favor of some imagined and homogenizing *proficiency* for an entire school.

Language and Identity Struggles

Buried silently within the standards for the children at MVE were the seeds of another struggle that grew at the school and was evident in both classrooms in which I studied, a struggle that could have easily become the central and driving theme of this book. That struggle was the one imposed on the children that came to MVE with Spanish as their first language. In the current educational climate, Spanish is viewed as a problem or a weakness to be overcome. Having English language learners (ELLs) as one category into which disaggregated data must be placed is a way of demonstrating that *those* Spanish speakers are the ones responsible for a school not making adequate yearly progress. Children from diverse, typically poor, non-English speaking homes are akin to some sort of pariah that needs to be transformed into English speakers. Officially, their knowledge of Spanish was viewed as a deficit in their reading, writing, and speaking. But our work became a place in which languages, cultures, and experiences were capital that mattered and could be used for profit (Lareau, 1989) in literacy work and in counterportrait work. Counterportraiture involves questioning policies about language, in our case particularly in light of the established knowledge base about bilingualism (Crawford, 2008 and Krashen, 1999, for example).

Roberta made it clear that the children could speak Spanish with her and write in Spanish when we worked on biographies. She legitimated a strength that they had as part of their identity—and the increase in the use of Spanish was noticeable, yet concomitant with the increased use of academic English. Translation has historically been an act that makes one and others vulnerable (Behar, 1993) and the bravery needed to cross linguistic borders was something that the children in this book mustered, not simply by moving words from one language to another, but by doing the work of authentic translators. They attempted to re-present identities that lived in one language and culture into another language and culture. In doing so, they teach us about strengths and struggles. Strengths were evident in their tenacity in going about this work. Struggles presented themselves as they got stuck working to figure out how to translate a world, not just a word. Katherine Paterson (1981), an author of many books for children and adolescents, moved to Japan for four years when she was a child. Years later, reflecting on her feelings when she first arrived in Japan, struggling with a new language and culture, she wrote that she "wanted to scream. If only you could know me in *English*, you would see at once what a clever, delightful person I am" (p. 7). Writing about her return to the US four years later she states, "The reason I thought my family didn't know me was that they didn't know me in Japanese" (p. 8). The struggles to translate self, words, and worlds remains very real in schools.

School as a Site of Struggle

The individual struggles and the larger contextual struggles within social groups, within each classroom, and within the school cannot be separated neatly. They are all contextualized within the district, state, federal, and global contexts that interact with each other. Nestled prominently among the children's work in the main hallway of MVE were the results of the previous year's testing. This was another school coerced into one official way of thinking about progress because of the realities that could be imposed upon them by federal legislation. We struggled to overcome the perceptions that were initiated as a "disinformation campaign to teach the public that their schools had failed" (Edelsky, 1999, p. 13). The use of language to create general consensus is referred to as framing (Lakoff, 2002). In education, a law named "No Child Left Behind" is difficult to oppose because the general public gets the impression that opposing the law means leaving some children behind. The framers of No Child Left Behind appear advantaged because they have been instrumental in the "installation of a regime of truth" (Foucault, 1972b, p. 242). That regime is about power that is used to enforce curriculum (and thus sell it, making money for publishers). Foucault points out that "we must produce truth in order to produce wealth" (pp. 93–94). However, titling a book *Many Children Left Behind* (Meier & Wood, 2004) is important because it suggests direct and bold challenges to the name, intent, and effects of the law. Reframing involves the re-appropriation of language, meaning, and activity. The contrast between the official portrait and counterportraits of the children is at the center of reframing as we strive to challenge the deeply enculturated beliefs about children from *a school like that.*

There is much money being made by publishers of curriculum and tests (often the same companies) (see Altwerger, 2005 or Poynor & Wolfe, 2005 for more on this), corporations that work to maintain their positions and enlarge their wealth. This is a major source of the feelings that teachers have of being controlled, especially as standards dissolve into standardized programs and tests. Control by a large corporation that functions far from the school site may make struggle seem futile because there is no one to face, challenge, or resist. It gives the sensation of a shadow over the school, a shadow that influences every activity and influences the possibilities for literate activity within each classroom. Corporate control dangles the possibility of success in front of hopeful teachers and families, but failure is what the public views and comes to know as the official portrait of places like MVE. There's more money to be made when things are this way and there is an underlying struggle that has to do with knowledge, how it is created, and how it is used as an instrument of power.

Knowledge/Power Struggle

Foucault (1972b) discussed the relationships between knowledge and power as a struggle over whose knowledge has worth, influence, and prestige. Roth (1992) offers that knowledge is "an activity, not a corpus, fixed body" (p. 686). He differentiates between Foucault's ideas of knowledge and "disciplinary technologies" (p. 687). The latter focuses on the use of power (from a privileged position) in order to engage in the "ordering of bodies in space and time ... [thereby] normalizing judgment which [means using] normalized data to rank people in terms of a mean" (p. 687). These ideas of normalizing people "over space and time underpin the control of bodies and minds at schools, penitentiaries, and factories" (p. 688). Ryan (1991), also relying upon a Foucauldian perspective, discusses schools as perpetuating inequality through this commitment to discipline and power. Discipline and power serve to portray knowledge as stationary, fixed, standardized, and complete, therefore it is something that is to be placed into a child's brain. This is activity that can be undertaken by a technician (Shannon, 1989), rather than a reflective practitioner (Schön, 1983). The evolution of *discipline* includes power over children and teachers in order to convey the idea that knowledge is known, non-changing, and originates within an 'other' more powerful, influential, and knowing source (Foucault, 1972b). The idea of 'discipline' in this view of teaching, learning, and power is twofold. It means the subject matter (**the** discipline, a noun) and it also refers to control (**to** discipline, a verb). This intimates that there is a constant push for control in order to impart pre-established knowledge. Knowledge in this sense is a struggle for power over another in order to have the other comply with content and the process for acquiring that content. These were the disciplines within which MVE lived; they were controlling, clearly defined, and not open to questioning.

Roth (1992) explains the tight grip that the teachers felt, even when that grip consistently does not *fix* the problem. Schools, he contends, are not controlled by one individual or group . . . both the structure and outcome of schools are products of a range of individual and group desires and actions. For example, although rhetorically committed to providing equal educational opportunity, schools contribute very little toward equalizing the life changes of students. In the face of this failure . . . educational reformers recurrently propose tightening the very disciplinary technologies that have generated the inequalities in the first place: higher standards (which stigmatize average performance), increased surveillance (which further restricts students' liberty through tougher codes of conduct), and more explicit punishment and reward systems . . . . As long as schools continue to use an organization scheme geared to watching, testing, and normalizing students, their efforts to reduce inequality . . . are bound to fail.

(pp. 690–691)

The reactionary stance of NCLB and the curricular and testing demands that flowed from it led to increased cognitive and physical surveillance. Tighter physical control is continuous with tighter mental control as state standards have led to standardized curriculum in the disciplines across the district, especially reading, language arts, and math—all closely monitored by various levels of administration. The knowledge/power struggle along with the other struggles explained earlier contributed to responses, which I call 'agency' a theme I articulate in the following sections.

Agency: Responding to Struggles

Counterportraiture is a political act. It may be political because of consciousness raising, learning more about the power dynamics and hierarchies of one's contexts, or because of acts that one commits in response to what one knows. Agency means acting upon one's world as an individual or collectively in some way in order to change the power dynamics, thus changing the nature of knowledge, the contexts in which it is constructed, the legitimacy of its sources, and its prestige. Counterportraits are struggles for complexity, identity, and recognition, so they are a form of agency. Rather than create a dichotomy of good versus evil, right versus wrong, or passing versus failing, counterportraits are meant to add multiplicity, specificity, and details. An official portrait using broad strokes that obfuscate individuality produces dichotomies that vilify, reduce, or in some way marginalize or disenfranchise groups by using means, standard deviations, and other quantitative generalizations that give the appearance of pinpoint accuracy but in actuality serve to make individuals invisible through homogenization.

Agency that is rooted in struggle involves addressing or even overcoming oppression, thus, not all struggles are 'bad' things. A struggling reader is working hard to make meaning. A struggling activist works for the rights of self and others. A struggling athlete works towards victory. So it is for struggling teachers and their student writers struggling to create places in which to compose. They are not necessarily in pain and they are exerting energy—life force—as a way of being more present and more real. They are drawing energy from their spirits to enhance the quality of their own and others' humanity and composing spaces for more possibilities. Agency, then, as a theme, is related to the other themes discussed so far. Agency means teachers and children acting upon the purposes of school, the search for joy, spirit, and struggles.

Personal acts of agency, particularly when individuals feel "discredited" (Goffman, 1959), may occur when an individual resonates with someone else, such as the sixth graders finding import in the Martínez poem. It may occur when a teacher wants her students to have an experience they remember for life, when she lets go of using rubrics that aren't working, or courageously (Palmer, 1998) explains to her colleagues in fifth grade that she was using time differently than they (and she) previously planned. The students also influenced their colleagues in the classroom as did language, gender, familial and friendship affiliations, and more, including me.

Any teacher acting as an individual faces barriers, knowing that she may have colleagues who "feel most disempowered in the institution [and] are also most likely to subscribe to . . . [the] notion that 'These kids can't be helped'" (Fine, 1996, p. 245). Such teachers tend to "shut down" (p. 246) students when they bring up issues about the neighborhood or their families or social equity, telling them to "leave it at the door." We found that naming events, experiences, and relationships in their lives had consequences for individuals. Fine concludes that not naming has consequences. "To not name is to systematically alienate, cut off from home, from heritage and from lived experience, and ultimately to sever from their educational process" (p. 246). She saw the "academically mute . . . who say nothing all day, who have perfected the mask of being silenced, who are never identified as a problem" (p. 247). In counter-portraiture, naming is a form of agency as it brings to consciousness ideas and events that are then open to scrutiny and subsequent action. It is about interrogating and recomposing *the mask of being silenced.*

Teachers acting out by retaking or taking control of curriculum and students acting out in different ways, such as being silent, talking back, fighting, arguing, ignoring, withdrawing, writing biographies, looking for answers to difficult questions, and sharing their work in small groups, large groups, and with outsiders were all ways in which they responded to struggles and struggled to resist. Acting out is a form of resistance and, as such, is a form of agency, though it may not always serve one well. Historically, people like Ghandi (2005) acted out; so did Alinksi (1946), although the latter suggested violent tactics. Considering and taking actions carries with it consequences that one considers when plans for agency are made. Or, sometimes we act and realize what happened after the fact, moving intuitively in some direction.

Obvious expressions of Patia's resistance were obfuscated by the over-powering presence of pressure from others, leaving her emotionally and physically exhausted. Her struggle was deep within herself, embedded in the conflict of faith she had in the state and publishers knowing what was best for her students in opposition to the information coming from her students. The conflicts that she lived as the collision between her belief in the authority of others and the realities presented to her by her students formed the essence of her struggle. Barbara and I probably contributed to her struggle by challenging and interrogating what she said she was forced to do. Patia struggled to come to terms with her students' consistently poor performances on state and local assessments, alternating between blaming the students, feeling let down by the district, and finding the demands of the state unrealistic for her students. She ended the year still deeply mired in this conflicted state, which was the struggle she took with her into summer break. This conflicted state is a form of agency because Patia agreed to take on the challenge as her own and that very consideration is a form of agency and demonstrates how emotional such work can be.

Resistance, active or passive, was a way of moving against standardized and prescribed curriculum, ideas, and relationships. It was evidence of the struggles that we were all experiencing. Some of the children (when they fought, yelled, or neglected assigned work) resisted school-imposed subjectivities (Moje, 2002) that demanded that they comply. Resistance in this sense was a socio-cultural construct that involved self, others (social contexts), languages, cultures, and ideologies. Some of the children resisted crossing the borders (Giroux & McLaren, 1994; Giroux, 1992) into being fully present and participating in school because of the cultural and linguistic uprooting to which they were forced to assent (Kohl, 1991). Others may have resisted assignments, especially sixth graders, that were presented as 'work' that needed to be done, like the factory work that Wolk (2007) described above. Still others resisted because of the social status that one maintained by othering the teacher, objectifying the work as useless, and sustaining relationships that viewed other affiliations as more important and urgent than schooling (girlfriends, gangs, church affiliation etc.).

Biography was a form of agency in which the children struggled with *world* issues such as facing themselves and being researchers into their families' lives and with *word* and textual issues such as: how to begin, how to evaluate an ending, spelling, audience, translation, grammar, and a concept of story (Applebee, 1978). They struggled with a writing state of mind, what that feels and sounds like, and how one talks about it. They put forth genuine and authentic efforts (agency) to face these issues and they outwardly resisted (also agency). And when resistance subsided in one area (realizing the benefits—even joys—of writing multiple drafts, for example), it emerged from another area. The work was tentative and fragile, with old ways of being seeming to wait in the wings for a cue to be reinstated, to be faced again. There were the struggles to express, understand, and meet expectations and the resistance to all of those as well. There were struggles over the use of tools, struggles to figure out why pieces weren't saved when we thought they were, resistance to technology, and loving technology. There were struggles with acting upon new relationships, redefining old ones, and changing subjectivities (finding confidence and strength in their understandings of their realities)—all parts of agency.

Hybridized spaces were fertile grounds for agency in which the children became "cultural workers" (Freire, 2005) as their work interrogated, challenged, and perhaps undermined some of the "ideologies on poverty" (Shannon, 1998) and race that were held by the children themselves, future teachers, and their own teachers (to some degree). Reading, writing, studying their own lives, and studying their families' lives helped the children understand ways in which they and others were positioned and could entertain ways to reposition themselves. Consider Verdad's writing about games involving killing Mexicans, played by children who were second generation Americans from Mexico equally as economically poor as, yet aimed at, their newly arrived peers. Verdad interrogated that game in her writing and again as she read it to the class. We talked about the game, others recalled seeing it, and we talked about the fights that followed. The in-class dialogic space for discussions about such issues was new (for school) and validated Verdad's experience, opening a place for her to think and consider other actions. Esperanza's "thank you" poem about having a brain with words suggested a shift—a hybridized leap—into a new way of seeing herself in the world. Now she has words to name her world and some power to shift who she is and what it means to have a brain with words. Hybrid spaces were organic locations in which children and their teachers composed counterportraits that more accurately portrayed who they were, what they thought, and what they could do. It was a space of and for voice, presence, honesty, struggle, resistance, agency, and the cultivation of writing and writers for better times.

Agency and Responsibilities in Composing Counterportraits

In this section I discuss some of the implications of, and possibilities for, the themes presented with the hope that they will inspire counterportrait work. Counterportraiture involves the assumption of responsibilities by teachers, researchers, and children—to themselves, their classmates, their families, and their community—rather than to compliance. If a counterportrait is accepted by some dominant group, such as a legislature, the work of counterportraiture must continue. Any official portrait—newly adopted or longstanding—must be interrogated in order to systematically and systemically question who has power and privilege and who does not; whose voices are heard or silenced; who is represented and who is not; how wealth is defined and distributed; and who has access to that wealth and who does not. At the present time, the official portrait of the children at MVE has a limited (and limiting) view of what is acceptable and 'right,' which necessitated the creation of counterportraits (plural) in order to open spaces for multiple perspectives as points of origin for discussions, writing, and actions. Educators in a democracy have the responsibility of constantly applying the pressure that can be felt from counterportraits as a way of maintaining a process of challenging, interrogating, hoping, critiquing, questioning, wondering, and acting upon the status quo. Such a process must be endemic to the organicity (Gramsci, 1992) of schools as living, growing, and changing places and as forums for the ongoing interrogation of any existing official portrait and the composing of counterportraits. This means a reconsideration of the way power is distributed in the classroom (Murray, 1999). Further, teachers, students, and researchers may assume responsibility to become agents of actions as Luke, O'Brien, and Comber (2001) explain:

> Too often, linguistic analysis and literary deconstruction are treated as instructional ends in themselves, rather than means for socially productive textual work. We would argue that text analysis and critical reading activities should lead to an action with and/or against the text. That is, there is a need to translate text analyses into cultural action, into institutional intervention and community projects.
>
> (p. 117)

When we assume these responsibilities as agents of change, classrooms and research sites may become thriving literary ecosystems (Gutiérrez, Baquedano-López, & Alvarez, 2001) that include the world within and beyond the school building in ways that honor differences, address inequities, and work for justice. As Bomer (2007) explained, such openings are possible only if teachers (and I would add researchers) are willing to work for them, by reimagining (Greene, 1995) possibilities for truth telling through oral and written conversations (Clark, 1990), using them as vehicles for thought and action collectives in which to compose counterportraits. But we were only beginning when the year ended. In the following paragraphs I offer some possibilities for reimagining our work with schools.

Agency and Responsibility: The Bigger Picture

In the film *Granito de Arena* (Freidberg, 2005), one of the teachers explains that, "Globalization and free trade control everything, and everything is subject to the laws of the market, and education is no exception." The film documents hundreds of teachers in Oaxaca, Mexico that rose up against the government who was controlling their union and preventing a democratic process for teachers. Teachers were kidnapped, tortured, and murdered, as they demanded the removal of the governor of their state, a man who allowed very little academic freedom and teacher decision-making. Salaries were so low that teachers had two or three other jobs in addition to their teaching responsibilities. Centrally controlled curriculum and Spanish as the primary (typically only) language of instruction (ignoring the many indigenous languages and calls for bilingual instruction) were the way schools were run because of the profit to be made by such an arrangement. At the end of the film, other countries in which teachers were central to uprisings against unfairness were briefly mentioned. Most teachers in the US have not heard of these uprisings, but we need to learn about them as exemplars of counterportraiture and agency that are responses to the larger socioeconomic and cultural issues teachers and students face.

At one point in the movie, the camera pans a crowd in which there are children and adults standing along the strikers' march route holding signs reading (in Spanish) "We support our teachers." They supported their teachers because those teachers supported their children, the community, and a deeply held conviction to multiple perspectives, languages, and voices. The teachers took responsibility for their students in ways far beyond complying with completion of a state mandated curriculum. Many US teachers feel as trapped in the global economy as the workers in a small village that was colonized by a large corporation for cheap labor (Gee, Hull, & Lankshear, 1996). Over time, the locals lost their families' skills at living off the land, in some ways analogous to teachers that are coerced to defer to scripted programs. Such teachers may not have the necessary skills for co creating curriculum (Short & Burke, 1991), pedagogically living off the land with children and families, which is part of agency. When the corporation left, the locals felt the impact of their reliance on the factory. When the scripted programs leave or are forced out, teachers will need to assume the professional responsibilities they've had in the past, enhanced by a deeper understanding of the political project in which they are involved.

It is not sufficient to rely upon teachers and their students to change things. Small spheres of influence certainly do have an effect, but the official portrait is composed within larger spheres of influence that often silence the type of work that the children at Mesa Vista Elementary did. Activist teachers' movements (Shannon, 1990) have a history of living pedagogically within the cracks or on the periphery of official views of education. Progressive education, as a grassroots movement, has not garnered sufficient inertia to make substantive sustained systemic changes, partly because we are only beginning to understand that pedagogy is connected to ideologies, knowledge and power, economic development, and views of cultural and linguistic differences. For example, one reason for the ongoing interruption of progressive pedagogic activity is the intrusion by corporations assuming curricular (and economic) control of schools (Altwerger, 2005). The oxymoronic 'whole language basal reading systems' that emerged when the whole language movement gained momentum is evidence of the economic drive and profit motive that work to appropriate the accomplishments, political realities, and pedagogic strength of such movements. Further, the corporate drive for standardization of programs serves their economic motives (one product for many consumers means significant profit with no new innovation) while marginalizing cultural and linguistic differences. Ever-increasing consciousness of such issues is foundational to counterportraiture.

Grassroots movements, such as whole language, are forums of hope and collectives of teachers thinking about the purposes of school in a democratic society (Flurkey & Meyer, 1994). Critical literacy is another such movement, learning from the past, and using that understanding to engage in schooling as a political project (Lewison et al., 2007). It remains extremely difficult to find a school committed to teaching children to learn, read, and write from a critical literacy perspective, but such inertial activity takes time and tenacity. Our hope may rest in our continued efforts within grassroots movements because it is there that teachers and children have presence and voice. However, we need to recruit more partners in our efforts because part of the work of agency in counterportraiture involves exposing and acting upon the inequities that exist in all realms of life, not just schools. I am still (continually) mystified by the global economy because I cannot conceptualize the amount of profit, typically rooted in greed (it seems), that companies make on the backs of children and teachers. I am not sure who will partner with teachers and children and the families from schools like MVE because, quite frankly, such families matter little in the larger global profit-based system in which we live. I cannot imagine any company willingly relinquishing profits in order to hire more workers, offer better benefits, and deeply care about the quality of their workers' lives. But that doesn't mean we should not try and we need to publicize our efforts so they appear in the media, blogs, websites, etc.

Rather than a government that steps in to support the work of large corporations in a global economy, we need a government that works for the diverse economically poor families that are increasing in number daily. Even as I write this chapter, two new reports have been published, one showing 24 percent of New Mexico's children under 18 living in poverty in 2007 (compared to 18 percent, nationally) (US Census Bureau, 2008a), up from just under 20 percent in 2006. The second report (US Census Bureau, 2008b) showed a significant increase in the number of New Mexico children that do not have health insurance. Teachers understand and are faced daily with the importance of healthy children. We need action plans to present to the public as we garner their attention. Consider the following example.

Karp (2004) suggests that rather than apply the principle of adequate yearly progress to scores on tests, apply it to the economy. 'Proficient' in this sense would mean a family's movement towards the median income, with the responsibility for the movement falling not upon the family, but upon employers. At present under the No Child Left Behind legislation, schools have until 2014 for all students to reach proficiency in certain academic disciplines. Instead, 2014 will be the year by which all families must have employers that will help them make progress towards median income. Further, they must make progress towards adequate health insurance and overall quality of life on measures we have yet to determine (but can certainly imagine). This seems much more reasonable that explaining to the public that our economy is falling apart because children didn't get a certain test score and that if those children would reach proficiency, then the economy would be better. I will refer to adequate yearly progress in income as *yearly increase in personal income* (YIPI for short). YIPI will hold corporations responsible for achieving goals that will bring all members of our communities to a decent standard of living. Mothers will not have to hold down two or more jobs. Children will not have to suffer with chronic infections, dental or mental health issues, and all the stresses that are part of living in poverty.

If the framers of NCLB were serious about 100 percent of students being (rather than merely scoring) proficient, we would need to re-imagine our country as a place in which all citizens are reading and thinking and making plans to act as informed cultural workers. That would probably lead to increased activism, the reappearance of strong unions, and the next iteration of gay, civil, workers, women's, children's, and immigrants' rights movements (and others I discuss later or that have yet to be invented). An informed proficient citizenry will take responsibility and assume agency, putting at risk the creators of the extant official portrait. It remains quite difficult to imagine those in power dreaming up a plan that would threaten their power and wealth to this extent, a fact that exposes the pernicious nature of NCLB. Teachers know that nature because they've been saddled with programs that do not teach reading, such as those using nonsense syllables or bizarre stories composed of phonetically regular words (Ruiz & Morales-Ellis, 2005). These programs exist for profit-making, not successful literacy learning that cultivates a citizenry that actively participates in the democratic process.

This bigger picture of responsibility and agency is about socioeconomic counterportraits that threaten the status quo. These pictures demand a reconsideration of wealth, power, and the distribution of those across all people living in the US and perhaps the world. This sounds naïve even to me, yet one child (now grown) worked to end child labor practices in third world countries (Kielburger, 1998). He didn't fully succeed, but he made inroads. He writes:

> Freeing children is never a question of money. We simply do not believe that world leaders can create a nuclear bomb and send a man to the moon but cannot feed and protect the world's children.
>
> (p. 297)

He poses an interesting challenge to our present priorities for funding and the permissions we give (for example, to relocate US corporations in third world countries) that perpetuate certain forms of taking advantage of, even abusing, others. Kielburger concludes that, "change starts within each one of us. And ends only when all children are free to be children" (p. 305). Again, I wonder about relying solely upon children (and their teachers) to change their own situation in schools and in the larger worlds in which they live. I rejoice that aberrations such as Keilburger exist and also know that larger, more systematic changes may be farther reaching.

Agency and Responsibility in Schools

The consideration of these larger socioeconomic issues is not intended to minimize the work that teachers, and students have done—including those in this book. The work of schools must move forward in the democratic project with (or in spite of) such larger socioeconomic work (or the lack of it), otherwise we become complicit in that hegemony. Yet there remains the nagging feeling that what happens in school isn't getting us much closer to the democratic ideals that so many of us envision. Stuckey (2002) wrote that curriculum (as cause) and ultimate success in school and life (as effects) are not as easily connected as some would have us believe. Later, Stuckey adds, "The most consistent feature of schools . . . is rampant insistent fragmentation. No real community could ever work this way" (p. 218). The suggestion that schools are not "real" communities and that they are kept in constant states of disruption or upheaval helps explain why a school or teacher or group of children may not be able to effectively compose counterportraits with credibility in official forums. Add to the lack of credibility that comes from a place of "fragmentation" the additional lack of credibility that poor and diverse children have, and we are left with a school that is silenced in official forums. Still, teachers with a commitment to student and teacher voice work to use writing "to make a difference" (Benson & Christian, 2002). Benson and Christian collected stories of teachers and students that worked to connect to their larger ("real") communities, by networking electronically with other communities. The writing of the teachers and students in Benson and Christian's book is action in the form of voices, of significance locally first, but spreading as those students and teachers talk, present, and write more and as they experience the personal and larger scale effects of having their pieces published. This is the work of smaller spheres of influence being connected to become slightly larger. It is the work that we must perpetuate in order to contribute to a tipping point (Gladwell, 2000) at which those in power in official forums look around and realize that multiple and increasingly present and listened-to voices are calling for changes in what is legitimate, whose voices count, and how wealth, knowledge, and power are created and distributed.

The International Reading Association (Lewis, Jongsma, & Burger, 2005) realizes the importance of advocacy work by teachers and their students. Lewis et al. help teachers understand advocacy, make decisions about when to advocate and for what, and offer print-based, multimedia, and in-person strategies for such work. They intuited an understanding that needs to be stated explicitly, which is that we must keep in mind that when we advocate by asserting some form of agency, we are facing "[t]raditionalists [who] are the status quo, opposed to democratic change from below . . ." (Freire, in Shor & Freire, 1987, p. 82). This means that there will always be pressure to maintain the status quo from those who benefit most from that status quo, those that are dominant and privileged. Advocacy work should not be approached naïvely, but rather it must be considered as the deeply political work it truly is. Teachers fearful of such work may want to consider the deeply political work of perpetuating the status quo by being compliant. Compliance is a political act of complicity that may seem easier in the short term, but leaves reflective teachers angry, withdrawn, bitter, isolated, or searching for alternative employment. Ideas for teacher activism do not need to jeopardize employment (see Meyer, 2008/2009), but they are typically beyond many teachers' comfort zones.

Even though we in the field of literacy research know of and have categorized ways in which content that we teach young adolescents, like the ones in this study, may be substantively part of curricular activity focused on justice (Moje, 2007), we have not determined ways in which to integrate that knowledge into the fabric of life in schools.

> Teachers often devalue, ignore or censor adolescents' extracurricular literacies, assuming that these literacies are morally suspect, raise controversial issues, or distract adolescents from more important work. This means that some adolescents' literacy abilities remain largely invisible in the classroom.
>
> (National Council of Teachers of English, 2007 p. 3)

When their abilities are "invisible," terms like 'achievement gap' are used to name poor performance on official assessments. It is time to seriously consider what will happen to the students of MVE if the real gap—the one between the portrait that is official and many counterportraits—is not addressed. The children at MVE may be conveniently tucked into 'at risk' or 'not proficient' categories of their official portrait, but their learning achievements over the course of less than one year put someone else at risk: those either in charge of or complicit in perpetuating the official portrait. They are at risk of having to face and deal with a whole new level of rights activists, not only those mentioned above but literacy rights, economic rights, access rights, and even spiritual rights. Counterportraiture exposes the fallacies of an achievement gap (because the kids at MVE and their families are achieving) as much as it demonstrates a discourse gap about the meaning of *achievement*. The children and their families have achieved as gang members, poor people, increasingly angry people, loving people, churchgoers, blue-collar workers, and people working to care for their children. These achievements intimidate, interrogate, and challenge much of what currently happens in school. The harder the school (as an agent of larger influential bodies) may push to keep these realities out, the larger the real gap grows. The more willing a school may be to welcoming the realities of the lives of students and their families, embracing those realities as the roots of what should happen in school, the greater the possibilities for school to be a meaningful place. It is in such meaningful contexts, the incubators of counterportraits, that authentic learning may take place, writing spaces may be composed, and hard times may be interrogated with a view towards better times.

The strength and power of the official portrait is apparent in the language that is found within that portrait. I responded to one instance of such language in one of my journal entries after I first heard some teachers discuss the impossibility of dedicating time to students working on biographies because of the need for *fidelity* to the reading program. I wrote:

> What the hell is it with 'fidelity' to a program? I thought fidelity was about sexual commitment and intimacy, not about dedication to a reading or writing program. Here's what the thesaurus in this computer offers as synonymous with 'fidelity': loyalty, faithfulness, reliability, trustworthiness, dependability, devotion, commitment, and conformity. I would argue that *conformity* is a rather remote synonym but the only one that makes sense in the context of a 'relationship' with a literacy program. And I wonder if a teacher does not follow the program with fidelity—if she is an infidel—can the teacher or the program file for a divorce? I know that teachers are being told that infidelity is punishable because it is a form of insubordination, which can lead to job termination.

Fidelity suggests sustained commitment and caring, things in which teachers pride themselves. Metaphorically (Lakoff & Johnson, 2003), linking intimacy and a reading program is a way of coercing teachers into compliance and being vehicles of complicity in the damage such programs do. The use of *fidelity* is a frame—an idea linked to a deeply held belief—that suggests no caring teacher would want to carry the weight of having caused the cognitive and emotional upheaval that accompanies a curricular divorce. The frame suggests that departing from the scripted program is departing from the sacredness of a relationship. *Divorce* suggests and carries the weight of another failure, coupled with the already-present frame of failing as a teacher of content as evidenced by failure on high-stakes tests. That other failure is the failure of some kind of intimate relationship, something sacred between teacher and student. Teacher agency is limited except when brave teachers understand their position and choose to act upon it, something typically done in unofficial ways beyond the borders of standardized curriculum. Fidelity (and fear) trumped the commitments, bravery, strength, demands, thinking, trust, honesty, and truthfulness associated with counterportrait work.

Agency and Responsibility in Partnerships

A redefined partnership between home and school began with the families as the children learned about their parents, relatives, and friends and shared their learning. In many schools, families are blamed for larger socioeconomic realities in which they live. The enmity between home and school is nothing new and was documented by Waller in 1932 (offered as one piece of evidence of the age of this tension):

> From the ideal point of view, parents and teachers have much in common, in that both, supposedly, wish things to occur for the best interests of the child; but, in fact, parents and teachers usually live in a condition of mutual distrust and enmity. Both wish the child well but it is such a different kind of well that conflict must inevitably arise over it. The fact seems to be that parents and teachers are natural enemies, predestined each for the discomfiture of the other. The chasm is frequently covered over, for neither parents nor teachers wish to admit to themselves the uncomfortable implications of their animosity, but on occasion it can make itself clear enough.
>
> (p. 68)

Partnerships with families are temporary and fragile because of the obvious reality that, at present, students disperse to different classrooms, teachers, and even schools at the end of a school year, fracturing the relationships they've formed and anticipating (or not) new ones. The cultivation of partnerships with families may require a school-wide effort coupled with a community-wide effort, things which are quite difficult in rural and economically poor schools.

The partnerships with preservice teachers and the Albuquerque Slam poetry team were also just beginning and are left to future work, perhaps siting a preservice program at MVE and bringing in the poets and other writers more regularly than our limited contact. The partnership with the district is not yet articulated, but one administrator at the district level asked that I present my work when it is finished, something that I will offer soon. The partnerships with chambers of commerce, business incubators, and other institutions that might support ideas for economic development also remain to be explored, but the need for these is clear.

Many of these partnerships suggest reaching into official forums, places in which the official portrait is composed. Entering such forums with dissent as one of the focal themes of the work may worry some of the stakeholders in these organizations. Partnerships are also political projects composed of individual subjectivities and the multiplicity of relationships that are possible. Slam poets love dissent, thriving on it as one source of their composing process. But businesses do not. Many families do not. Chambers of commerce do not. On the surface, we think of the *American Dream* as something within everyone's reach, but digging deeper and living alongside writers like the children at MVE reveal that dreams may turn out to be lies because of conflicts of interest, economics, racism, xenophobia, and a host of other conditions described in the preceding pages. Profit for one party but not the other cannot be the driving force. Partnerships must be mutually beneficial with no party held hostage, oppressed, or disenfranchised. Finding those willing to participate under these terms is our challenge, but it is the only way that all those involved will have legitimacy and true access.

Changing the Course of History

Approaching the end of a work of this nature, I wonder about its eventual influence and find myself conflicted, much the way Elie Wiesel seemed as *Night* (1958/2006) was first published. In the preface, he wrote:

> I am not so naive as to believe that this slim volume will change the course of history or shake the conscience of the world . . . . Books no longer have the power they once did . . . . Those who kept silent yesterday will remain silent tomorrow.
>
> (pp. xii–xiii)

The newer version also includes his acceptance speech for the Nobel Prize:

> As long as one dissident is in prison, our freedom will not be true. As long as one child is hungry, our life will be filled with anguish and shame. What all victims need above all is to know that they are not alone; that we are not forgetting them, that when their voices are stifled we shall lend them ours, that while their freedom depends on ours, the quality of our freedom depends on theirs . . . . Our lives no longer belong to us alone; they belong to all those who need us desperately.
>
> (p. 120)

There is such an interesting contrast in these two quotes. One seems to be about powerlessness and the other about power and responsibility. One is about little agency to do and the other is about acting on someone else's behalf. This pretty much articulates what it has been to write this book. Some days, it didn't seem like it would matter much. Other days, the urgency I felt in getting the students' voices and lives out to the larger world was about my freedom depending on theirs and my life not belonging to me alone, but to the quiet and unarticulated desperation that I sensed many days driving to the school, working with the students, and talking with teachers, children, and families. The more that I learned about their lives, the greater the urgency of this book became as they reminded me of Taylor's (Taylor & Yamasaki, n.d.) work with children of trauma. The trauma here is a slow and nagging kind that steeps throughout a lifetime, and leaves me wondering about what such steeping will yield. I am not convinced that working in a classroom and considering teaching and learning as political projects for part of one day a week for a school year is sufficient time for young writers to understand the depth of their work and the intensity of their voices. Although Bell (1992) was referring to black people, his description fits many children at MVE:

> Black people are the magical faces at the bottom of society's well. Even the poorest whites, those who must live their lives only a few levels above, gain their self-esteem by gazing down on us. Surely they must know that their deliverance depends on letting down their ropes. Only by working together is escape possible. Over time, many reach out, but most simply watch, mesmerized into maintaining their unspoken commitment to keeping us where we are, at whatever cost to them or to us.

> (p. 89)

In the sixth grade, we spent much time building trust and in both classrooms we spent much time exploring how writing works and what it is for. These features of writers' lives are crucial and demand sustenance over time and space and were somewhat lost as the kids moved to the next year in school. Jesus was failing every subject in seventh grade at the time of this writing. Verdad moved to a different town and school after her father's suicide. But mostly I've lost them, lost contact because they are emerging as middle school students who, in sixth grade, already behaved like high school students. They explored their sexuality, relationships, and the world as adolescents coming into their own. They grew up too fast in order to fit in. My life belongs to the children in this book and the growing number of immigrant and new or longtime citizen children like them. They are the children lost in the economic, literacy, legislated, corporate-based, and even spiritual poverties in our country and they are the ones that we must increasingly fear because they are smart and they have less and less to lose.

The children's sense of agency as authors involved them in composing counterportraits that inspired them as writers, strong individuals, family members, and people who have brains "with words." Still, their futures remain the true test of our work together. To some degree, we were NCLB outlaws, writing beyond the margins of an oppressive and repressive legislated context. Therein may rest some hope. The children knew we were doing things that were not previously done in school during their school lifetimes. We weren't moving to the next level of a prescribed and very linear curriculum, rather we appropriated *curriculum*, using time in school in new-to-us ways that involved understanding through naming.

> Naming things, breaking though taboos and denial is the most dangerous, terrifying, and crucial work. This has to happen in spite of political climates or coercions, in spite of careers being won or lost, in spite of the

fear of being criticized, outcast, or disliked. I believe freedom begins with naming things. Humanity is preserved by it.

(Ensler, 2006, p. 64)

We explored, interrogated, and named things as a way of composing better times by writing, preserving, or carving out a piece of humanity during hard times. We did that by working at the borders of Discourses (Gee, 2000–2001) with an eye towards other possibilities. We initiated something that became part of their minds and experience (Dewey, 1938), upon which they will draw when conditions allow or the need arises with an urgency that forbids silence. Counterportraits change who we are, what we know, how we come to know, and what we do with our knowledge, and, as such, they are a part of the power shift that constitutes a larger shift towards a more just world.

Microeducational Economies

I opened this book with a brief discussion of Yunus' (2006) work with economically poor individuals in very small spheres of influence. Loaning a woman the equivalent of a few US dollars to purchase a cow allowed her to feed her family better, sell extra milk and milk products, and repay the loan. This entrepreneurial activity by one woman may not shift the world, but it is the work of hundreds of such small spheres that may. The work of each woman as a family member most certainly did shift those individuals' quality of life. Paralleling the work of Yunus, perhaps we as teachers and researchers along with children and families will enhance the educative (Dewey, 1938) lives of children by working similarly in our local places, cultivating hybrid spaces that influence the quality of lives in those locales, at first, and then reaching more official forums as legitimate ways to teach and learn. Yunus didn't begin as a Nobel Prize winner; he took many years and so must we. It took a long time to reach the levels of academic and scholastic poverty in which many poor, diverse, English language learning children are going to school. It will take us years to get out and it is time to begin, for some, and to continue and renew the efforts of others.

The fifth and sixth grade students' words and worlds were shifted and as such work is carried out in locales across the globe, we might expect a shift in the official portrait because the very nature of legitimacy could change. We need to follow Yunus' model by building trust in the communities in which we work, gaining credibility, and looking beyond the hostage situation in which high-stakes tests and restrictive curriculum place teachers and their students. We need to show families our faith and trust in them, as Yunus did and does. We need to find or take small (almost unnoticeable) loans of cognitive and emotional capital—creating microeducational economies paralleling Yunus' work—and invest that in the children we teach, our research, and ourselves and we need to show them and ourselves the gains that are made. The children at MVE did not make adequate yearly progress, but for teachers, future teachers, principals, and their families to be moved (an inertial force) by the children's writing makes a difference (a profit) in the quality of their lives and their senses of agency, at least for some moments of a school year. That's the local payoff and it was a beginning of the microeducational economy in which we invested time, energy, and truth. One possible next step is involving the children, teachers, researchers, and future teachers in projects that grow from what we learn in doing counterportraiture work. For example, Consuelo's mom wants to earn her GED, but is worried about safety at the site at which the program is run. Working to understand her feelings means changing the portrait of Consuelo's mom as someone that misses many classes to a counterportrait in which, for example, a group of students might engage in a needs assessment of such a specific problem and then search for ways to address the needs they identify. The reading and writing inherent in such work would be a context in which to learn literacy in a way consistent with Freire's (1970c) ideas about literacy teaching and learning. The power of Freire's and Yunus' work is that they listened to their contexts, incorporated individuals from those contexts in assessing needs, and acted with those individuals to influence small spheres.

I end this book in the same place I started, thinking of the work of Yunus, but with a deeper understanding of the threats that are involved when we seek to disrupt others' profiting, the potentials that are diminished when profiteers flourish, and wondering about the democratic possibilities in a country that has allowed teaching to deteriorate into a search for secret places in which teachers can teach what students need by supporting them in finding and telling their truths. The countries following Yunus' model are saturated with corruption at the local levels as loan sharks keep people in debt for life. Yunus' model disrupted that and now there are banks that follow his lending model, marking a shift in the use of capital and the nature of investments. We need a shift from a high-stakes testing educational economy—one that consistently yields high risks to our cognitive, cultural, linguistic, emotional, and spiritual capital—to an educational economy in which multiplicities of capitals within a school and its communities are valued, engaged, and welcome as the points of origin of legitimate literacy activity.

Our work in the two classrooms was a literacy microeconomy with efforts rooted in the children's changing sense of agency within self, the classroom, their families, and beyond. We made a beginning, an initial investment—one that may be cultivated, but more likely will be bankrupted by a middle school model that historically excludes the kind of work we did. Yet the seeds of hope have been planted and the kernel of possibilities has been set in the minds of two classrooms of children. A tiny investment has been made, the work to disrupt the corrupt education economy in which some students attend school was somewhat influenced, and the yield remains to be seen.

Counterportraiture as Method/Method as Political Work

This appendix is an overview of the research methods I employed in this study. In Chapter 1, I explained how I gained access to the site. I also discussed the way that portraiture (Lawrence-Lightfoot & Davis, 1997) is used to present lives. Originally, I considered case study as a method (Merriam, 1998; Stake, 1995), but as the work progressed, I found that we were countering someone else's arguments about the children, their teachers, the school, and the community. I realized that I could not write a narrative (Clandinin & Connelly, 2000) that was not political because I finally understood that all texts and contexts are political. I wanted to develop a way of portraying lives in and out of school in some partnership with the *stuff* of the children's writing and knew their writing needed to be included as centrally and fully as possible, not simply represented. I wanted to include the stories behind their writing as well as the contexts in which they composed, so I invented counterportraiture as a method that is based upon the legitimation of multiple truths, particularly those in opposition to curricular, economic, social, psychological, cultural, and linguistic policies that perpetuate the concentration of power in the hands and minds of some at the expense of others.

Relying on Dyson's (1997) idea of "official curriculum," and using that as a part of the semantic relationship of a domain analysis (Spradley, 1980), I reached the idea of 'official portrait.' Fitting demographic and assessment data into this analysis was relatively swift because of the hard nature of numbers and the weight that they carried (spheres of influence came out of that notion of weightiness, meaning influence and inertia within and across contexts). The next analysis involved using unofficial portraits in opposition to the official portrait. I decided to use 'the' official portrait, rather than a plural form, because the oneness of the official portrait felt like a massive omnipresence that influenced each day's work, thinking, and ethos at Mesa Vista Elementary. Again, using domain analysis (Spradley, 1980), I found instances in the data that demonstrated work in opposition to the official portrait. Some of these were conscious efforts, as when Barbara made certain decisions, and other instances were intuitive or child-identified, such as when Esperanza found her brain with words.

The creation of an official/unofficial dichotomy oversimplified what I was finding at the school, so I moved to the idea of counterportraits, in the plural form, as a way of bringing forward the individuality of each child, each group, each classroom, each family etc. At this point, portraiture resonated with the artistic metaphor whence it came as I pictured one canvas with the official portrait and multiple canvases (and eventually films or movies because they are more suggestive of ongoing action and change) of counterportraits. The themes that I presented in Chapter 11 are rooted in the tensions between official and counterportraits.

I followed traditions of qualitative research, taking field notes at the site and elaborating those as soon as I could, rarely ever exceeding a 24-hour time period between the visit and the elaboration (Spradley, 1980). I read and reread the notes in search of teaching ideas (that the teachers or I might present or discuss with the children or amongst ourselves), teachable moments taken or missed, and to gain insights into the students' thinking about themselves as writers, their actual writing, and the ways in which they composed and discussed their writing. The focus on these particular ideas emerged from constant comparison (Glaser, 1965; Glaser & Strauss, 1967) of elaborated field notes and photocopies of students' work. I typed the sixth graders' writing and returned it to them, along with their originals, when I returned the following week. I wrote responses to their writing and kept copies of those for analysis as well. I copied participating students' computer files, including their interviews as sound files, as part of the data set. Sadly, some of the students' files including their biographies and other writings were lost because of technological glitches or intentional deletion.

During the elaborations, I had "aha!" moments that would serve in the organization of chapters and support the location of themes. These ideas were rooted in the ongoing analysis and recorded in a separate word processing document. Further, there were times when emotions welled up and I needed to vent. At these moments, I wrote "observers' comments" (Bogdan & Biklen, 1982) within the flow of the elaborated field notes, denoted them with "begin OC" when I started and "end OC" at the conclusion of the venting. During our lunch sessions, I discussed categories (Glaser, 1965) and themes that were emerging and asked the teachers for their responses and thoughts. They clarified things I didn't understand, filled in details about the community (especially Roberta), and we argued about our perceptions about writing events and pieces of writing. My notes on these sessions were treated as field notes and were used to place tension upon the categories I identified as I analyzed the data.

When the school year ended, I catalogued the entire data set. Each set of raw and elaborated notes was put into a separate folder that also contained any writing that the students had completed that day (photocopies and/or my typed versions). As we moved into the biography part of the year, the students were much more active as partners in data collection. I purchased the digital voice recorders so that they could tape each other and eventually the focus adult of their biography. The fifth grade students worked with their teachers (Barbara and Roberta) and me to develop interview questions, initially for each other and then for their adult-focus. The sixth graders and I developed interview questions for their biographies of each other and Roberta and Patia developed their questions for adults when I was not present. Portions of some of these interviews were translated (if they were in Spanish) and transcribed by the students for use in their biographies. I transcribed other sections for use in understanding the decisions the students made about what to include in the biographies they wrote. All of this data was included in what was catalogued.

The children's writing was a large part of the database and I originally analyzed the pieces by considering their lengths, conventions, and other fairly traditional ways of examining writing. I abandoned this line of analysis and began using the content and contexts (spaces) of their writing to confirm and disconfirm the categories, and eventually themes, that I was finding. I looked for shifts to student-identified truths, such as being afraid that their father was going to get shot, their parents might divorce, or that their grandmother was going to die. I studied truthfulness by interrogating children's willingness to present themselves and those that they loved over the course of the year. I looked for writing strategies that would provide opportunities for them to compose in truthful ways, and I compared their pieces over time, not only to themselves but also to each other as a way of understanding each classroom context as a place to write and the ongoing presentation of truths. I certainly was witness to the unevenness of the presentation of truths, such as the otter pop and pickle experience in Chapter 7.

The categories that I found posed a challenge in terms of locating relevant and informing literatures. Finding Goffman was very important because of his work on relationships and institutions; Foucault was also useful in this regard. I was inspired by the work of other researchers whose endeavors are consistent with counterportraiture because they interrogate the official portrait of the participants in their studies. Gutiérrez et al.'s (1997) work with spaces helped me develop categories for the students' writing by considering first, second, and third space evidence. Rogers' (2003) use of critical discourse analysis helped me examine the ways in which power is perpetuated in institutional settings, Valdés' (1996) elaboration of caring and respect in the classroom and community, and Anzaldúa's (1999) passionate explication of life at the borders helped in the construction of 'counter' as a legitimate method and political activity. I chose to use each chapter's literature as a lens for what I found chronologically over the course of the year in ever-deepening layers of analysis. It was in looking across the chapters that I found the themes presented in Chapter 11. Counterportraiture demands the use of multiple literatures (Willis et al., 2008) as a way of interrogating borders between those literatures and to shed light on the taken-for-granted, assumed, and appropriated borders between official and counter.

I will state the obvious here: method is political work. Each part of it, from gaining entry into the site to collecting, from analyzing to writing, all of it is political as the work to understand and re-present (Mortenson & Kirsch, 1996) is undertaken. Language and culture are political because they are inextricable from power, position, and prestige. I knew I was and still am an outsider to the community of children, their teachers, and their families. I regretted that I couldn't know the children in Spanish, yet the work was important because it helped the children understand that they were living translated lives and supported their interrogation of "multiple discourses in their lives" (Martínez-Roldán & Fránquiz, 2009, p. 338) in a way that honored language, culture, and history (Nieto, 2002). Our discussions about borders and living in two worlds sometimes folded into Spanish because that was the only way they could explain to each other what they needed to say. Our discussion of English as a language of power at the present time in the US grew out of our study of the Martínez (1991) poem (Chapter 2). The struggle in this process was with the idea that one language is more powerful and carries greater prestige in the US than another. This topic re-emerged when we prepared to present to the largely monolingual English speaking preservice teachers. The struggle for language dominance was not resolved in this work, but it was named, made public, and brought to consciousness. Monolingual teachers may struggle to access some of the cultural capital (Bourdieu & Passeron, 1990) that diverse and multilingual children bring to school, a condition true for some researchers, too. In contrast, it remains easier for a government to view the children as deficient or not proficient, rather than understand the struggles some students face at the borders between languages, cultures, and the possibilities for learning. This is an issue for the method discussion because working across languages means working across cultures, which means that certain things are misunderstood—by me. For that, I apologize and emphasize that these interpretations are mine alone. Method is sociolinguistic, cultural, cross-cultural, and advocative—all facets of its political nature.

In Chapter 11, I discussed partnerships as ways of helping teachers, children, and schools have a sense of agency. My partnership with MVE allowed the teachers to carve out some space for a study of children's writing with those children as partners in the journey. Partnership in research that is action- and classroom-based inquiry is also part of the political nature of counterportraiture. The teachers and I, sometimes with the children, engaged in lofty discussions of what we were finding, learning, and doing. Our partnership also buffered some of what the teachers experienced in the larger school context, a political activity with me as a shield in an effort to avoid having "the research-practice connection . . . appropriated by those whose purpose is to control teachers and teaching" (Richardson, 1989, p.16). Our work was a vehicle to deviate from the prescriptions and the method was political activity when it was enacted in this capacity.

Inherent in the method were questions of consciousness because mine was increasing along with the students' and teachers'. Making our learning conscious and being articulate about it was a process to which I was open, sharing my understandings and searching for the understandings of others. Quite often we were engaged in the work—writing, sharing, and thinking—and didn't stop to engage in the metapolitical work that a year of analysis afforded me. However, in future work such activity will remain more central as we work, understand our work, and study the impact of the work on ourselves and others more systematically as a way of deepening agency.

There are methodological implications of this study and I was relieved to find support for these in other scholars' work (Cherland & Harper, 2007; Moje, 2002; Willis et al., 2008). Understanding that research is political work means that we need an increasing cognizance of how the work shifts power so that the marginalized and disenfranchised are heard. For example, the themes of "purposes of school, the search for joy, and the spirit of the child," need to resonate with our research in schools and communities. We need to consider the deeper purposes in operation at the site and how we might interrogate and challenge them as part of our work. We have to work to understand the multiple layers of contexts within which the site exists. In the case of the MVE community, at the end of the study I was just beginning to learn about the Spanish land grant activity within the area (Dunbar-Ortiz, 2007) and how that led to some of the present configurations of land ownership. Such historical analyses are important because their effects are still being lived and felt today. Counterportraiture is a sociopolitical, economic, psychological, transactional (Rosenblatt, 1978), historical, and even spiritual method employed while it was being developed in this study. The research activity, from meeting the teachers through writing this report of our work, helped to further articulate the method as my own awareness of what we were doing and how we were doing it grew with each successive meeting with the teachers and the students. Counterportraiture is research that is action based because its very essence involves changing individual minds and thought collectives both locally and beyond. It is a way to collaboratively challenge, interrogate, and act upon the suffering inflicted by the official portrait.

Full Text of Some Biographies

The following biographies included extensive clipart and coloring of slides/pages, which were not included because of copyright and other technical issues. I regret that some of the children's work loses its intensity but celebrate the inclusion of their words. Most photographs are not included to protect confidentiality, a decision for which I assume full responsibility. I apologize to any young authors that wanted those included. The space between portions indicates a new slide/page. The grade level of the author is included after their name. — indicates names omitted for confidentiality. Biographies are separated by a line of asterisks.

Javier —
An Unknown Hero
By Estevan — [Fifth Grader]

To Javier — , a real hero
Copyright © 2007 Francis co.

Birth
Estevan Javier — was born on March, 29, 1962. His parents called him by his middle name.

As a Kid
He went to school like a normal boy until he quit in the 9th grade, because his family didn't have money to pay for school.

The U.S. Trip
He set off to the United States at age 16. He came to America with his brother in a van. He hid under the van's carpet when they passed the border because he didn't want them to not let him pass.

Texas
After that he went to Texas where Javier started to install carpet. He got his permanent residence card. Then a few years later he came back to Mexico for a while.

Love

One day he was driving and passed by a woman. It was love at first sight for both of them. They became pen pals and Javier headed back to the United States.

Marriage

He went back to Mexico to marry L— —. Both of them went to Denver, Colorado.

A Son

Nine months later they had their first son in Denver, Colorado. He was named after Javier.

Life

Javier kept installing carpet and working hard for his family. As he said, "I had always installed carpet and I'm going to die installing carpet."

The Trip

Years later Javier went to Philadelphia, Pennsylvania, to install more carpet and earn money for his family. Three months later, he went back to Denver, Colorado.

Another Son

A year later he had his second son in Brighton, Colorado. His name is — — .

Moving

A few months later Javier moved to [town], New Mexico.

A Good Person

Javier got his wife's permanent residence in November, 2006. Now L— is an American citizen.

A Hero

Javier works hard for his family. He may not be famous, but he is a hero for his wife and his son.

[Poem, see Chapter 7]

About the Author

Estevan was born in 1995, in Denver, Colorado. As he grew up he loved his dad. When his dad got his mom's residence Estevan thought his dad was a hero, so Estevan wrote this story.

****

A Boy in the Desert turns into a Hardworking Man!

By Chuck C— [Fifth Grader]

Page 2 © 2007
I dedicate this book to my dad.

Table of Contents [Lists the following slides' titles with page numbers.]

Eugene was born December 21, 1966.
He became a little boy in the desert with his homemade bow and arrow chasing snakes and rabbits.

In the Desert
Eugene spent most of his time riding his dirt bike or fixing it. With a family of six, Eugene had to do most of the work like mowing the lawn, watering the trees, and cleaning.

Got ya!
In school, my dad was the class clown. One time he had a plastic bag and blew it up and bang! The teacher ran out screaming.

Glued
Another time my dad super glued an apple to the teachers' desk.

Ouch!
Then my dad cut off the wings of some bees and put them into roses and gave them to his teacher and you can guess what happened, right?

Bang! Bang! Bang!
The funniest story was when a kid told on my dad so he put firecrackers on the bottom of the kid's chair and lit them and bang—the kid peed in his pants!

Suspended
The last story is when my dad got suspended and then climbed on the roof of the school and put smoke bombs in the vents and every one came out and saw him sitting there.

Ending
Eugene finally got married the second time after getting divorced. Now he's 40 years old and has 2 boys, a wife, 2 dogs, and a cat. He works as a locater of under ground utility lines. He still enjoys the outdoors.

All About the Author
Chuck was born in New Mexico. He was born on February 1, 1996.

He wants to be a cop when he grows up. His cousin Nick is his big hero. His favorite hobby is football and soccer. His favorite rappers are Akon, M&M, 50cent, Young Jock, and Nelly. Chuck has 2 dogs and 1 cat. He wants to go to Denver to play for the Denver Broncos. His artifacts are his four wheeler, Play Station 2, basketball court, and his stereo.

He went to Denver in 2005 for the biggest fan and the Broncos signed his book. He saw cheerleaders. He even hugged the cheerleaders. There were a lot of games in the new stadium. He played this game where you have to sit in a chair and make the football in a hole, but the chair moves. He played a football player and Chuck won him. Chuck was ten years old when he played him. He got pictures with the cheerleaders and the football players. He got his face painted orange, white, and blue. In back of his head, he got the logos.

****

The Life of a Mexican Child
Written by Marisol, — [Fifth Grader]

Dedication
I dedicate this book to my family, because they love me and because I love them, and because they always support me. Take care and I love you, loving family.

Table of Contents
[Lists the following slides' titles with page numbers.]

How it All Got Started
In the old times a child named Gregorio — was born. And as he grew up with all his brothers and sisters they began to not have enough money or enough toys to play with. Now it's time to go deeper into 'The Life of a Mexican Child.'

My dad's life was exciting, but it was too big of a family, so they didn't have enough money to buy what they wanted. They had enough food on the table and enough clothes but no extras, so it was good in a bad way. When they couldn't get toys they would build their own toys.

A Sad Moment
When my dad was still a little kid he had three sisters that died. My dad's sisters were three or four years old when they died. Two of my dad's sisters were older than him and one sister was younger than my dad.

Remembering
The first thing that my dad can remember when he was a kid is Christmas because that was the only time they would get toys.

When He Took an Interest in Horses
My dad took an interest in horses when he was a little kid because he used to have horses. Since his brothers and sisters liked horses too what they did for fun was race horses.

His Heroes
My dad's hero will always be his dad because he loves what his dad did for him when he was a little kid like helping him when he couldn't do something, or when my dad couldn't spell a word right my grandpa would help him. His other heroes are cowboys because he admires how they ride and rope.

What He Can Remember
My dad's favorite moments are when my family gets together and has fun and talks and gets along with everybody and shares whatever we have.

His Goal
What my dad always dreamed of being when he grew up was a veterinarian, but as he grew older as an adult his goal didn't come true. His other goal was to save enough money to buy a car of his own and he did get a car of his own.

His Favorite Color and Favorite Holiday
My dad's favorite color—and still is his favorite color—is blue, and his favorite holiday—and still is his favorite holiday—is Christmas.

He Was Never a Bad Kid
In my dad's entire life he was not a bad kid, well not that he can remember. Back in the neighborhood where he lived was good because there were lots of kids my dad's age and they would have a ton of fun.

His Regret
My dad did not finish school. He dropped out in the 12th grade. The regret that he most hates was not finishing school.

Another Thing He Can Remember
One other thing that he can remember is that they used to go fishing and used to go to the state fair once in awhile, not every time but once in awhile.

The Best Adventure
The best adventure my dad has been on was on a horseback trail ride, and they went to places they had not gone to. "It was pretty exciting to let the wind go through my hair when it was as hot as the sun," said my dad about their riding adventure. When my dad and his sisters and brothers went on the horseback trail ride, my dad and his brothers and sisters followed the train tracks, and it took them somewhere they had not been to in their lives.

Where He Was Born when It was His Birthday
My dad's birthday is on May 9, 1957. My dad was born in Chihuahua, Mexico, and he will be half a century on May 9, 2007.

My Dad's First Job
My dad's first job was here in the United States in a print factory for telephone books.

His Favorite Dog and His First Gift
My dad likes Rottweilers because they are smart and sensitive dogs. My dad says they're good watch dogs. My dad's first pet was a German Shepherd and he liked it because it was a gift.

His Favorite Song and Where He's Been To
My dad's favorite song is *Una Pagina Mas* which mean's, "One More Page." My dad is an adventurous person and likes to go to a lot of places like almost all around the United States. He can start from New York and name all the states between Canada and New York. The states my dad has lived in are Texas, Illinois, and in New Mexico because of his job.

How He Came to America and How He Met My Mom
My dad came to America when he was 18. He had been in America before, but the last time they walked about 7 weeks to get to a place in Texas.

My dad met my mom in Chihuahua, Mexico, and that was about 15 years ago. They met because my uncle's girlfriend introduced my mom to my dad.

I Hear Wedding Bells
Gregorio and G— got married by law not by church, and had three beautiful children. G— is the oldest. She was born in 1992. Then four years after that Marisol was born in 1996. When Marisol was 1 year old the youngest came along who is Gregorio Jr., and he is 9 years old.

Booooooooom . . . My Dad Was Shot And What He Likes About His Life

When my dad and my mom were barely married, and still didn't have children, my dad got shot in the stomach.

The things that my dad likes about his life are: the family he has, where he lives, where he works, and the animals that he has.

What My Dad is Afraid Of
My dad is afraid that we are going to leave him alone and never come and visit him or anything, but we all said, "that is never ever gonna happen because we love you and my mom with all our hearts." All his family gave each other a big hug.

Ending
And that is the life of a Mexican child which is my loving dad.

Best Father Ever
[See poem in Chapter 8]

All About the Author

Marisol began her life in Albuquerque in the Presbyterian hospital. When she was a baby she lived with her mom's friend, a very close friend. Marisol has one brother and one sister. Their names are Gregorio Jr. and G—. She also has one mom and one dad. Their names are G— and Gregorio. Her sister G—, likes to play around with them.

Marisol likes basketball, soccer, volleyball, tennis, a little bit of football, and any sport that could make her run. She wants to be a scientist, basketball player, soccer player, and a lawyer. She wants to be a scientist because a scientist has fun doing experiments. She wants to be a basketball player because she's been playing for three years, and she wants to play more because it's pure fun. She wants to be a soccer player because she likes running and she likes to be healthy. And the last thing she wants to be is a lawyer because they get good money.

Marisol's afraid of people when they escape from jail because they can go anywhere and maybe even to your house. She's also afraid of driving in the snow because when her mom is in a hurry she drives fast and when her sister is driving she gets frustrated and then she drives fast.

****

A Good Long Life
By Rosa [Fifth Grader]

Dedicated to my parents:
Nancy and Jon,
the best parents in the whole
world!!!!

☹ Copyright©2007 Rosa ☺
Table of Contents
[Lists the following slides' titles with page numbers.]

Birth
Jon was born on January 13, 1963, in — —.

The First Job
Jon's first job was cutting grass. He had to go to a lady's house and get the lawn mower and cut her grass, clean the yard up, and he would get $10. The lawn mower made a lot of noise, so he didn't have to listen to anything and just think about school and what he had to do.

Meet the Family
Jon has 2 brothers and 2 sisters. His brothers are Anthony, Andy, and his sisters are Rosalynn and Patty.

Jon's Mother

Jon's mother's name is Mary Lou. She is a good mother to him. In the past few years she has been good to Jon 's children, Rosa and Michael. When they are sick and Jon's wife Linda can not take care of them, Linda will call Mary Lou to see if she is available to take care of Rosa or Michael, so Ms. Linda does not have to miss work.

Good Adventures

Jon's adventure was to jump bikes and find things to jump off of. He used to go on his dirt bike and go find a hill and find new tracks to go on. He liked to go and ride his bike to cool down or sit on a rock in the shade.

He had about 40 teachers in his school life. He liked the teachers that told interesting stories.

The Race Family

Linda, Jon, and Rosa love the number 20 car. Its sponsor is Home Depot. It is driven by Tony Stewart.

Dune Buggy

Sometimes Jon goes to the shop to watch TV when he is working on his dune buggy. He loves that car a lot. He made it out of another car he had got. But when it is winter, he can't drive the car, because he does not want the car to freeze up in the cold. Jon loves to go on bumps a lot in the summer. He has the car washed a lot because he goes to places he finds in the paper to show the car in the best car shows. It has a roll cage so we do not get hurt in a crash. Rosa helped Jon work on his car for two years.

Meet the Dogs

These dogs are well-trained to do a lot of things. They will help you take care of kids, because they will keep your kids amused. They will not fight other dogs. They will play rough with other dogs but they will not hurt them. Jon likes his dogs because they keep him company.

Bear

Jon had about 5 dogs that loved him. The first dog was Bear. Bear was a Saint Bernard mix. Bear was trained to be a good dog to Jon. When you opened the gate he would not get out of the gate, unless you said he could go out of the gate. He would not hurt you. If you left him outside of a building he would stay outside until you went out to get him.

Bunny

Bunny was the oldest dog in the family. She was a Lhaso Apso, with gray and black fur and long ears. Bunny and Bear were the best sister and brother ever.

Indy

Indy was a good dog. Linda found him when she was walking down a path by the road. She saw a shadow on the path. Linda looked at the object. It was a dog that made the shadow on the path Linda was walking on. Rosa and Michael were coming from school and saw the dog. Rosa saw the dog and said how cute that dog is. Linda said that we can keep it until we can find its owner. No one called so my dad said that we could keep it.

"We miss them very much and we would love to see them again."

—The voices of the people who love them very much. ☺

Doise [Doce]
Doise is a good and sometimes bad dog, because he will get under the gate or the fence, and when he gets out he will get chained up for the rest of the day so he will learn not to go out the gate again. He is a golden retriever and a chow mix. He has the purple tongue with some pink in it too. He has some black on the bottom of his ear. When Bear died we were worried that Bunny was going to be alone. So we went to the pound to find a dog for Bunny. My dad had just remembered that it was his 12th anniversary with Linda. He said that we can name him Doise (a Spanish name for 12). I said that is a good name for a dog, but we need to find a dog for that name. Then we found Doise in one of the cages in the back of the long room.

Tika
When Bunny died Doise was alone. We went to the pound where we got Doise. We saw a chow mix just like Doise but very brown. Tika was a good name because my mom saw the name in a book that she was reading. It was the first name in the book and Rosa said that was a good name for her.

The Army
Enlisted in the Army National Guard as a machinist in August,1990.

Served overseas in Kuwait, 1993, and again in Germany, 1994. Highest rank of E4 Specialist.

Honorable discharge March, 1996.

How He Saw Her
Upon separation from his first marriage, he went out for fun and spirits and found himself dancing the night with Linda. They agreed to have a dinner date to get to know each other and a bond was formed. He has been grateful and content since that moment.

Hobbies
Home yard landscapes
Custom fabrication and assembly
Automotive racing of all kinds (spectator & driver!)
Involved in Cub Scout and Boy Scout leadership
Metal art with the potential to be a career.

Career
24 years in the Welding/Fabrication. Involving 15 of those years supervision and past 3 years as mechanical design and computer drafting capabilities.

His career was fencing, produce processing plant, mobile high-tech units for government, race cars, aero space and Intel clean room equipment furnishings.

Jon's Poem
[See Chapter 8]

About the Author
Hey! Let me tell you about the most curious person. Her name is Rosa Kay. She has hazel eyes and red hair. She has been part of the girl scouts for six years (WOW!!!). She would like to be a race car driver when she grows up because her dad was once a race car driver. He won an award for the 5th place. Rosa has two brothers and one sister. They are M—, D— and B—. Her mom's name is Linda and she works at Mesa Vista Elementary as a teacher's assistant. Her dad, Jon, works at —. Furthermore, she has a great grandma, Nina, and lots of other relatives who love her!

****

My Favorite Grandpa, Robert D—
By Andres [Fifth Grader]

Dedicated to Mary
☹ Copyright© 2007 Andres ☺

The Table of Contents
[Lists the following slides' titles with page numbers.]

It's Just the Beginning
Robert D— was born June 2, 1948. He was hurt in the Vietnam War when he was 19. He was in a helicopter accident. He was cleaning the fans when his friends were filtering the helicopter and one of his friends punched the wrong button and the helicopter exploded on him.

His legs caught fire and his friends rolled him in dirt. When the fire went out, they rushed him to the hospital. His legs were fine but his shoulder was not. Now he has scars but he recovered from the accident.

How He Met His Wife
Robert met his wife, Mary Lou at his friend's house. Why was she there? She was there because she was my grandpa's friend's sister.

How He Met his Friends
My grandpa and his friend both went to school together. My grandpa grew up in San Jose. He used to go on top of a hill and play cowboys with his friends. He used to find arrowheads.

Figure A. 2.1 One of the many photos Andres brought in and scanned of his grandfather.

What He Built
My grandpa used to have a small house but then he made it into a big house. He built more than half his house with help from his dad.

His First Pet
His first dog was Casper. He named it Casper because his dad got it in Casper, Wyoming, and he loved it so much—even after it died.

What He Said He Will Do
He said when he finishes the garage, he will paint the 1994 Chevy pearl white and give it to me when I get my license, but he hasn't had time.

His Favorite Parts in Life
He has had a Siberian Husky from 1999 until now. He is allergic to cats. He loves his wife, kids, and grandkids very much.

His first job was as a dish washer in a restaurant. And he is very, very smart (to me any way). That is my grandpa's adventure in life.

Ol' Gramps
By Andres
Long legs
Wants massager
Fears war because it kills
"You guys shut up"
Gives time for me
Makes cool stuff
Very friendly
Thoughtful

About the Author
Andres was born 1996 in New Mexico. His hobby is playing guitar. He loves Chinese food. He has a great family and he loves to play board games.

****

My Mom's Life
By: Lorenzo [Sixth Grader] [Translation in brackets but original was only in Spanish.]

Chihuahua, México
Mi mama nació en un pueblito de Chihuahua, México que se llama Las Varas. Es un pueblito muy bonito pero muy falto de trabajos. Dice que le gustaria que existieran mas trabajos para una vida mejor. Su niñez fue muy bonita.

[My mom was born in a small town in Chihuahua, Mexico named Las Varas. It's a very pretty little town, but very short on jobs. She says that she would like it if there were more jobs for a better life. Her childhood was very nice.]

Una Vida Mejor
Ella vino pensando en sus hijos. Para buscar una vida mejor y porvenir mejor para ellos. Que ellos puedan tener un mejor progreso económicamente y para que tengan éxito y a que logren sus propósitos.

[A Better Life
She came (to the US) thinking about her children. To look for a better life and to better provide for them. That they could have better economic progress and that they would have success and that they achieve their goals.]

Cruzando
Ella vino ilegal a los Estados Unidos. Una de las experiencias que tuvo fue cuando cruzaron el río ya se andaban ahogando.

[Crossing
She came illegally to the United States. One of the experiences that she had
was when they crossed the river and were walking drowned (this may be
an expression that I don't really understand...but I picture them walking
up to their necks in water.).]

U.S.
Una de las razones principales por las que se vino a E.U es para progresar y
salir adelante con sus hijos. A ella le asusta la inseguridad en el mundo para
ella misma y sus hijos, "Porque hay mas maldad que bienestar" dice ella.

[US
One of the principal reasons that she came to the US is to progress and
come out ahead with her children. The insecurity in the world scares her
for herself and her children, "Because there is more badness than well-
being," she says.]

Vida Mejor
Ella piensa que la vida en EE.UU. ha sido bonita porque en México no hay
trabajos y aquí se puede salir adelante mas fácil.

[Better Life
She thinks that life in the US has been nice because in Mexico there are not
jobs and here one can get ahead more easily.]

Memoria Feliz
Su memoria mas feliz fue cuando se dio cuenta que estaba embarazada de
su hijo el más pequeño después de siete anos de no tener familia.

[Happy Memories
Her happiest memory was when she realized that she was pregnant with
her smallest son after seven years of not having family.]

Acerca Del Autor
Mi nombre es Lorenzo I— y yo soy el autor. A mi me gustan los caballos.
Mi materia favorita es matematicas. Yo siempre me paseo en los caballos.

[About the Author
My name is Lorenzo and I am the author. I like horses. My favorite subject
is math. I like to spend time with my horses.]

****

Alicia
By Corazon [Sixth Grader] [Translation in brackets but original was only
in Spanish.]

Mi mama Alicia R— nació en un pueblo junto a Chihuahua llamado
Delicias. Ella vino a los Estados Unidos porque le fue mal en su primer
matrimonio, y huyó moviéndose a [town] Nuevo México con su hermana.

[My mom Alicia R— was born in a town near Chihuahua named Delicias. She came to the United States because her first marriage went badly, and she moved to [town] New Mexico with her sister.]

Ella fue muy pobre hasta que se caso por primera vez pero dice que nunca cambiaria su niñez a cambio de cómo vive ahora.

[She was very poor until she got married the first time but she says that she would never change her childhood to change how she lives now.]

Un encuentro que tuvo con la inmigración fue pasando la frontera donde traía muchas cosas ilegales y unas de las principales fue una pata de halcón cuales animales están en extinción y tuvo que pagar 500 dólares de multa.

[One encounter she had with immigration was passing the border where many illegal things are brought and one of the first things was a hawk foot which are extinct (endangered) animals and she had to pay 500 dollars in fines.]

Dice haber trabajado con papeles chuecos en—donde hacen tortillas y productos de Nuevo México. Su primer experiencia al llegar a los Estados Unidos fue miedosa porque dice que tenia miedo que mis hermanos no tuvieran lo necesario para vivir en los Estados Unidos.

[She says that she had worked with false papers in [name of a factory] where they make tortillas and New Mexican products. Her first experience arriving in the United States was timid because she said that she was afraid that my brothers would not have what they needed in order to live in the United States.]

Pero aparte de todo mi mama dice que toda su vida ha sido muy especial.

[But apart from everything, my mom says that her whole life has been very special.]

The Storyboard Protocol

First read through your biography and circle or in some other way (highlighters, perhaps, or sticky notes) note which chunks are going to go on a page. Label them 1 (for first page after the introductory stuff, like title page), 2,3, etc. Then use the storyboard format to sketch your layout.

Storyboard Sheet # 1 This storyboard belongs to:_____

Sketch your cover, quick and simple without much detail.	What information do you want on your title page?	What information will you put on the next page (look at the page after a title page: copyright, publisher etc)?
See NOTE # 1 to learn what to do here.	See NOTE # 2 to learn what to do here.	See NOTE #3 to learn what to do here.
See NOTE #4 to learn what to do here.	See NOTE # 5.	NOTE: There are more blank boxes on subsequent pages.

NOTE # 1: Write a number 1 here to show which chunk of text you'll put here. Then make a note to yourself that you will either insert a photo (write which one) or a drawing. If you are doing a drawing, put a very rough sketch of it here (in the box, back up there!)

NOTE # 2 Write a number 2 here to show which chunk of text you'll put here. Then make a note to yourself that you will either insert a photo (write which one) or a drawing. If you are doing a drawing, put a very rough sketch of it here.

NOTE # 3: Write a number 3 here to show which chunk of text you'll put here. Then make a note to yourself that you will either insert a photo (write which one) or a drawing. If you are doing a drawing, put a very rough sketch of it here.

NOTE # 4: Write a number 4 here to show which chunk of text you'll put here. Then make a note to yourself that you will either insert a photo (write which one) or a drawing. If you are doing a drawing, put a very rough sketch of it here.

NOTE # 5: You get the idea . . . finish as many boxes as you need. Remember to insert the chunk number. Use as many storyboard sheets as you need to lay out your entire story.

For more storyboard space, use the second sheet because there are no directions because you know what to do. Remember to number the boxes to go with the chunk you'll cut and paste onto the page of your book.

Editorial Checklist
Biography Project Spring 2007

You will need to listen to your partner's piece twice. The first time you listen to the whole thing. The second time, you go one sentence at a time and you have to SEE the sentences as they are read (because writers sometimes think something is there, but it's not).

Part I

Listen to the whole piece. After you hear it, you read each question below out loud. Then discuss it with the writer before you answer it. If you sign your name on the first line, it means you think the author or poet has this whole part correct.

1   Does the piece make sense? _____

2   Is the piece in the right order? _____

3   Are you sure that every part of it makes sense? _____ (If you answer 'no' then go back and find the parts that don't so you can help your partner).

4   Does the piece tell a story? _____ (If you answer 'no' then help the author make it right.)

I listened to the piece and answered each question 'yes.' If I did not answer 'yes,' then I helped the writer fix the piece. By signing my name, I am showing that I did this work with my partner seriously, honestly, and kindly.

Listener signs here:_____

I worked with the person that signed above. By signing my name, I am showing that I listened to ideas, made any needed changes, and tried to improve my piece of writing.

Author/Poet signs here: _____

Part II This may be done with a new partner.

Now go sentence by sentence. The author or poet reads each sentence and you answer these questions after studying each sentence. You have to be close enough to see the sentences and comment on each one. Ask the questions for each sentence. Write the answers AFTER you have worked on every sentence.

1   Is each sentence a good sentence? _____ (If you answer 'no' then help the author make it right.)

2   Is the punctuation correct? _____ (If you answer 'no' then help the author make it right.)

3   Do the details describe what happened to the person? _____ (If you answer 'no' then help the author make it right.)

4   Did you check for grammar?_____Punctuation?_____ Capitalization?_____ Spelling?_____ (If you answer 'no' then help the author make it right.)

5   Is the title a good grabber? _____ (If not, help the author or poet develop a good one.)

6   Are photos used well?_____ Are sounds?_____

7   What else will help the author or poet? Give other ideas. List here any ideas you offered: _____
_____
_____
_____
_____

The editor signs here, after agreeing to this: I went through this piece very slowly and carefully with the writer. I tried to help make corrections and changes that would improve the piece.

Editor:_____

The author or poet signs here, after agreeing to this: I worked with the editor and tried to make corrections and changes so that my piece is improved and clearer.

Author or poet:_____

References

Alinsky, S. (1946). *Reveille for radicals.* Chicago: University of Chicago Press.

Allen, J. (1989). Introduction: Risk makers, risk takers, risk breakers. In J. Allen & J. Mason, (Eds.), *Risk makers, risk takers, risk breakers: Reducing the risks for young literacy learners* (pp. 1–16). Portsmouth, NH: Heinemann.

Allington, R. (2004). Setting the record straight: Federal officials are holding schools to impossible standards based on misinterpretations of research. In K. Goodman (Ed.), *Saving our schools: The case for public education saying no to 'no child left behind'* (pp. 210–217). Berkeley, CA: RDR Books.

Allington, R., & Woodside-Jiron. (1998). Thirty years of research in reading: When is a research summary not a research summary. In K. Goodman (Ed.), *In defense of good teaching: What teachers need to know about the reading wars* (pp. 143–157). York, ME: Stenhouse.

Altwerger, B. (Ed.). (2005). *Reading for profit: How the bottom line leaves kids behind.* Portsmouth, NH: Heinemann.

Annie E. Casey Foundation. (2007). Retreived on September 17, 2007, from http://www.aecf.org.

Anzaldúa, G. (1999). *Borderlands/La Frontera: The new mestiza* (3rd edition). San Francisco: Aunt Lute Books.

Applebee, A. (1978). *The child's concept of story: Ages two to seventeen.* Chicago: University of Chicago Press.

Atwell, N. (1998). *In the middle.* Portsmouth, NH: Boynton/Cook.

Au, K. (1993). *Literacy instruction in multicultural settings.* Belmont, CA: Wadsworth/Thompson Learning.

Augusto, C., Allen, R. L., & Pruyn, M. (Eds.). (2006). *Reinventing critical pedagogy.* Lanham, MD: Rowman & Littlefield.

Bakhtin, M. (1981). Discourse in the novel. In C. Emerson & M. Holquist (Eds.), *The dialogic imagination: Four essays by M. Bakhtin* (pp. 259–422). Austin, TX: University of Texas.

Bakhtin, M. (1984). *Rabelais and his world.* Bloomington, IN: Indiana University Press.

Behar, R. (1993). *Translated woman: Crossing the border with Esperanza's story.* Boston: Beacon Press.

Belenky, M., Bond, L., & Weinstock, J. (1997). *A tradition that has no name.* New York: Basic Books.

Bell, B., Gaventa, J., & Peters, J. (Eds.). (1990). *We make the road by walking: Conversations on education and social change, Myles Horton and Paulo Freire.* Philadelphia: Temple University Press.

Bell, D. (1992). *Faces at the bottom of the well: The permanence of racism.* New York: Basic Books.

Benson, C., & Christian, M. S. (2002). *Writing to make a difference: Classroom projects for community change.* New York: Teachers College Press.

Berliner, D., & Biddle, B. (1995). *The manufactured crisis: Myths, frauds, and the attack on America's schools.* Reading, MA: Addison-Wesley.

Bloome, D. (1983). Reading as a social process. *Advances in Reading/Language Research, 2,* 165-195.

Bogdan, R., & Biklen, S. (1982). *Qualitative research for education: An introduction to theory and methods.* Boston: Allyn and Bacon.

Bomer, R. (2007). The role of handover in teaching for democratic participation. In K. Beers, R. Probst, & L. Reif (Eds.), *Adolescent literacy: Turning promise into practice* (pp. 303–310). Portsmouth, NH: Heinemann.

Bomer, R., & Bomer, K. (2001). *For a better world: Reading and writing for social action.* Portsmouth, NH: Heinemann.

Bourdieu, P., & Passeron, J. (1990). *Reproduction in education, society, and culture* (2nd ed.). London, UK: Sage.

Bracey, G. (2003). *On the death of childhood and the destruction of public schools: The folly of today's education policies and practices.* Portsmouth, NH: Heinemann.

Calkins, L. (1994). *The art of teaching writing.* Portsmouth, NH: Heinemann.

Cambourne, B. (1984). Language, learning, and literacy. In A. Butler & J. Turbill (Eds.), *Towards a reading-writing classroom* (pp. 5–10). Rozelle, Australia: Primary English Teaching Association.

Carger, C. (1996). *Of borders and dreams: A Mexican-American experience of urban education.* New York: Teachers College Press.

Cherland, M., & Harper, H. (2007). *Advocacy research in literacy education: Seeking higher ground.* Mahwah, NJ: Lawrence Erlbaum.

Christensen, L. (1994). Whose standard? Teaching standard English. In B. Bigelow, L. Christensen, S. Karp, B. Miner, & B. Peterson (Eds.), *Rethinking our classroom: Teaching for equity and justice* (pp. 142–145). Milwaukee, WI: Rethinking Schools.

Christensen, L. (2000). *Reading, writing, and rising up: Teaching about social justice and the power of the written word.* Milwaukee WI: Rethinking Schools.

Christensen, L. (2008). Putting out the linguistic welcome mat: Honoring students' home languages builds an inclusive classroom. *Rethinking Schools, 23(1),* 19–23.

Clandinin, D. J., & Connelly, F. M. (2000). *Narrative inquiry: Experience and story in qualitative research.* San Francisco: Jossey-Bass.

Clark, G. (1990). *Dialogue, dialectic, and conversation: A social perspective on the function of writing.* Carbondale and Edwardsville, ILL: Southern Illinois University Press.

Clarke, L. (2005). A stereotype is something you listen to music on: Navigating a critical curriculum. *Language Arts, (83)2,* 147–157.

Coles, G. (2000). *Misreading reading: The bad science that hurts children.* Portsmouth, NH: Heinemann.

Coles, G. (2003). *Reading the naked truth: Literacy, legislation, and lies.* Portsmouth, NH: Heinemann.

Comber, B. (2001). Classroom explorations in critical literacy. In B. Comber & A. Simpson (Eds.), *Negotiating critical literacies in classrooms* (pp. 90–102). Mahwah, NJ: Erlbaum.

Crawford, J. (2008). *Advocating for English learners: Selected essays.* Clevedon, UK: Multilingual Matters Ltd.

Damico, J. S. (2005). Evoking hearts and heads: Exploring issues of social justice through poetry. *Language Arts, (83)2*, 137–146.

Delpit, L. (1988). The silenced dialogue: Power and pedagogy in educating other people's children. *Harvard Educational Review, 58(3)*, 280–298.

Delpit, L. (1995). *Other people's children: Cultural conflict in the classroom.* New York: The New Press.

Dewey, J. (1938). *Experience and education.* New York: Collier Books, Macmillan.

Draper, S. (1999). *Romiette and Julio.* New York: Simon Pulse.

Dunbar-Ortiz, R. (2007). Roots of resistance: A history of land tenure in New Mexico. Norman: University of Oklahoma Press.

Dyson, A. (1997). *Writing superheroes: Contemporary childhood, popular culture, and classroom literacy.* New York: Teachers College Press.

Dyson, A. (2001). Relational sense and textual sense in a U.S. Urban classroom: The contested case of Emily, girl friend of a Ninja. In B. Comber & A. Simpson (Eds.), *Negotiating critical literacies in classrooms* (pp. 3–17). Mahwah, NJ: Lawrence Erlbaum Associates.

Dyson, A. (2003). *The brothers and sisters learn to write: Popular literacies in childhood and school cultures.* New York: Teachers College Press.

Edelsky, C. (1996). *With literacy and justice for all: Rethinking the social in language education.* Bristol, PA: Taylor & Francis.

Edelsky, C. (Ed.). (1999). *Making justice our project: Teachers working toward critical whole language practice.* Urbana, Ill: National Council of Teachers of English.

Elbow, P. (1981). *Writing with power: Techniques for mastering the writing process.* Oxford: Oxford University Press.

Ensler, E. (2006). The power and mystery of naming things. In J. Allison & D. Gediman (Eds.), *This I believe: The personal philosophies of remarkable men and women* (pp. 62–64). New York: Henry Holt.

Espada, M. (1994). *Poetry like bread: Poets of the political imagination.* Willimantic, CT: Curbstone Press.

Filbrandt, T. (1999). Poetry and transformation. *Primary Voices 8(2)*, 11–18.

Fine, M. (1996). Silencing in Public Schools. In B. Power & R. Hubbard (Eds.), *Language development: A reader for teachers* (pp. 243–254). Englewood Cliffs, NJ: Merrill/Prentice Hall.

Flurkey, A., & Meyer, R. (Eds.). (1994). *Under the whole language umbrella: Many cultures, many voices.* Urbana, Ill: National Council of Teachers of English; Bloomington, IN: Whole Language Umbrella.

Foucault, M. (1970). *The order of things: An archaeology of the human sciences.* New York: Pantheon.

Foucault, M. (1972a). *The archaeology of knowledge and the discourse on language.* New York: Pantheon.

Foucault, M. (1972b). *Power/knowledge: Selected interviews and other writings, 1972–1977.* New York: Pantheon.

Frankl, V. (1978). *The unheard cry for meaning: Psychotherapy and humanism.* New York: Touchstone.

Freidberg, J. (Writer/Producer/Director). (2005). *Granito de arena.* United States: Corrugated Films.

Freire, P. (1970a). The adult literacy process as cultural action for freedom. *Harvard Educational Review, 40(2)*, 205–225.

Freire, P. (1970b). Cultural action and conscientization. *Harvard Educational Review, 40 (3)*, 452–477.

Freire, P. (1970c). *Pedagogy of the oppressed.* New York: Seabury Press.

Freire, P. (1991). The importance of the act of reading. In B. Power & R. Hubbard (Eds.), *The Heinemann reader: Literacy in process,* (pp. 21–26). Portsmouth, NH: Heinemann.

Freire, P. (2005). *Teachers as cultural workers: Letters to those who dare to teach.* Bolder, CO: Westview.

Freire, P., & Macedo, D. (1987). *Literacy: Reading the word and the world.* South Hadley, MA: Bergin & Garvey.

Gandhi, M. (2005). *All men are brothers: Autobiographical reflections.* Compiled and edited by Krisna Kripalani. New York: Continuum.

Gardiner, M. (1993). Bakhtin's carnival: Utopia as critique. In D. Shepard (Ed.), *Bakhtin carnival and other subjects: Selected papers from the Fifth International Bakhtin Conference, University of Manchester, July 1991.* Critical Studies vol. 3, No. 2–vol. 4, No. 1–2. Amsterdam: Rodopi.

Gee, J. (2000–2001). Identity as an Analytic Lens for Research in Education. In W. Secada (Ed.), *Review of Research in Education, 25,* 99–125. Washington DC: American Educational Research Association.

Gee, J. (2006). *An introduction to discourse analysis: Theory and method.* New York: Routledge.

Gee, J., Hull, G., & Lankshear, C. (1996). *The new work order: Behind the language of the new capitalism.* Boulder, CO: Westview Press.

Geertz, C. (1973). *The interpretation of cultures.* New York: Basic Books.

Gilyard, K. (1996). *Let's flip the script: An African American discourse on language, literature, and learning.* Detroit, MI: Wayne State Press.

Giroux, H. (1992). *Border crossings: Cultural workers and the politics of education.* New York: Routledge.

Giroux, H., & McLaren, P. (1994). *Between borders: Pedagogy and politics of cultural studies.* New York: Routledge.

Gladwell, M. (2000). *The tipping point: How little things can make a big difference.* Boston: Little, Brown.

Glaser, B. (1965, Spring). The constant comparative method of qualitative analysis. *Social Problems,* Vol. 12, No. 4, 436-445.

Glaser, B., & Strauss, A. (1967). *The discovery of grounded theory: Strategies for qualitative research.* New York: Aldine De Gruyter.

Goffman, E. (1959). *The presentation of self in everyday life.* New York: Anchor Books.

Goffman, E. (1961). *Asylums: Essays on the social situations of mental patients and other inmates.* Chicago: Aldine.

Goffman, E. (1969). *Strategic interaction.* Philadelphia: University of Pennsylvania Press.

González, N. (2005). *I am my language: Discourses of women and children in the borderlands.* Tucson, AZ: University of Arizona.

Goodlad, J. I. (1984). *A place called school: Prospects for the future.* New York: McGraw-Hill.

Goodlad, J., Mantle-Bromley, C., & Goodlad, S. (2004). *Education for everyone: Agenda for education in a democracy.* San Francisco: Jossey Bass.

Goodman, K. (2006). *The truth about DIBELS: What it is: What it does.* Portsmouth, NH: Heinemann.

Goodman, K., Shannon, P., Freeman, Y., & Murphy, S. (1987). *Report card on the basal readers.* Katonah, NY: Richard C. Owen.

Goodman, Y., & Marek, A. (1996). *Retrospective miscue analysis: Revaluing readers and their reading.* Katonah, NY: Richard C. Owen.

Gramsci, A. (1992). *Prison notebooks* (J. Buttigieg & A. Callari, Trans.) New York: Columbia University Press.

Graves, D. (1991). *Build a literate classroom.* Portsmouth, NH: Heinemann.

Greene, M. (1995). *Releasing the imagination: Essays on education, the arts, and social change.* San Francisco: Jossey Bass.

Greene, M. (2000). The ambiguities of freedom. *English Education, 33(1),* 8–14.

Grumet, M. (1988). *Bitter milk: Women and teaching.* Amherst, MA: University of Massachusetts.

Guerra, J. (1998). *Close to home: Oral and literate practices in a transnational Mexicano community.* New York: Teachers College Press.

Gutiérrez, K., Baquedano-López, P., & Alvarez, H. (2001). Literacy as hybridity: Moving beyond bilingualism in urban classrooms. In M. Reyes & J. Halcón (Eds.), *The best for our children: Cultural perspectives on literacy for Latino students* (pp. 122–141). New York: Teachers College Press.

Gutiérrez, K., Baquedano-López, P., & Turner, M. G. (1997). Putting language back into language arts: When the radical middle meets the third space. *Language Arts, 74(5),* 368–378.

Gutiérrez, K., Rymes, B., & Larson, J. (1995). Script, counterscript, and underlife in the classroom: James Brown versus Brown v board of education. *Harvard Educational Review 65(3),* 445-471.

Hagood, M. (2002). Critical literacy for whom? *Reading Research and Instruction, 41(3),* 247–266.

Halliday, M. A. K. (1978). *Language as social semiotic: The social interpretation of language and meaning.* London: Edward Arnold.

Harjo, J. (1994). *The woman who fell from the sky: Poems.* New York: W.W. Norton.

Harjo, J., & Bird, G., with Blanco, P., Cuthand, B., and Martínez, V. (1997). *Reinventing the enemy's language: Contemporary native women's writings of North America.* New York: W.W. Norton.

Harste, J., Woodward, V., & Burke, C. (1984). *Language stories and literacy lessons.* Portsmouth, NH: Heinemann.

Harwayne, S. (2000). *Lifetime guarantees: Toward ambitious literacy teaching.* Portsmouth, NH: Heinemann.

Heath, S. B. (1983). *Ways with words: Language, life, and work in communities and classrooms.* New York: Cambridge University Press.

Hernstein, R. & Murray, C. (1996). *The bell curve: Intelligence and class structure in American life.* New York: Simon & Schuster.

Holland, D., Skinner, D., Lachicotte, W. & Cain, C. (1998). *Identity and agency in cultural worlds.* Cambridge, MA: Harvard University Press.

Hughes, L. (1969). *Black misery.* New York: Paul S. Eriksson, Inc. Retrieved September 23, 2006 from http://www.poetryfoundation.org/archive/poem.html?id=177021.

Jackson, P. (1968). *Life in classrooms.* New York: Hold, Rinehart and Winston.

John-Steiner, V. (2000). *Creative collaboration.* New York: Oxford University Press.

Jordan, W. (1996, December). Bringing college within reach: Critical interveners in the schooling of the poor. *Educational Researcher, 25(9),* 29–30.

Kahn, S. (1991). *Organizing: A guide for grassroots leaders.* Silver Spring, MD: National Association of Social Workers.

Karp, S. (2004). NCLB's selective vision of equity: Some gaps count more than others. In D. Meier and G. Wood (Eds.), *Many children left behind: How the No Child Left Behind Act is damaging our children and our schools* (pp. 53–65). Boston: Beacon Press.

Kidd, S. M. (2002). *The secret life of bees.* New York: Viking.

Kielburger, C. (1998). *Free the children: A young man fights against child labor and proves that children can change the world.* New York: Harper Collins.

Koch, K. and the students of P.S. 61 (1970). *Wishes, lies and dreams: Teaching children to write poetry.* New York: Chelsea House.

Kohl, H. (1991). *I won't learn from you: The role of assent in learning.* Minneapolis, MN: Milkweed Editions.

Kohl, H. (1998). *The discipline of hope: Learning from a lifetime of teaching.* New York: Simon & Schuster.

Kozol, J. (2007). Letters to a young teacher. *Phi Delta Kappan, 89(1),* 8–20.

Krashen, S. (1999). *Condemned without a trial: Bogus arguments against bilingual education.* Portsmouth, NH: Heinemann.

Krogness, M. (1995). *Just teach me, Mrs. K: Talking, reading, and writing with resistant adolescent learners.* Portsmouth, NH: Heinemann.

Kujunkzic, D. (1994). Review of D. Shepard (Ed.), Bakhtin carnival and other subjects: Selected papers from the Fifth International Bakhtin Conference. *Slavic and Eastern European Journal, 38(4),* 697–698.

Ladson-Billings, G. (1994). *The dreamkeepers: Successful teachers of African American children.* San Francisco: Jossey-Bass.

Lakoff, G. (2002). *Moral politics: How liberals and conservatives think (second edition).* Chicago: University of Chicago Press.

Lakoff, G., & Johnson, M. (2003). *Metaphors we live by.* Chicago: University of Chicago Press.

Lareau, A. (1989). *Home advantage: Social class and parental intervention in elementary education.* London, UK: Falmer.

Lave, J., & Wenger, E. (1991). *Situated learning: Legitimate peripheral participation.* New York: Cambridge University Press.

Lawrence-Lightfoot, S. & Davis, J. D. (1997). *The art and science of portraiture.* San Francisco: Jossey-Bass.

Lee, C. (2008). The centrality of culture to the scientific study of learning and development: How an ecological framework in education research facilitates civic responsibility. *Educational Researcher, 37(5),* 267–279.

Lemke, J. (1995). *Textual politics: Discourse and social dynamics.* Bristol, PA: Taylor & Francis.

Levine, A., & Nidiffer, J. (1996). *Beating the odds: How the poor get to college.* San Francisco: Jossey-Bass.

Lewis, C. (1999). The quality of the question: probing culture in literature-discussion groups. In C. Edelsky (Ed.), *Making justice our project: Teachers working toward critical whole language practice* (pp. 163–190). Urbana, Ill: National Council of Teachers of English.

Lewis, C. (2001). *Literacy practices as social acts: Power, status, and cultural norms in the classroom.* Mahwah, NJ: Erlbaum.

Lewis, C., Enciso, P., & Moje, E. (2007). *Reframing sociocultural research on literacy: Identity, agency, and power*. Mahwah, NJ: Lawrence Erlbaum.

Lewis, J., Jongsma, K. S., & Berger, A. (2005). *Educators on the frontline: Advocacy strategies for your classroom, your school, and your profession*. Newark, DE: International Reading Association.

Lewis, T., & Solórzano, E. V. (2006). Unraveling the Heart of the School-to-Prison Pipeline. In C. Augusto, R. L. Allen, & M. Pruyn (Eds.), *Reinventing critical pedagogy* (pp. 63–76). Lanham, MD: Rowman & Littlefied.

Lewison, M., Flint, A. S., & Van Sluys, K. (2002). Taking on critical literacy: The journey of newcomers and novices. *Language Arts 79(5)*, 382–392.

Lewison, M., Leland, C., & Harste, J. (2007). *Creating critical classrooms: K-8 reading and writing with an edge*. New York: Routledge.

Lincoln, A. (n.d.). Abraham Lincoln Quotes. Retrieved December 22, 2007, from http://www.brainyquote.com/quotes/quotes/a/abrahamlin107482.html.

Liston, D., & Zeichner, K. (1996). *Culture and teaching*. Mahwah, NJ: Lawrence Erlbaum Associates.

Lorde, A. (1984). The master's tools will never dismantle the master's house. Retrieved May 9, 2007, from http://lists.econ.utah.edu/pipermail/margins-to-centre/2006-March/000794.html.

Luke, A., O'Brien, J., & Comber, B. (2001). Making community texts objects of study. In H. Fehring & P. Green (Eds.), *Critical literacy*. Newark, DE: IRA/S. Australia: Australian Literacy Educators' Association.

Macedo, D., & Bartolomé, L. (1999). *Dancing with bigotry: Beyond the politics of tolerance*. New York: Palgrave.

Martínez, O. (1994). Chicano Borderlander in *Border people: Life and society in the U.S.-Mexico Borderlands* (pp. 116–117). Tucson: University of Arizona Press.

Martínez-Roldán, C. & Fránquiz, M. (2009). Latina/o youth literacies: Hidden funds of knowledge. In L. Christenbury, R. Bomer, & P. Smagorinsky (Eds.), *Handbook of adolescent literacy research* (pp. 323–342). New York: The Guilford Press.

McIntosh, P. (1990). *White Privilege: Unpacking the invisible knapsack*. Retrieved December 24, 2006, from Arizona State University site, http://mmcisaac.faculty.asu.edu/emc598ge/Unpacking.html.

McLaren, P. (2007). *Life in schools: An introduction to critical pedagogy in the foundations of education* (5th ed.). Boston: Pearson/Allyn and Bacon.

McQuillan, J. (1998). *The literacy crisis: False claims, real solutions*. Portsmouth, NH: Heinemann.

Mehan, H. (1982). The structure of classroom events and their consequences for student performance. In P. Gilmore & A. Glatthorn (Eds.), *Children in and out of school: Ethnography and education* (pp. 59–87). Washington, DC: Center for Applied Linguistics.

Meier, D., & Wood, G. (2004). *Many children left behind: How the No Child Left Behind Act is damaging our children and our schools*. Boston: Beacon Press.

Merriam, S. (1998). *Qualitative research and case study applications in education*. San Francisco: Jossey-Bass.

Meyer, R. (1996). *Stories from the heart: Teachers and students researching their literacy lives*. Mahwah, NJ: Lawrence Erlbaum Associates.

Meyer, R. (2001). *Phonics exposed: Understanding and resisting systematic direct intense phonics instruction.* Mahwah, NJ: Lawrence Erlbaum Associates.

Meyer, R. (2005). Invisible teacher/invisible children: The company line. In B. Altwerger (Ed.) (pp. 96–111). *Reading for profit: The commercialization of reading instruction.* Portsmouth: Heinemann.

Meyer, R. (2008/2009). Strategies for activism: Taking a stand. In K. M. Paciorek (Ed.), *Annual editions: Early childhood education* (pp. 28–31). New York: McGraw Hill.

Miedema, S. (1992). The end of pedagogy? A plea for concrete utopian acting and thinking. *Phenomenology + Pedagogy, (10),* 28–37.

Moje, E. (2002). Re-framing adolescent literacy research for new times: Studying youth as a resource. *Reading Research and Instruction, 41(3),* 211–227.

Moje, E. (2007). Developing socially just subject-matter instruction: A review of the literature on disciplinary literacy. In L. Parker (Ed.), *Review of research in education,* (pp. 1–44). Washington, DC: American Educational Research Association.

Moll, L., Amanti, C., Neff, D., & Gonzalez, N. (1992, Spring). Funds of knowledge for teachers: Using a qualitative approach to connect homes and classrooms. *Theory into Practice 31(1),* 132–141.

Mortenson, P., & Kirsch, G. (1996). *Ethics and representation in qualitative studies of literacy.* Urbana, Ill: National Council of Teachers of English.

Murray, D. (1985). Writing and teaching for surprise. *Highway One, 8(1–2),* 174–181.

Murray, D. (2004). *A Writer Teaches Writing.* Boston: Heinle.

Murray, R. (1999). Power, conflict, and contact: re-constructing authority in the classroom. In K. Gilyard (Ed.), *Race, rhetoric, and composition* (pp. 87–103). Portsmouth, NH: Heinemann.

National Council of Teachers of English. (2007). Adolescent Literacy: A Policy Research Brief. Retrieved September 5, 2008, from http://www.ncte.org/collections/adolescent literacy.

National Reading Panel. (2000). *Report of the National Reading Panel: Teaching children to read: An evidence-based assessment of the scientific research literature on reading and its implications for reading instruction: Reports of the subgroups.* Washington DC: National Institute of Child Health and Human Development.

Nieto, S. (2002). *Language, culture, and teaching: Critical perspectives for a new century.* Mahwah, NJ: Erlbaum.

Noddings, N. (1984). *Caring, a feminine approach to ethics and moral education.* Berkeley, CA: University of California Press.

Norton, N. (2005). Permitanme hablar: Allow me to speak. *Language Arts, 82(2),* 118–127.

Ochoa, A., Franco, B., & Gourdine, T. (2003). *Night is gone, day is still coming: Stories and poems by American Indian teens and young adults.* Cambridge, MA: Candlewick Press.

Ohanian, S. (1999). *One size fits few: The folly of educational standards.* Portsmouth, NH: Heinemann.

Ohanian, S. (2001). *Caught in the middle: Nonstandard kids and a killing curriculum.* Portsmouth, NH: Heinemann.

Palmer, P. (1998). *The courage to teach: Exploring the inner landscape of a teacher's life.* San Francisco: Jossey-Bass.

Park, R. E. (1950). *Race and culture.* Glencoe, IL: The Free Press.

Paterson, K. (1981). *Gates of excellence: On reading and writing books for children.* New York: Lodestar Books.

Paull, I. (1972). To die among strangers. In M. Greer & B. Rubinstein (Eds.), *Will the real teacher please stand up? A primer in humanistic education* (pp. 6–10). Pacific Palisades, CA: Goodyear Publishing.

Pedraza del Prado, R. (2008). Oh, Beautiful? The son of two Cuban exiles experiences the ugliness of prejudice in America. In L. M. Carlson (Ed.), *Voices in first person: Reflections on Latino identity* (pp. 48–51). New York: Atheneum.

Peterson, R. (1992). *Life in a crowded place: Making a learning community.* Portsmouth, NH: Heinemann.

Peterson, R., & Eeds, M. (1990). *Grand conversations: Literature groups in action.* Ontario, Canada: Scholastic.

Philips, S. (1971). Participant structures and communicative competence: Warm Springs children in community and classroom. In C. Cazden, V. John, & D. Hymes (Eds.), *Functions of language in the classroom* (pp. 370–394). New York: Teachers College Press.

Pierce, C., Carew, J., Pierce-Gonzalez, D., & Wills, D. (1978). An experiment in racism: TV commercials. In C. Pierce (Ed.), *Television and education* (pp. 62–88). Beverly Hills, CA: Sage.

Polakow, V. (1993). *Lives on the edge: Single mothers and their children in the other America.* Chicago: University of Chicago Press.

Poynor, L., & Wolfe, P. (Eds.). (2005). *Marketing fear in America's public schools: The real war on literacy.* Mahwah, NJ: Lawrence Erlbaum.

Public Law 107–110. (2002). The elementary and secondary education act. Retrieved October 15, 2006, from http://www.ed.gov/policy/elsec/leg/esea02/index.html.

Richardson, V. (1989). Significant and worthwhile change in teaching practice. *Educational Researcher, 19(7),* 10–18.

Rogers, R. (2003). *A critical discourse analysis of family literacy practices: Power in and out of print.* Mahwah, NJ: Lawrence Erlbaum.

Romano, T. (1995). *Writing with passion: Life stories, multiple genres.* Portsmouth, NH: Boynton/Cook.

Rosen, H. (1986). Politics of English education in the face of bilingualism and multiculturalism. Paper presented at the International Teachers of English annual conference, Ottawa, Canada.

Rosenblatt, L. (1978). *The reader, the text, the poem: The transactional theory of the literary work.* Carbondale, ILL: Southern Illinois University Press.

Roth, J. (1992). Of what help is he? A Review of *Foucault and Education. American Educational Research Journal,* (Winter 1992), *29(4),* 683–694.

Ruiz, N., & Morales-Ellis, L. (2005). 'Gracias por la oportunidad, pero voy a buscar otro trabajo . . .' A beginning teacher resists high-stakes curriculum. In B. Altwerger (Ed.), *Reading for profit: How the bottom line leaves kids behind* (pp. 199–215). Portsmouth, NH: Heinemann.

Ryan, J. (1991). Observing and normalizing: Foucault, discipline, and inequality in schooling. *The Journal of Educational Thought, 25(2),* 104–119.

Sarason, S. (1972). *The culture of the school and the problem of change.* Boston: Allyn and Bacon.

Schön, D. (1983). *The reflective practitioner: How professionals think in action.* New York: Basic Books.

Shannon, P. (1989). *Broken Promises: Reading instruction in twentieth-century America.* Granby, MA: Bergin & Garvey.

Shannon, P. (1990). *The struggle to continue: Progressive reading instruction in the United States*. Portsmouth, NH: Heinemann.

Shannon, P. (1998). *Reading poverty*. Portsmouth, NH: Heinemann.

Shor, I., & Freire, P. (1987). *A pedagogy for liberation: Dialogues in transforming education*. Granby, MA: Bergin & Garvey.

Short, K., & Burke, C. (1991). *Creating curriculum: Teachers and students as a community of learners*. Portsmouth, NH: Heinemann.

Short, K., Harste, J., with Burke, C. (1996). *Creating classrooms for authors and inquirers*. Portsmouth, NH: Heinemann.

Slavitz, H. (1992). Introduction. In J. S. Baca, *Working in the dark: Voice of a poet of the barrio* (pp. ix–xii). Santa Fe: Red Crane Books.

Smith, F. (1983). Demonstrations, engagement, and sensitivity. In F. Smith (Ed.), *Essays into literacy* (pp. 95–106). Portsmouth, NH: Heinemann.

Smith, F. (1988). *Joining the literacy club: Further essays into literacy*. Portsmouth, NH: Heinemann.

Smith, D., & Whitmore, K. (2006). *Literacy and advocacy in adolescent family, gang, school, and juvenile court communities: 'CRIP 4 LIFE.'* Mahwah, NJ: Lawrence Erlbaum.

Solórzano, D. (1998). Critical race theory, race and gender microaggressions, and the experience of Chicana and Chicano scholars. *Qualitative studies in education, 11(1)*, 121–136.

Solórzano, D., Ceja, M., & Yosso, Y. (2000). Critical race theory, racial micro-aggressions, and campus racial climate: The experiences of African American college students. *Journal of Negro Education, 69(1/2)*, 60–73.

Spradley, J. (1980). *Participant observation*. New York: Holt Rinehart and Winston.

Spring, J. (2002). *Political agendas for education: From the religious right to the Green Party*. Mahwah, NJ: Lawrence Erlbaum Associates.

Stake, R. (1995). *The art of case study research*. Thousand Oaks, CA: Sage.

Street, B. (1995). *Social literacies: Critical approaches to literacy in development, ethnography and education*. New York: Longman.

Stuckey, J. E. (1991). *The violence of literacy*. (Chapters 1 and 4). Portsmouth: Boynton Cook/Heinemann.

Stuckey, J. E. (2002). Reader refunds. In C. Benson & S. Christian (Eds.), *Writing to make a difference: Classroom projects for community change* (pp. 215–228). New York: Teachers College Press.

Tan, A. (2003). *The opposite of fate: Memories of a writing life*. New York: Penguin.

Tapahonso, L. (1998). *Sáanii dahataal: The women are singing*. Tucson, AZ: University of Arizona Press.

Taylor, D., (1998). *Beginning to read and the spin doctors of science: The political campaign to change America's mind about how children learn to read*. Urbana, Ill: National Council of Teachers of English.

Taylor, D., & Yamasaki, T. (n.d.). *Children, literacy and mass trauma: Teaching in times of catastrophic events and ongoing emergency situations*. Unpublished manuscript.

Tolle, E. (2006). *A new earth: Awakening to your life's purpose*. New York: Plume.

US Census Bureau. (2008a). *American community survey*. Washington, DC: US Census Bureau. Retrieved August 29, 2008 from http://factfinder.census.gov/servlet/GRT Table?_bm=y&-geo_id=null&-_box_head_nbr=R1704&-ds_name=ACS_2007_1 YR_G00_&_lang=en&-format=US-30&-CONTENT=grt.

References 281

US Census Bureau. (2008b). *Current population survey.* Washington, DC: US Census Bureau. Retrived August 29, 2008 from http://www.census.gov/cps/.

US Department of Education (DOE). (2001a). Elementary and Secondary Education Act: Public Law PL 107-110, the *No Child Left Behind Act of 2001.* Retrieved November 16, 2005, from http://www.ed.gov/policy/elsec/leg/esea02/index.html.

US Department of Education (DOE). (2001b). Elementary and Secondary Education Act: Public Law PL 107-110, the McKinney-Vento Homeless Assistance. Retrieved September 23, 2007, from http://www.ed.gov/policy/elsec/leg/esea02/pg116.html≡ c1031.

Valdés, G. (1996). *Con respeto: Bridging the distance between culturally diverse families and schools.* New York: Teachers College Press.

de Valenzuela, J. S., Copeland, S., Qi, C., & Park, M. (Summer, 2006). Examining educational equity: Revisiting the disproportionate representation of minority students in special education. *Exceptional Children, 72(4),* 425–441.

Van Manen, M. (1991). *The tact of teaching: The meaning of pedagogical thoughtfulness.* Albany, NY: State University of New York.

Van Manen, M. (2002). *The tone of teaching.* University of Western Ontario, London, Ontario, Canada: Althouse Press.

Volosinov, V. N. (1973). *Marxism and the philosophy of language* (L. Matejka & I. R. Titunik, Trans.). New York: Seminar Press. (Original work published in 1930).

Vygotsky, L. (1978). Mind in society: The development of higher psychological processes. In M. Cole, V. John-Steiner, S. Scribner, & E. Souberman (Eds.) Cambridge: Harvard University Press.

Walker, A. (2006). *We are the ones we have been looking for: Inner light in a time of darkness.* New York: New Press.

Walkerdine, V. (1990). *Schoolgirl fictions.* New York: Verso.

Waller, W. (1932). *The sociology of teaching.* New York: Russell & Russell.

Weaver, C. (2002). *Reading process and practice.* Portsmouth, NH: Heinemann.

Wenger, E. (1998). *Communities of practice: Learning, meaning, and identity.* New York: Cambridge University Press.

Wiesel, E. (1958/2006, translated in 2006 by M. Wiesel). *Night.* New York: Hill and Wang.

Wild, M., & Brooks, R. (2000). *Fox.* St. Leonards, Australia: Allen and Unwin.

Willis, A., & Harris, V. (2000). Political acts: Learning literacy and teaching. *Reading Research Quarterly, 35(1),* 72–88.

Willis, A. I., Montavon, M., Hall, H., Hunter, C., Burke, L., & Herrera, A. (2008). *On critically conscious research: Approaches to language and literacy research.* New York: Teachers College Press.

Wolk, S. (2007). Why go to School? *Phi Delta Kappan, 88(9),* 648–658.

Yunus, M. (2006). Nobel Lecture, Oslo, December 10, 2006. Retrieved December 27, 2006, from http://rantingsbymm.blogspot.com/2006/12/poverty-is-absence-of-all-human-rights.html.

Zizek, S. (2007). Fear Thy Neighbor as Thyself. Presentation at the University of New Mexico on November 30, 2007.

Index of Children's Work

Index